Dave Simpson is a *Guardian* [...] mainly on music. His first [...] monumental quest to track down everyone who had ever played in Mark E Smith's legendary band. He is now applying those same forensic and possibly certifiable skills to his football team, Leeds United.

Living in Yorkshire, he has supported Leeds since the early 1970s, man and boy, which has brought about a small amount of pleasure and a great amount of pain. He also wrote for the *LeedsLeedsLeeds* magazine which documented United's rise and fall from 1998 to 2011.

THE LAST CHAMPIONS

Dave Simpson

BANTAM BOOKS

LONDON • TORONTO • SYDNEY • AUCKLAND • JOHANNESBURG

TRANSWORLD PUBLISHERS
61–63 Uxbridge Road, London W5 5SA
A Random House Group Company
www.transworldbooks.co.uk

THE LAST CHAMPIONS
A BANTAM BOOK: 9780857501011

First published in Great Britain
in 2012 by Bantam Press
an imprint of Transworld Publishers
Bantam edition published 2013

Addresses for Random House Group Ltd companies outside the UK
can be found at: www.randomhouse.co.uk
The Random House Group Ltd Reg. No. 954009

The Random House Group Limited supports the Forest Stewardship
Council® (FSC®), the leading international forest-certification
organisation. Our books carrying the FSC label are printed on
FSC®-certified paper. FSC is the only forest-certification scheme
supported by the leading environmental organisations, including
Greenpeace. Our paper procurement policy can be found
at www.randomhouse.co.uk/environment

Typeset in 11/14pt Berling by Falcon Oast Graphic Art Ltd.
Printed and bound by CPI Group (UK) Ltd, Croydon, CR0 4YY.

2 4 6 8 10 9 7 5 3 1

To the memory of Gary Andrew Speed, 1969–2011

Where does the power come from, to see the race to its end? From within.

Chariots of Fire

Contents

English First Division, 1991/92

	P	W	D	L	F	A	Pts
LEEDS UNITED	42	22	16	4	74	37	82
Manchester United	42	21	15	6	63	33	78
Sheffield Wednesday	42	21	12	9	62	49	75
Arsenal	42	19	15	8	81	47	72
Manchester City	42	20	10	12	61	48	70
Liverpool	42	16	16	10	47	40	64
Aston Villa	42	17	9	16	48	44	60
Nottingham Forest	42	16	11	15	60	58	59
Sheffield United	42	16	9	17	65	63	57
Crystal Palace	42	14	15	13	53	61	57
Queens Park Rangers	42	12	18	12	48	47	54
Everton	42	13	14	15	52	51	53
Wimbledon	42	13	14	15	53	53	53
Chelsea	42	13	14	15	50	60	53
Tottenham Hotspur	42	15	7	20	58	63	52
Southampton	42	14	10	18	39	55	52
Oldham Athletic	42	14	9	19	63	67	51
Norwich City	42	11	12	19	47	63	45
Coventry City	42	11	11	20	35	44	44
Luton Town	42	10	12	20	39	71	42
Notts County	42	10	10	22	40	62	40
West Ham United	42	9	11	22	37	59	38

Prologue

It was a Monday morning in July, and I was ringing a Sheffield branch of a popular travel agency.

'Hello,' I began. 'Can I speak to Mr Shutt?'

'I'm afraid the assistant manager isn't available at the moment,' replied the female voice at the end of the line. 'Can I help? Are you looking to book a holiday?'

I wasn't looking to book a holiday, but I couldn't admit, 'I'm looking for Shutty! Who won the last ever First Division title with Leeds United! The tireless South Yorkshireman who ran his bloody legs off and scored one of the greatest goals in the history of the club when he came on against Stuttgart in the European Cup and ran the full length of the pitch to put it past the keeper with his first touches of the game!'

I'd first begun my quest to meet Carl Shutt by skulking around the shop, hoping to bump into him; now I'd started ringing them up, which meant I'd gone from being a weirdo stalker to a telephone pest. Why was I doing this?

It started a few weeks earlier, in May, when I'd been

sat at Leeds United's Elland Road ground watching my beloved team limp towards another false dawn. Leeds had yet again managed to miss out on promotion to English football's top flight, where – as one of the best-supported clubs in England, if not the world – they surely belonged. As another season bulging with promise had fizzled out like a damp firework, I'd found my thoughts drifting to a similar spring day almost two decades earlier, when a Leeds United team assembled by manager Howard Wilkinson had stood as proud champions at the summit of domestic football.

I remembered the glorious day when the title was won, Sunday, 26 April 1992, when Leeds were 3–2 victors in a bizarre, windy, fluke-ridden noon kick-off game at Sheffield United while Man U went down at Liverpool that afternoon, continuing England's biggest club's quarter-century wait to win the league. Manager Howard Wilkinson – dubbed 'Sergeant Wilko' by fans and players for his dour military air and inscrutable, almost unknowable persona, which seemed to shroud a bone-dry humour – was then doorstepped by the media during his Sunday dinner, and had been so atypically overcome by emotion – or something stronger – that he could barely manage a word.

In three and a half astonishing seasons, the former schoolteacher from South Yorkshire had taken the ailing West Yorkshire giant from the bottom of the old Second Division to the top of the First, the speed of the ascent even outstripping the achievement of the legendary Leeds United manager Don Revie, who'd taken eight years to accomplish the same thing in the 1960s.

The triumph was all the more remarkable because forty-eight-year-old Wilko, then seen as the most brilliant manager in English football, had beaten Sir Alex Ferguson's more lavishly funded Manchester United to domestic football's top honour with players often picked up on the cheap. Some of Wilko's troops – the likes of Scottish internationals Gordon Strachan and Gary McAllister – were top players (Strachan had in fact been snapped up for a modest fee after being surplus to requirements at none other than Manchester United). But many players followed Wilko from Sheffield Wednesday, or had been signed from lowly clubs; he had even taken two players from non-league football and turned them into League Championship medal winners, which would be unthinkable, if not impossible, now.

Those Leeds United players weren't just champions but the Last Champions, the final winners of the Football League before the formation of the Premiership brought wall-to-wall Sky TV, all-seater stadiums, fancy foreign players, multi-million-pound transfer deals and wages, and billionaire owners. Wilkinson remains the last English manager to win the league, with players who for the most part weren't paid that much more than the people in the stands. It was the last title won by ordinary people, and the end of an era.

From almost the moment Wilkinson held up the trophy, English football was in revolution. From then on, battles for the title would be as much about contests between financial muscle as management or tactics. Things would never be the same again.

Looking back on it all that day in May 2011, it felt like some distant, almost mythical era of muddy pitches, cheap tickets and players you could bump into in the city centre. I recalled the amazing citywide celebrations even before the following week's game at home against Norwich City, the last league fixture of the season. On the way up to Elland Road, four of us had crammed into a tiny car, our pal Tim hanging out of the window shouting 'Campioni! Campioni!' at passers-by amid a cacophony of car horns.

The game itself, which Leeds began as champions and won 1–0, was surreal, like a practice match; even the Norwich players seemed in awe of the occasion, or the achievement, or the fact that a giant stuffed panda was partying with the players on the pitch. I particularly remembered the post-match title celebrations, when everybody, including the mayor, turned out to honour the manager and his triumphant players, who stood on a balcony outside the Town Hall as mercurial French centre-forward Eric Cantona uttered his comically worded but instantly memorable 'Why I love you, I don't know, but I love you' pronouncement to thousands of cheering supporters. Back then, it felt like the entire population of Leeds had turned the city into a beautiful display of white, yellow and blue.

For the players, it was the defining moment of their lives. For me, a typical supporter, it was the culmination of almost twenty years supporting the club and the proudest, most exhilarating moment I'd ever known in football.

But now Leeds United were back where they were

before Wilkinson came to the club, struggling in the second tier with falling crowds, and it was starting to feel like 1991/92 was a mirage, some distant, almost-forgotten dream that may or may not have happened.

The bookshelves rightly bulged with tomes – including the one made into the film *The Damned United* – honouring the Revie-era triumphs: a Second Division title, two League Championships, two Fairs Cups, the FA Cup, the League Cup and the Charity Shield. But Wilkinson had won the Second Division title inside eighteen months (to Revie's three years), and had also won the Charity Shield alongside the First Division title. His 411 games (more than any other Leeds manager since The Don) also included a League Cup Final, and even in the Premiership he notched up two more top-five finishes before he was unceremoniously sacked in 1996. By then he'd set up the Leeds youth academy, which produced a glittering stream of future internationals even though the man who conceived it all was no longer at the club to see them play.

For me, and a generation like me, too young to have seen The Don barking out his orders and players like Billy Bremner and Jack Charlton in their prime, the Wilko years were the 'Glory Years'. Title-winners like Strachan, Lee Chapman, Chris 'Huggy' Whyte, Shutty and Mel 'Zico' Sterland were our heroes. It felt like their story had been written out of history, or lost in a welter of acrobatic camera angles and tabloid stories about players on £250,000 a week who didn't fancy getting on the pitch, and managers who could barely control their players and were lucky to make it into a second season.

When he managed Leeds, Sergeant Wilko was an inescapable, dominant presence, our Great Leader, feared yet loved by players and fans alike. Most of us instinctively thought he was a genius. How else could he have taken good ol' Shutty from Spalding or Micky Whitlow from Witton Albion and managed them into picking up the greatest medal in domestic football? Coaching? Tactics? Black magic?

Wilko was certainly unlike a normal football manager. Unashamedly futuristic and intellectual – he was a sports science graduate who introduced good nutrition to players reared on beer and chips years before Arsenal's Arsène Wenger, and spoke to Eric Cantona in French – he was also a gruff South Yorkshireman with something very quaint, even awkward about him which I found tremendously endearing. He was like a cross between a great philosopher and Brian Glover's disciplinarian PE teacher in *Kes*. With none of the social skills of today's media-savvy modern managers, with their official web-sites and sponsored television channels, Wilko would address the faithful via a crackling Tannoy, expounding his thoughts like a footballing Chairman Mao. 'Today we host Notts County, the oldest professional football club in the world . . .'

In those days, before the internet, fans would ring Leeds United's Clubcall service for that urgent piece of breaking news, like the latest information on Mel Sterland's ankle injury, to be greeted by the Sergeant, 'the official voice of Leeds United'. One Saturday, after a game, in my days as a young, struggling music journalist, I'd rung Clubcall, as you do, then gone out, been beaten up by a band to whom I'd given a negative review, woke up the next morning covered in bruises, picked up the phone to call the doctor, only to hear 'Hello. This is Howard Wilkinson. The official voice of Leeds United . . .' The previous call hadn't been disconnected: Clubcall had been on all night. It was a very expensive phone call. Still, at least I knew the condition of Mel Sterland's ankle.

But with the passing years, you couldn't help wondering whether the Sergeant had really been a genius or just a good manager who got lucky.

It didn't help, of course, that it had all gone badly wrong. Within months of those glorious celebrations, Cantona was sold amid rumours of extra-curricular physicals including players' wives, LUFC were humiliated home and away in the European Cup by Rangers, and the players we chanted 'Sergeant Wilko's Barmy Army' at made such a hash of defending the title that they failed to win a single game away from home the whole season. In fact, they were almost relegated, which would have made them the first defending champions to go down since Manchester City in 1938. Even the group of friends I went to games with dissipated and would never attend a match together again. One of them went so far as to leave the country – although I'm not sure these facts are related.

But even at the time, the Sergeant and his loyal soldiers never received the credit they deserved. In particular, there was a notion that Leeds hadn't won the title, Manchester United had lost it, which isn't borne out by events. Yes, Ferguson's players wobbled in the run-in, losing three games in a row to Leeds' one in the final nine matches of the season, but Leeds won the title with a week to go, taking thirteen points from the last five games to their rivals' four and finishing four points clear. That season they lost just four games, weren't beaten in the league by any of the top clubs – including Manchester United, Liverpool and defending champions Arsenal (the defeats came at Crystal Palace, Oldham, QPR and Man City) – and scored more goals (seventy-four) than anyone except the Gunners, keeping twenty clean sheets and not losing a single game at Elland Road.

It's also been said that Cantona won the title for Leeds, before departing for Manchester United, enabling Ferguson to dominate English football in the nineties. His impact at Manchester is undeniable, and his arrival at Elland Road towards the end of the title season certainly cemented a mood that something incredible was happening, but at Leeds he started just six games and scored three goals. Wonderful as those goals were – especially the one at home against Chelsea, when he audaciously flicked the ball on his right foot like a ballet dancer before blasting it into the top corner – none of them was a match winner. Cantona wasn't involved in the two most notable performances of the 1991/92 season, the 4–1 and 6–1 away demolitions of Aston Villa and Wilkinson's old club Sheffield Wednesday (then high-flying: they finished third in the table) respectively.

No. Even without the gifted Frenchman, Wilkinson

had created a momentum over three seasons and assembled teams that by 1991/92 were unstoppable, even unplayable. I remember how the two centre-halves, the Chrises Whyte and Fairclough, would marshal the halfway line while the rest of the team bar the goalie set up camp in the opposition's half, steam-rollering them into submission. More often than not a Sterland cross would meet Chapman's head, or a Tony Dorigo centre would be guided goalward by Gary Speed, and the game would be over as a contest inside twenty minutes. It's been called long-ball football. It wasn't. It was brutally, efficiently, beautifully direct.

Whatever happened later, Wilkinson surely created worthy champions – a perfectly balanced side of super-fit footballing cybermen with brains. At the back, goalkeeper John Lukic was solid and unspectacular, but when needed could pull off astonishing feats like the double save from Ian Rush and Michael Walters to keep a clean sheet at Anfield in the run-in. The two full-backs, Sterland and Dorigo, were blessed with oodles of pace and the ability to pass a ball and read the game, and formed a Maginot Line of a defence with Whyte and Fairclough, both centre-halves who could play the ball.

Central to the club's success was the Sergeant's pre-ferred midfield of Strachan, McAllister, Speed and David Batty, an almost perfect combination of brawn, talent and youth (Batts and Speedo) with two states-manlike footballing Rolls-Royces. Up front, big Lee Chapman and elfin Rod Wallace were a devastating striking partnership, a perfect little and large combination.

Six foot three Chapman notched up sixteen league goals in thirty-eight games, while his nimble attacking partner was capable of exquisite chips and explosive running at defences and was rewarded with eleven league goals in the victorious campaign. Chapman was a well-travelled goalscorer, but under Wilkinson (first at Sheffield Wednesday and then at Leeds) he was a goal machine.

Less heralded but just as vital were the squad players who stepped up to the breach when the first choice XI were unavailable – the Steve Hodges, John McClellands, Jon Newsomes, Shuttys and Whitsies who all played crucial roles for Wilkinson by somehow playing out of their skins in game after game against the top sides in the country.

As I sat in my shiny blue, outrageously expensive seat at Elland Road in May 2011 – a far cry from the over-crowded stands and cheapish admission prices of the Wilko era – I started not just to pine for those days but to become more and more fascinated by how Wilko had assembled players with some special quality that made them champions, and wondered what had become of those players we idolized so much.

Strachan and McAllister (who went on to win trophies at Liverpool, but not another championship) were high-profile pundits and had had varying success in management, and Speed was, of course, manager of Wales. Chapman had spent the intervening years more on front pages than back ones. Chris Kamara, who laid on the vital cross for Chapman to head the goal that secured promotion from the Second Division in 1990 and who was still featuring in 1992, was a popular Sky

Sports reporter/presenter. Cantona, who'd sealed Wilkinson's fate in almost Shakespearean manner when he scored the final goal in a 4–0 hammering by Man U at Elland Road on 7 September 1996, had enjoyed a film career and become Director of Football at New York Cosmos.

But most of them, even once high-profile players like Batty, seemed to have disappeared. I kept hearing dark rumours that some of those players – who missed out on the Premiership windfall, the huge sums now paid to footballers some of whom are not fit to lace those Leeds players' boots – had fallen on hard times. I was curious, too, about other key figures in the Sergeant's mission, like commercial director/wheeler-and-dealer Bill Fotherby, an Arthur Daley-type character who once claimed to be signing Diego Maradona for LUFC and who is still the subject of unflattering graffiti near the ground.

So I set myself the task of finding them, sure in the knowledge that Sergeant Wilko's troops not only held the stories of the club's rise and fall, but that they were sitting on a piece of social history: a period of enormous transformation in English football seen through the eyes of those on the ground – or, rather, the pitch.

Which is why, on that balmy July Monday morning, I was ringing a travel agency after reading on an internet messageboard that that was where Carl Shutt worked. I knew none of them were getting any younger and that memories might already be fading. Wherever they all were, I needed to find them. While there was still time.

ONE
The Rise

CHAPTER 1

Howard Wilkinson – 'Sergeant Wilko'

You can't say why you're doing anything because it will
destroy the effect. They'd work it out eventually, but by
that time it's too late.

I start not with Shutty but with Howard Wilkinson,
without whom none of it would have happened,
although it's not immediately obvious how to get in
touch with a man who hasn't managed in this country
for a decade. Wilkinson recently stepped down from the
board of his old club, Sheffield Wednesday, and these
days is chairman of the League Managers Association,
although their website seems to list a contact for every
single member of staff except him. In recent years,
Wilkinson has been conspicuous by his public absence.
Even his 1992 autobiography *Managing to Succeed*
hasn't been updated since, as if his life had ended as
soon as he held up the trophy.

Eventually, contact is made via Leeds United, who
seem to be belatedly honouring Wilkinson's achievements with a new restaurant called Howard's, which

serves 'free-range Soames farm chicken liver parfait with red onion marmalade and homemade brioche', which I suspect wasn't on the pre-match menu for Mel or Shutty. As my green MG hurtles towards an address in Sheffield, I find my thoughts drifting back to autumn 1992, and my previous encounter with the Sarge.

It was a few weeks into the season, the wheels were still on the 1992/93 campaign, and the great man was in the city centre branch of WHSmith in Leeds, autographing copies of *Managing to Succeed*. I recall a bright, sunny day – for some reason, most of my memories of that time seem set in bright sunshine – and piles upon piles of books, decked in Leeds United white, blue and yellow. The queue to get his signature stretched out of the store – the sort of thing you'd normally see with a teenage boy band, not a forty-eight-year-old football manager in a suit.

And yet, at close quarters, I saw something in Wilko that day I'd never imagined from row X of the Spion Kop. In his suit and tie, the normally agitated track-suited man on the touchline looked positively radiant, as if he had somehow gained an invisible aura or halo from the brilliant achievement of winning the Football League with a club he had dragged up by its bootlaces from the edge of the abyss. I was twenty-eight years old and as in awe of him then as I have ever been of any pop star I've seen live or interviewed in my day job as a pop journalist. We all were. As his gold pen glided over the page, the subject of our affections barely acknowledged us. He was as inscrutable, unknowable, as ever. When I suggested he sign my copy 'I manage very well' he looked up for a millisecond – was that even a flicker of a smile? – before staring down impassively and inevitably merely putting 'To Dave'. This is the Sergeant Wilko I remember and still cherish.

What on earth is he like now?

I drive through electric gates towards a large but not ostentatious family home. The door opens before I ever knock on it, as if whatever dark powers turned Micky Whitlow into a title-winner extend to seeing through solid wooden doors. 'Hello,' he says, and the voice is exactly the same as Clubcall, 'the official voice of Leeds United'. Wilko is sixty-seven years old, but with almost as much hair as he had in 1992; he looks eerily as if he has just strolled in from the touchline after rollocking Cantona. He is wearing a pink polo-type shirt and tracksuit bottoms, and were it not for the slightly incongruous flip-flops he could easily be about to embark on another of his infamous cross-country runs, which were said to have had players vomiting and crying 'No more, gaffer!'

The greatest Leeds United manager of the modern era makes me a cup of tea and produces two small, individually wrapped biscuits, like you'd get at a seaside B&B – no sweet treats for the nutrition pioneer – and the atmosphere initially is as awkward as I'd expected. Wilkinson never did suffer fools gladly (he once described a Leeds fanzine as 'like issues of *Private Eye*, pre-war') and doesn't do small talk.

I break the ice by asking about the house, which he reveals he's lived in with his family for twenty-five years. 'We used to live over the road, but I acquired a plot of land,' he explains, as gruffly as if he were addressing Mel or Shutty, gazing impassively through French windows over a long, plush lawn. While he's speaking, the significance of the twenty-five-year reference hits me as hard as a McAllister free kick: from this suburban new-build, Sergeant Wilko conquered the Goliaths of English football.

We begin with the celebrations, specifically with the photograph on the front of *Managing to Succeed* which captures the Sergeant as he gazes into the trophy and at the reflected image of thousands of cheering supporters.

What went through your mind at that moment?

'Relief,' he replies, and there's a tiny chuckle before he explains that he was already worrying about the future. His title-winners – 'Speed, Batty, McAllister, to name a few' – had become attractive to other clubs. He'd only won the blessed title ten days before but can still remember the cold start to the morning as his thoughts turned to the enemies trying to topple him from his perch. 'But of course you enjoy it,' he admits, and there's another flicker of a smile as he remembers the 'fantastic' feeling of pipping Man United to the title and the subsequent two parties.

'But you can't physically celebrate for ever,' he insists, although among the supporters the celebrations seemed to go on so long – years, really – that to this day I half expect drunken fans to be rescued from pubs in Wakefield in the way that Vietnam vets were found in the jungle years after the war ended.

'I think what was also going through my mind that day was taking in the huge number of people that were there. It was packed, and the streets all around were packed. That in itself was an event.' By the end of the celebrations – attended by a crowd estimated at 150,000, a fifth of the city's population and greater than anything in the Revie era – he was 'breathless'.

The title marked the pinnacle of what he calls a three-year 'whirlwind sort of rise. From moving there in October '88, [at the] bottom, going on an unbeaten run of games, in many respects fortunately missing out on the playoffs . . . then Second Division championship, then finish fourth [in the First Division], then say, "Let's achieve what we can next season."'

In winning the championship in 1992 he was two years ahead of schedule: his initial goal that season was just to get one point more than in 1990/91.

Wilkinson had arrived at Leeds after realizing in his fourth or fifth year at Sheffield Wednesday that 'different clubs have different ceilings', and that in terms of the make-up of the club and the revenue coming in, the Sheffield club's was lower than it should have been. 'That's not to criticize anyone at Sheffield Wednesday,' he adds. 'It's just the way it is.' He got a call from a journalist friend, David Walker at the *Sunday Mirror*, saying, 'You're going to think this is a crazy phone call. Would you be interested . . . in Leeds?'

On the face of it, it was pretty crazy. The ambitious young manager had just taken Wednesday from the Second Division to the top half of the first and yet was being asked to consider a club where a succession of Revie players – Allan Clarke, Eddie Gray and Billy Bremner – had failed as managers to revive a slumbering giant now better known for ruckuses around the ground. 'It had become a sort of beaten-up old picture of the Revie days with this frame around it of bad behaviour,' Wilkinson exhales, bluntly. 'The club didn't own the ground and were in debt. The training ground was shit and we were [at the] bottom of the league.'

However, he did know that a one-club city and a bigger one than Sheffield had a much greater untapped potential than Wednesday. After mulling over the approach for a week he outlined, to LUFC chairman Leslie Silver, the remarkable conditions on which he'd take the job. In a brief but glorious nutshell, he wanted to take Leeds back to where it was in the Revie era 'in terms of the team', set up an academy to produce young players (an idea years before its time) and renovate the ground into the sort of stadium that 'encourages people to be proper fans'. With the attention to detail that Silver realized would become his trademark, Wilkinson had put all this into a ten-year plan.

Wilkinson was proposing nothing less than a total revolution of a football club by its manager – unthinkable now, and even then about as radical as a new Prime Minister striding into the House of Commons and announcing free beer for all.

'You wouldn't contemplate it now,' Wilkinson admits, 'where you can't plan for five months let alone five years and then ten. Maybe Wenger did at Arsenal and I'm sure Alex did when he went to Manchester United, but to sit down and say to the chairman, "Yeah,

I'm interested, but only if we enter a partnership which involves rebuilding the club . . ."'

He doesn't need to finish the sentence – you'd be laughed out of the room. But in Silver, Wilkinson had a 'real fan' who had sold his paint business and had the time and resources to fund the new project. Not the kind of finances modern football sucks up – Dave Whelan spent £48m taking Wigan Athletic from League Two to the bottom of the Premiership, and Manchester City spent £380m to finish third in 2010/11 – but, in 1988, enough to mount a challenge. For his part, the chairman was fascinated to discover that Wilkinson already knew everything about Leeds United, from the young players to the boardroom power structure to, perhaps, the size of the individual director's shoes.

He shrugs dismissively: 'I made it my business to find out.'

One of the first things they did together was re-organize the United board, a huge, unwieldy beast dominated by the council, who also owned the ground. 'You couldn't run an organization with a board that big, where everyone has a say and an opinion,' snorts Wilko. 'I don't disagree with that,' he adds, taking care not to come over like Chairman Mao. 'All I'm saying is that in football it doesn't work, because sometimes you have to make quick decisions so it's essential the chain of command is kept as small as possible.'

Thus, from then on Leeds would be controlled by Silver, managing director Bill Fotherby and director Peter Gilman. It was an important victory for the Sergeant before his teams even stepped on the field.

He transformed the football side in an equally audacious manner. Arguably his most controversial act was removing all mementoes of the Revie era from inside the ground – 'unfortunately', he says, even Norman 'Bites Yer Legs' Hunter from the coaching staff. The Glory Years had become, in his words, 'A weight. A comforter. Players can take refuge in the past. I knew it would cause ripples, but I told them, "When we've got a team worthy of them, we'll put 'em back up."'

Another inspired early move was to place microphones above the Kop to amplify the crowd noise, to the extent that the visiting Oldham manager Joe Royle once compared Elland Road to a cross between a Hitler rally and the Roman Colosseum when the Christians were on the menu. Central to the Sarge's masterplan was the idea of establishing a new culture 'which identifies the place, and by which people are moulded, if you like,' he explains, sounding almost like the leader of a cult, although his role models weren't crazed religious sects but Arsenal, Manchester United and Barcelona. 'When you sign for those clubs, you're instantly aware that the people in that place reflect that culture in the way they think, behave, the things they believe in.' He's now sounding ever so slightly impatient, in the way many great thinkers are in a hurry to get their ideas across. 'It's not about going in and getting a lecture from the manager. It's a hidden set of rules and expectations which everyone understands. As I heard anecdotally once – either Rio Ferdinand or Gary Neville once said to a new player after a game, "We don't do that here." Which prompts the question, "Who says so, and why?" And of course nobody does. You just don't do it!

'Very few people inherit a position in football where the chairman or whoever says, "It's terrific as it is, keep things as they are,"' he argues. 'Mostly you go to make things better, and that means change, and when you go somewhere new you want quick wins, so you make people aware that things are going to change. The only place I ever went as a manager where I wasn't able to change anything was Sunderland [where, four years after leaving Leeds, he won just two out of twenty games], because my hands were tied. But if you don't take quick measures, people settle back into the old habits. So, yeah, things like messing with the training games, coming in on a Saturday telling them they're in on Monday, then ending the session on a Monday telling them we're in at noon tomorrow. It was important to keep them on their toes.'

I'm starting to see why his players ran through the proverbial brick walls for him, but would never have guessed such a Machiavellian side to his management style when I gazed down from the Kop as he marshalled Mel and Shutty. And this is just the tip of the iceberg. He reveals other extraordinarily fiendish gambits, including, before he arrived, finding out who the social stars and cliques were, so he could split them up in training. 'You learn who has a lot of influence, some good, some not so good. You can't say why you're doing anything because it will destroy the effect. They'd work it out eventually, but by that time it's too late.'

He looks thoroughly contented, recalling how his revolution began.

There weren't many signs in his early life that Wilkinson would make a manager, although he reveals that a former schoolmate recently reminded him that in class he would never take the teacher's word for anything, and kept on asking question after question until he got what he believed was the right answer.

I bet you were popular, I say.

'I was, actually,' he grins, now exactly the kind of fearsome but funny character I'd hoped to find. 'Some twats,' he blasts, in pure Brian Glover mode, 'but four or five teachers took a genuine interest in me as a person.'

From a staunch working-class Sheffield family, Wilko was a child of the 1950s meritocracy that meant a bright kid could win a scholarship to a top grammar school without having to be posh. 'I was the only one in our class to do it, and I hated it at first,' he admits of his time at Abbeydale Boys. 'You get there and the kid next to you has two names [a double-barrelled surname] and speaks French in the first lesson. You're thinking, "Shit, I shouldn't be here." But I have to say, it made a huge difference to me. After about a week I realized that the form teacher was speaking to me in something other than a classroom manner. So you think, "Well, he's a teacher, and he's all right . . ."'

Adopting exactly the work ethic he'd later demand from his troops, Wilkinson threw himself into schoolwork but was particularly interested in running and football. He became an England youth international, but his league playing record wasn't remarkable: an unsuccessful stint at Sheffield United, twenty-two appearances for Wednesday, and 129 on the wing for Brighton, whom he helped get promoted to the Second Division in 1972. It was when he was living away from home on the south coast that, bored out of his head, he signed up for a coaching course, and was 'hooked instantly'.

A degree at Sheffield University, while he was also player-manager at Boston, enabled Wilkinson to 'go deeper' into sports science, sports medicine, psychology and sociology. He wanted to keep playing at the same time as learning about all aspects of management, but on one course a man called Alan Lee, the FA's Director of Coaching, told him that there were no courses specifically for football management, only coaching. However, Lee then gave him some very sage advice: '"Go do a PE course – teacher training. Cos there's a lot of stuff there that's related." And he was right.'

While Wilkinson downplays any notion that teaching (for two years, at his old school) groomed him for the peculiarities of instructing much older pupils on football grounds, he concedes that he emerged from the period with 'definite ideas, about a lot of things'.

He first put them into practice at Boston, setting new records by going 'fifty or sixty' games unbeaten, toppling future Man U manager 'Big' Ron Atkinson's Kettering Town to become the best non-league team in the country, and winning the Northern Premier League, twice. Coaching at Notts County in the eighties under Jimmy Sirrel, he helped the venerable old club to promotion, managed it himself for a season, and then took his wizardry to Wednesday. By the time he arrived at Elland Road in the autumn of 1988, he was at the peak of his powers.

Wilkinson introduced pioneering ideas at Hillsborough, but at Elland Road he went much further. He reveals that with the help of Leeds University, his fabled but mysterious vitamin and hydration drinks were even tailored to suit individual players.

When I wrote for the club's now defunct *LeedsLeedsLeeds* magazine in the 2000s, I remember being bamboozled when one of the coaches demonstrated their fab new-fangled ProZone gadgets, a computerized system that enabled them to measure precise things like the amount of kilometres Lee Bowyer ran during a game. But along with his new diets and ahead-of-their-time training techniques such as interval running, Wilko was doing this a decade earlier, using stopwatches and bits of paper. 'We worked out ways of measuring the players' KPIs,' he beams. 'Key performance indicators! People were suspicious, especially the media. Players? You get one or two find it difficult for them to subjugate themselves to something that makes sense, because they've got a personality.' Again, a flash of cult leader. The voice softens. 'But most players want to get better.'

So did the manager. He worked punishing hours. 'Leaving home at six forty-five a.m., rarely back before seven p.m. if I was coming back; obviously if you're away for a game you get back when you get back.' He sighs. 'No different to Alex [Ferguson].'

But he was different in that he achieved more with less.

Michael Whitlow, his first signing, epitomizes the strange magic of this period: a Witton Albion left-back who over three years Wilko somehow 'moulded' into a championship medal winner at Leeds. 'Got a tip-off about a kid, Neil Parsley,' he tells me with a shrug, recalling how assistant manager Mick Hennigan – his old youth coach at Wednesday – was dispatched to run his seasoned eye over the potential recruit. 'Micky comes back and says, "Hmmm, he's OK. But there's a guy at the back with a left foot: quick, controlled, good athlete. I think we can make a player out of him, gaffer."'

The desire for quick impact led the Sarge to re-hire troops he'd had at Wednesday – Mel Sterland and Shutty, Imre Varadi and Lee Chapman. 'Which isn't always ideal, but in some circumstances needs must. You don't have to spend six months getting to know what they're capable of.'

Key for the Sergeant wasn't just a footballer's ability, but his character. He needed mentally strong individuals capable of performing in the Elland Road cauldron, where high expectations and an unforgiving home support can destroy a player, and 'games get tight, the crowd gets tense, and you can feel the elastic getting tighter'.

Few characters came bigger than Vinnie Jones, most recently seen by television viewers fronting a CPR campaign for the British Heart Foundation to the accompaniment of 'Stayin' Alive' by the Bee Gees, but who in the promotion season became almost a talisman for the city of Leeds. Wilkinson remembers an incident on the opening weekend of the first season back in the top flight, away at Everton, when the charismatic midfield enforcer was dismayed to discover he wasn't in the team.

'It was a glorious day, that Friday. I got on the coach last, and sat in the front. We hadn't got out of the car park and this shotgun appears next to my temple.' The South Yorkshireman's talents extend to an impeccable cockney accent: "'Do yah want to have anothah fink about the team tomorrah, gaffah?'"

We both erupt in laughter.

What did you do? I ask.

'Told him to piss off, I think.' He smiles contentedly. 'But that was one of the good things about Vinnie. Another person would have sulked at the back of the bus, but he turned it into a positive.'

Jones, while he was there, and Strachan ('in his thirties, yet still wanting to win everything in training') were born leaders who epitomized the new culture. Strachan was an experienced Scottish international who, under Alex Ferguson, had won European honours with Aberdeen and an FA Cup with Manchester United, but his relationship with his former mentor had gone pear-shaped. Even so, persuading a player like that to drop a division was a major coup. 'I had to sell the club to him, yeah. Big time. Gordon, in his typical [contrary, combative, I think he means] fashion, says it was all about money. It wasn't! For the first time in a long time he was involved in more than just winning the next game. He had a role mapped out for him for five years on the bridge of the ship.

'It was part driven by economics,' Wilkinson reasons. 'Like you say, at Man U it had gone pear-shaped, but what you saw at Man U in the latter stages of his career was no reflection on what he could do. So you think, "Right, we can't go out and spend £600,000 but there's a player there who for half that, with a bit of massage, can deliver the goods."'

Like finding a Rolls-Royce in a barn?

'Exactly.'

By the start of the 1991/92 campaign he'd honed his team to the point where he fielded the same eleven players for a lot of games. That first XI, especially the midfield, was almost flukishly well balanced. Was that designed or did it come together organically, with a bit of luck?

'Bit of both. There was a lunatic at the club called Batty,' he explains, referring to the now reclusive midfielder, 'who had an enormous capacity in terms of winning the ball, intercepting and so on. He did a lot wrong, but he got away with it. I saw Speed playing in the kids, at left-back I think. Recognized that he had a good left foot, tremendous ability in the air . . .'

As the squad took shape, his management became even more nuanced. In those far-off days when Saint and Greavsie were on the telly, four different balls were used in the league, so he'd find out which one they'd be playing with on the Saturday so they could train with it all week. When Leeds scored, they were instructed to get the ball back within four passes to regain focus. If they lost, they were instructed to 'not lose two on the trot'; they responded to one of the four defeats in

1991/92, a 4–1 setback at QPR, by destroying Wimbledon 5–1. He set targets – first goal, first point, first win. They'd spend hours practising identical free kicks and corners. A favoured mantra – picked up from Arsenal and Leeds coach Don Howe, although it's also the motto of veteran Salford rock group The Fall – was 'Repetition, repetition, repetition'.

'I knew it was boring,' admits the Sergeant. 'But I had choices. Do I sacrifice efficiency for enjoyment? Everyone says training should be enjoyable, and it should. But no one says training *must* be enjoyable.' He is clearly still enormously proud that LUFC were 'consistently the best team in the league on set pieces. For and against!'

He became devoted to the point of obsession to finding that extra two or three per cent to give his team the edge. 'Take one of those increments away and it won't make a difference,' he says. 'Take three or four away and it will make a huge difference. The trouble is . . .' He groans. 'In trying to cover as much detail as possible . . .' He emits a little laugh. 'It's ****ing hard!'

Very occasionally he would have to resort to more primitive methods of getting a point across – which you could never do in the modern game, when players get on their mobiles to their agents if there's a problem with their turkey sandwich. His schoolteaching days were in the era of corporal punishment, and one ex-pupil has posted a wonderful anecdote on the internet about the time he forgot his gym kit and was admonished by the Sarge. 'Howard went into a cupboard and pulled out the sole of a slipper which was nice and smooth from a lot of use,' writes one Stephen

S. (Abbeydale, 1976–81). 'With a mighty run up he gave us the slipper. I never forgot my kit again.'

At Leeds in 1990, John Pearson, a cheery striker Wilko eventually sold to Barnsley, was clouted around the face.

'That was to instil aggression,' insists Sergeant Wilko, firmly.

So you slapped him round the face?

'It didn't work. He just kept smiling.'

We're both chuckling, but I remind him that in the game he's talking about, a 2–0 win at Sheffield United, Pearson scored.

The psychology of football management fascinates me, particularly as it's shrouded in so much secrecy. It's the sort of stuff managers rarely talk about, and it can't be analysed with the help of fancy gadgetry on Sky. When a team wins a game, how much of it is won by the team talk in the dressing room compared to the preparation?

'Lot of bullshit about team talks,' Wilkinson snorts, Glover once again. 'Ninety-nine per cent of your team talk is done in the week, and it's done in the year, and it's done in the two years or, if you're there, three years.' However, he admits that while his admired Barcelona has created 'animals, who take it in their stride', even the most hardened players can lose their focus in big games, in which case 'there's nearly always something you can use to bring the focus in'.

In the Second Division promotion season of 1989/90, as Leeds prepared for a crucial game at Sunderland – not at today's glistening Stadium of Light but at the notorious old Roker Park where the 'Roker roar' could have opponents soiling their underpants – the Sergeant informed his players, 'We're going into the lions' den and we're going to remove its teeth.' In a sentence he'd summed up that this was not a place to be taken lightly, but one that could be conquered. 'There was a lot of hostility between Leeds and Sunderland, possibly going back to the FA Cup,' he says, acknowledging the twenty-year resentment that dated back to the 1973 final when Revie's heroes found opposing goalkeeper Jim Montgomery in inspired form. 'I remember their chairman got involved. Thankfully! Because it had rattled him.' He grins. 'Fear is a very toxic emotion. We knew how hostile it could be. But once you've dealt with the hostility it can't hurt you.'

He marvels at the stupidity of coaches who dispense 'detailed instructions an hour before a game. Because the last piece of information you're given is the first piece you'll forget. I hear about these managers walking in and telling the team, "We're going to play with a sweeper."' His tone changes to absolutely aghast. '"Boss, what's a ****ing sweeper?"'

Wilkinson's techniques and ideas came together beautifully in the final weeks of 1991/92, by which time he'd started using golfing metaphors, such as 'trust your swing', to encourage his players to keep on doing what they'd been doing. But the title came after a serious jolt. After a goalless draw at West Ham at the end of March – after which Ferguson commented that Leeds were succumbing to nerves (although he had not yet coined his famous 'squeaky bum time' phrase at that point) – came a shock 4–0 defeat at Manchester

City, with just five games left to play and Man U with a game in hand. Even the most optimistic supporter feared the dream was over.

Wilkinson admits his troops were 'walloped, mullered' by City, and says that within fifteen minutes of the start he knew the outcome and was already formulating his response. Eric Cantona – signed in January 1992 to cover for an injured Chapman, but whom he blamed for one of the City goals – would be dropped as he reverted to his tried and trusted first eleven. He told the players to shun the press, knowing that the papers would be crowing that LUFC had blown their title chances, then spent the next day analysing the statistics. Of Leeds' five remaining games, three were at home; Man United had six in the same period. If Leeds won the home games and drew at Liverpool (which they did), Man United would have to go to Anfield and win.

Two decades later, the recollection finally brings a glimpse of the passion beneath the Sergeant exterior: 'We knew there was no way Liverpool would let them ****ing win.'

He was spot on. On 26 April, three hours after Wilkinson's side triumphed at Sheffield United, Liverpool's 2–0 victory at Anfield over their fierce rivals sent the title to West Yorkshire for the first time since 1974.

We will talk more – much more – but I'm intrigued by this strange talk of 'moulding'. Had Wilko really manufactured champions? What's it like to go through such a process? And, not least, what on earth do you do next?

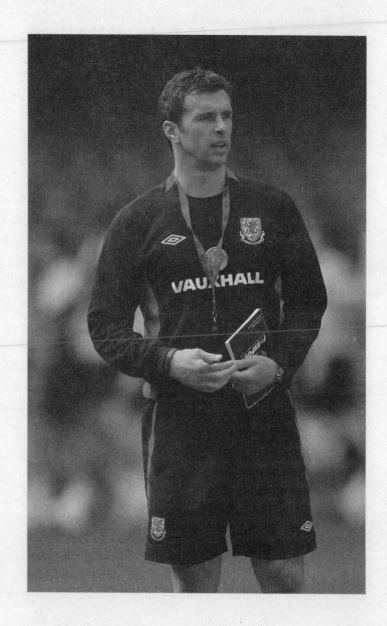

CHAPTER 2

Gary Speed – 'Speedo'

I thought that it would always be like this – that we'd always be that successful. It was only years later, after I'd left Leeds, that I realized the magnitude of what we'd done.

Only two of the championship-winning players were at Leeds before Wilkinson arrived and thus could give me the full lowdown on how he transformed the club. Alas, David Batty has turned into football's Lord Lucan ('You've no chance, mate, we've been trying to get hold of him for years,' sighs a beleaguered LUFC press office), and the other is, well, Gary Andrew Speed.

As I begin my quest in August 2011 – knowing, of course, nothing of the tragic events that lay ahead – it's approaching two decades since this youthful, fresh-faced midfielder drove around Leeds city centre in an open-topped car with 'Batts', celebrating the title. The player we dubbed 'Speedo' for his high-pace rampages from left midfield went on to play for Everton, Newcastle, Bolton and Sheffield United, becoming one of the most highly regarded figures in the game. He held the record for the most Premiership appearances (535, until he was pipped by David James and Ryan Giggs) and became the most-capped outfield player for Wales ever, with eighty-five caps.

Gary Speed is a very busy man who as Wales manager has taken his nation from 117th to 45th in the world rankings, mostly with lower-league international equivalents of Whits and Shutty. He even has an MBE to prop up on the mantelpiece alongside that championship medal. However, as international managers rarely give one-to-ones and Speedo doesn't know me from Adam, I suspect I have as much chance of getting an interview with him as landing an audience with the Queen.

It doesn't happen overnight, but after an email to his agent I hear back that not only is Speedo up for the interview, he would like to do it in person. The next thing I know I'm hurtling to Chester, where he lives with wife Louise and sons, the arrangement being to meet one of the greatest Leeds United players in living memory in a Holiday Inn. He's even provided his personal mobile number in case I get lost along the way.

This, it turns out, is Speedo's style; it's why he has a reputation as one of the nicest, most selfless guys in football. Not for him the minders, paparazzi, image rights, appearance fees and hangers-on of the stereotypical modern football icon. He is a national football manager, yet strolls in unaccompanied and chats for two hours in a public area to someone he's never met before in his life, only the discreet Wales badge on his polo shirt and a fan's request (instantly granted) for a photo of Speed with his son hinting that he's anything other than an ordinary fan whiling away the afternoon talking football. But then, for all his years in the game, this gently spoken model professional from Wilko's football factory is the product of a bygone, more innocent and approachable era, far removed from the glitz, WAGs and Hummers of the modern game, which he concurs has made footballers 'more detached' than in the First Division era that ended in 1992.

'Everything fell into place that year,' he tells me with a smile on his face, considering his happiest time in football. 'The age and character of the squad, the team spirit. At the time, people didn't realize what a phenomenal achievement it was – to get promoted in 89/90 and win the league in 91/92. It just wouldn't happen now. For me, at the age I was then, I thought that it would always be like this – that we'd always be that successful. It was only years later, after I'd left Leeds, that I realized the magnitude of what we'd done.'

He was just twenty-two, a year younger than 'the lunatic called Batty', when LUFC won the title. That year, if you'd asked any male fan which Leeds United player they would most like to be, the chances are it would have been this one. He had everything – there was so much in his game that Fabio Capello once said he was the only British player who would get into his Milan side – and Wilko played him in every position bar goalie. The Sergeant once declared that Speed's only flaw was not realizing how good he was. When he occupied the left-hand slot of the Sergeant's famous midfield, the versatile Welshman was an early example of what managers now call the 'box-to-box' midfielder – full of running, tackling, crossing and always likely to pop up at the far post at a corner or rifle in a goal from twenty-five yards.

But his gifts had not come naturally. Like Kevin Keegan a generation before, he had hauled himself to the top of the game by sheer hard work and effort – qualities Leeds fans particularly admire in their heroes – spending hours on the training field when the other players were tucked up in front of the telly.

While swashbuckling midfielders are often bruisers – think of Lee Bowyer and Roy Keane – Speed was beautiful, nicknamed 'Gorgeous Gary' by female supporters for the darkly romantic film-star looks that saw him modelling for LUFC sponsors Top Man and Burtons. But he wasn't arrogant; he was in fact shy and reflective, even in his early twenties. Yet in the penalty box – especially in the air, where he would risk those handsome features every time he played – he was fearless. He was everywhere, but elusive.

'My dad used to say to me, "Yeah, you're a lot better than I was, but you'll never be as good in the air,"' Speed chuckles. Roger Speed was a part-time factory worker and fireman, but played for Wrexham and Walsall for a while. 'He didn't make the first team, but he was good locally. People say, "I've still got the bruises from your dad!" So I think it is that inbred fearlessness – all you see is the ball. I got clattered a lot – I've had tons of stitches – but none of it matters if you score.'

Speed experienced that unique thrill seven times in

forty-one appearances in the championship season, by which time he'd become one of the most noticeable beneficiaries of Wilko's revolution. Prior to 1988, when he was still playing in the youth team, he used to sit at the back of the stand at Elland Road. 'The crowds were twelve thousand, thirteen thousand. We weren't doing that well, to be honest.' He sighs, boyishly, only his first few grey hairs betraying his forty-two years. 'But when you're a kid you're just glad to be there. Saturday morning, we'd play on Fullerton Park in the Northern Intermediate League and watch the first team in the afternoon. It was the perfect Saturday.'

But suddenly, within three years, the stadium was full to the rafters.

'Some things stick in your mind,' he says, revealing that when Shutty scored the only goal at the far post in an away win at Chelsea in September 1991 Mick Hennigan had announced, 'Right, that's it. We're not going to get out of the top two all season.'

'Everyone said we snatched it from Man United, but we never saw it like that,' Speed insists. 'We won it by four points. We were top before Christmas; then they were, then we were. There's big rivalry there, they were a huge club, and we had just come up. But towards the end we were all playing so well we didn't think about it.'

Typically, he deflects credit to Wilkinson, explaining that his manager was 'amazing' in taking the pressure off the players in the final, crucial weeks but still showing the sort of insight that made him such a promising manager himself. For the fans, the arrival of Eric

Cantona in January 1992 provided goals (three) and Gallic flair, but Speed saw something else. 'Everyone thinks Eric came and won it,' he says, tackling the great myth. 'He didn't, but his charisma galvanized the crowd, which took the pressure off us. All of a sudden the crowd forgot about winning the league, all they bothered about was Eric! It was perfect timing.'

Equally, with four weeks to go, when Man United were breathing down Leeds' necks, Wilko switched training from the old pitch at Fullerton Park, opposite the West Stand, to leafier Adel Cricket Club, a change of scenery designed to deflect creeping tensions. 'I remember him getting us together and saying, "Look, you've achieved more than anyone could ever have imagined. All the pressure is on them. Just go and enjoy it." And we did.'

Most amazingly, Speed reveals that were it not for an eerie twist of fate, he might not have been at Leeds – or even playing professional football.

Five years earlier, when Billy Bremner was manager, Speed hadn't impressed and at the end of the season found himself in a group of 'also rans' who were to be discarded. There was one last game on Fullerton Park against the boys who were being kept on, among them his friend and future Leeds manager Simon Grayson. The game was about to start when Speed glimpsed Bremner in a window at the top of the old façade of Elland Road – which housed the trophy cabinet, as recreated in the *Damned United* film – and dipped into the reservoir of steely determination which perhaps distinguishes a champion. 'I played really well, and at half time he came down and said "You go with them" and put me with the kids who had made it,' he tells me, aware of the significance. 'If I hadn't had a good game, or he hadn't looked out of the window, it could all have been very different.'

Speed grew up in Mancot (pop. three thousand), a tiny football hotbed that produced Ian Rush, Michael Owen, Ryan Shawcross, Danny Collins and Kevin Ratcliffe (whose papers Speed delivered as a boy) within a two-mile radius. Wales captain Ratcliffe and England captain Owen even grew up on the same street. 'It's a tiny place, but there's nothing else to do. Everyone just kicks a ball against a wall.'

When he was just eight he played in the district Under 11s in a side that were Welsh youth champions three years on the trot, but after four years as a school-boy player at Manchester City he was told he wasn't going to make it. He was then scouted by Leeds, signing schoolboy forms when Eddie Gray was manager. He arrived with a tenner in his pocket from his dad, to a reception that hardly suggested he'd become one of the city's favourite adopted sons. 'I remember getting on the bus to go to Elland Road and the fare was ten pence,' he chuckles. 'I said, "That's all I've got." The bus was really full and the driver hammered me – "You sit there!" – while he was gathering up all his change. It was so embarrassing.'

After being kept on by Bremner, he signed up under the Thatcher government's Youth Training Scheme for school-leavers, on the same day in June 1988 as Grayson. For the kid from a Welsh village, being placed in digs in Seacroft felt like moving to New York. 'Burned-out cars everywhere – my mum was afraid to drop me off,' he recalls, laughing. 'But the people were great. Two buses to work every day? I loved it.'

Speed has never been a moaner, but his development was a world away from the experience of many of today's young players, wrapped in cotton wool in club academies. Writing for *LeedsLeedsLeeds* magazine in the 2000s, I interviewed young prospects who were on hundreds of pounds a week and drove sports cars, many of them never getting anywhere near the bench, never mind the first team. Back then, Speed felt 'lucky' to be asked to clean Ian Snodin's and John Sheridan's boots because 'there were other people you wouldn't have wanted to have'. He paints a picture of an unforgiving environment of initiation ceremonies, kangaroo courts and daily 'slaughterings' by senior pros.

'You'd shudder at it now, the things that went on, especially when you're an apprentice. Being made to run around naked. It's funny at the time, but it's bullying really, almost Deepcut. Gary Kelly [who went on to make over five hundred appearances for the club] was one who was homesick. But in a funny sort of way, it makes a man out of you. My mother said that when I came home after six months I was a different person.

'But it was brilliant as a kid, y'know, playing with Billy Bremner.' He smiles at the memories. 'If something wasn't right in training he'd go "Right, give me a bib" and the next thing you knew he was playing in his suit and his shoes with a fag hanging out of his mouth and he'd be the best player on the pitch.'

But suddenly he was gone, and in came Wilkinson. Speed admits that the players knew of the ex-Wednesday boss's reputation as a disciplinarian, but weren't prepared for the full horror of cross-country runs that felt more like marathons. 'The first six months under Howard was horrible, cos he was nasty. Which he had to be, but everyone was really scared.' The militarily strict new gaffer was soon dubbed Sergeant Wilko.

Overnight, players who had been enjoying the glamour associated with playing for Leeds United, without earning it, found themselves fearing for their futures after being bawled out for coasting in training regimes, like something straight out of *It Ain't Half Hot, Mum*. Speed remembers a typical incident when Wilkinson had wanted the ball played at a quick tempo, but it had gone out of play. 'Howard picked the ball up and he's going, "Get a grip! Get a grip!" And just booted Neil Aspin up the arse!' He chuckles. 'If a manager did that nowadays a player would clock him. But everyone was terrified of making a mistake. Looking back, he had to do it. There were a lot of old pros he had to get rid of.'

Mel Sterland would soon replace right-back Aspin. Sheridan, who repaid the boot cleaning by loaning the young Speed and Batty his beloved Escort XR3, was similarly bombed out for what Speed calls a 'couple of stupid things'. Meanwhile, players who didn't fit in or who moaned about being subjected to interval running or fat-free pasta were dubbed 'the leper colony', to be marshalled by the Sergeant's new attack dog, Vincent Jones. In his autobiography *Vinnie*, the Hollywood superstar recalls punching striker Bobby Davison in the face for a perceived slight.

'He just confronted them all and said, "If you've anything to say, say it to my face,"' Speed confirms. 'He was a tough lad, Vinnie, but a team player. I was scared stiff of him, but once you got to know him, he'd do anything for you.' Speed reveals that Jones insisted on cleaning his fellow players' boots, even much later when they were full Welsh internationals. 'His dad had told him, "Son, no matter how much money you have or haven't got, make sure you've got clean shoes." If you ever meet Vinnie, look at his shoes. They'll be sparkling.'

I make a mental note.

Although he roomed with Gordon Strachan, Speed's big mate Batty would end up sleeping on their floor. Batts was hardly a typical Wilkinson disciple. He lived on fish and chips, helped his dad out on the bins in the close season and ran out on the pitch without such trifles as warm-ups or stretches.

'Batts was a one-off,' chuckles Speedo, before revealing how his teammate particularly moaned about the Sergeant's endless tactical meetings. 'In the end Howard just gave him a ball and let him go off booting it around on his own, because otherwise he'd just mess the session up. Batts was a team player. He just didn't like training. He didn't like football! That's why he has walked away from the game now. He was always gonna.'

As a child, Batty had been virtually press-ganged into playing by his fanatical Leeds-supporting father, and when they played together Speed would be bemused to see his teammate staring up into the stand. 'You'd think,

"What's he looking at?" And it'd be his father, having a go at him!' While Mrs Batty supported the team home and away, the midfield terrier eventually took the extreme step of banning his father from the ground. 'If I lived my life like he did, with fish and chips and all that, I'd never have lasted. But only Leeds fans and people who played in the same team knew how good he was.'

By his second year at Leeds, Speed was bigger, stronger and seriously impressing, scoring in thirteen consecutive games for the youth team. 'I'd think, "How does that happen?"' he says, showing the insecurity that Wilkinson felt was his only flaw. 'Did I just get lucky? Suddenly I was getting above people. Corners would come over and I would just run and head them in.'

Although he made the bench under Bremner he didn't play. He made his Leeds debut against Oldham in May 1989, but then didn't feature again for months, only as sub. Then when he played against West Bromwich Albion in February 1990 he fluffed a scoring chance, to the fury of the Sarge. 'He slaughtered me,' Speedo remembers, but with a grin, not a grumble. 'It was so bad that every player came up afterwards and said, "Are you OK? Don't worry about it." It's very difficult to do that to young players now because they've never had it before. They've never even had it at school.'

He insists Wilkinson's hairdryer treatment did the trick. He played again in a 4–2 win over Oxford in March 1990 and points out, 'When I got back in, I stayed in.'

Occasionally, Speed the manager sounds eerily like his mentor, in pointed asides such as 'If you look at kids today, they don't head the ball. They look at it like this . . .' His boyish features scrunch into an expression of unadulterated fear. But he has an intriguing take on what playing under Wilkinson was like, portraying him as an old-fashioned, almost Victorian father figure.

'He's distant,' he ponders. 'There's no love there, but . . . you know he thinks a lot of you. He just doesn't show it often.'

So you want those glimpses?

'Yeah . . . yeah.'

One of Speed's most vivid recollections of the Wilkinson effect is a game he didn't even play in – the televised 4–1 demolition of Aston Villa at Villa Park in the title season. He was nursing a rare ankle injury, but unlike Batts – 'who wouldn't have bothered; he'd have stayed at home' – decided to travel with the team. When Chapman scored from a Strachan back-heel after a corner – something they'd worked on all week – the entire bench jumped up and down. 'And Howard grabbed me,' Speed recalls, revealing that until then, if he was injured, he'd always felt Wilkinson felt that he was no use. 'So that really struck a chord. I realized that even if I wasn't playing, I was part of it. That was the first time I'd felt like that.'

In fact, unusually for a footballer, personal, rather than overtly sporting, recollections dominate Speed's memories, like team bonding nights out with Vinnie, Batts and Chappy in city pizza restaurant La Comida, when Batts didn't have a steady girlfriend and Speed sat quietly in the corner with his future wife, Louise.

On the pitch, he cemented his role in club folklore on 16 April 1990 with a marvellous goal against Sheffield United at home, when Chris Kamara slipped him the ball and he ran the length of Elland Road as the TV commentator uttered the memorable line, 'Go on Gary Speed, get yourself one, son.'

But the player himself doesn't remember much about the Second Division period beyond crumbling stadiums and a young apprentice called Kevin Noteman getting 'dog's abuse' at Millwall in the forgotten Zenith Data Systems Trophy for simply being black. On a brighter note, he does recall playing particularly well – and earning Jones's effusive praise – in a 3–2 win over promotion rivals West Ham, after which he finally overcame his nerves. 'Suddenly I thought, "I can do this."'

He remembers the first game the next season – a division higher, against Everton, his boyhood team – particularly fondly. 'We battered them first half and you're thinking . . . not "This is easy", but that we belonged. The team spirit was so good, we just kicked on.' Speed scored in that 3–2 win, which showed that Leeds were truly back in the big time.

Another vivid memory is the way Wilko suddenly dispensed with Jones, bringing in Gary McAllister from Leicester. 'Massive decision,' admits Speed, perhaps speaking from his own experience in management. 'Vinnie was a terrific lad, and the amount he contributed [to the promotion season] and the club in general was incredible. To then say "That's it" – that takes some balls.'

Of the title season, he deflects attention from the much-heralded midfield by pointing out that the balance of the whole team was perfect, and also gives credit to the squad players who stepped into the breach, like Whits and Shutty. He goes on to reveal an unlikely friendship between Yorkshire lad Batty and Cantona, the philosophical Frenchman whose interests included fine wine, art and the poet Arthur Rimbaud. 'But they had the same outlook on life,' Speed argues. 'They just didn't care. Which is a great way to be, I think,' he adds, momentarily sounding miles away.

There was another eerie curveball. Midway through the title season he got into the only scrape of his playing career, when after a few drinks in La Manga on a mid-season club break he wrapped a Fiat Panda round a lamppost. He confessed all to Mick Hennigan, but the coach didn't tell the Sergeant. Perhaps if he had, Speed would have been bombed out. And perhaps the title would not have been won. 'I didn't even tell the wife,' he admits now. 'But in a way it was the best thing that could have happened. I was twenty-one, twenty-two, and I never even thought about doing anything stupid like that again.' Which doesn't stop him still beating himself up about the incident. 'I'm still really embarrassed about it, to be honest,' he says, and his sensitivity about something so long ago is really quite endearing.

He has happier memories of the run-in. When Leeds lost at Manchester City, the home fans were so gutted that their team had won – because they feared they had just handed Manchester United the title – that they boarded the Leeds bus. 'They came up and said, "Come on, Leeds, win it!"' And then came the turnaround: the 3–0 and 2–0 home wins over Chelsea and Coventry respectively, and there was 'That feeling when you're in the zone. Everything feels right and you feel so fit and quick, it's almost like slow motion. The Coventry game at home was massive. We had to win that game, but it was easy. No disrespect to Coventry, but I knew we were going to win it.'

He remembers the crucial game against Sheffield United at Bramall Lane at the end of April as strange and really windy. The first goal deflected off him, hit Rod Wallace and went in. 'And Mel Rees, bless him, who's dead now [tragically, from cancer, aged just twenty-six], was in goal and I've never hit a ball so sweetly in my life. It was going in and then it's smashed him right in the face! Then Jon Newsome, who's my mate, he's scored . . . and if you look at me on the video I'm going mental, because I'd said to him, "You're gonna score here."'

After the game, Speed went to Newsy's Mum and Dad's to watch Man United's game at Anfield. Meanwhile, miles away, the Liverpool players arrived at the ground with no idea of the Leeds result because there were no televisions on team buses in those days. Much later, Liverpool's Dean Saunders told Speed how their fans had come out of the pubs where they'd been watching Leeds to tell their players 'Go on!' and beat Man United. 'He said he knew then that they were going to win.'

That night, Leeds United Football Club, the Last

Champions of England, got on their mobiles and all met up at the Flying Pizza in Roundhay for impromptu celebrations that went on all week. The open-topped car was Steve Hodge's new Mercedes. Batty stood up in the sunroof and horns beeped around City Square. The players went out every night that week, before turning up for the meaningless celebratory game against Norwich.

Speedo howls with laughter at the memory. 'We're all still the worse for wear, and Howard's come in an hour before kick-off with a crate of champagne!' After the game, which he still can't believe Leeds won, the Norwich keeper came up and asked for his shirt. 'I said, "No, you ****ing can't!"' He still treasures it, he says.

Speed played for Leeds for another four seasons, asking for a transfer after Batty and Strachan had gone and he'd started feeling stale. But he was sad when Wilkinson was sacked soon afterwards and reveals that he'd once asked his manager why he always kept him in the team. 'He said, "You're brilliant in the air, set pieces for and against. You give a hundred per cent, always tackle and work hard. If you didn't have that I'd have dropped you."' The Sarge cited a game at Crystal Palace in 1990/91 when Speed played so poorly he felt like his shoes were on the wrong feet, but scored from a Strachan corner. 'He said that's why he never dropped me.'

All these years later, Speed credits Wilkinson for the league and the academy, but also for shaping him as a player and a person. 'Without that grounding, I wouldn't have been anything in life,' he says – the highest praise a player could possibly give a manager. He also honours Strachan, whose curious diet of seaweed and bananas complemented Wilko's own ideas. 'He was thirty-two, which to me at that time meant an old man, but he was ahead of me every time. So that struck a chord with me very early. I'd think, "When we're back for pre-season, there's no way he's going to be ahead of me." When I was thirty-five, thirty-six, I was still ahead in training. That's why I played as long as I did.'

He hasn't seen Batts for six years, he says, and reveals that football's Lord Lucan doesn't even have a mobile, but he knows that whenever or wherever they meet again, the bond will be the same.

The texts from Louise are piling up so I let him go. Two hours have passed by in a flash. He's been lovely and unusually candid, even admitting to stresses from football management and suggesting fears for Simon Grayson, unless he receives more transfer funds at Leeds. The only awkward moment came when I suddenly found myself blurting out how much we really loved that team, more than any group of players we've had since, and he changed the subject, as if he didn't want to hear it, or perhaps had heard it too many times.

'If you need anything else, you've got my number,' he says as we shake hands and say goodbye. Then he walks out of the hotel and melts into the sunlight.

CHAPTER 3

Marching On Together

You are my sunshine, my only sunshine. You make me happy, when skies are grey.

I never really liked football. As a child, football for me meant being jostled in the playground by older, bigger boys and hoping in vain for a touch of the ball before the whistle went for the end of playtime and saved me from further ritual humiliation. I much preferred the children's game of blow football, the ancient art of putting a straw in your mouth and blowing as hard as you can to propel a small brown plastic ball past a small cardboard goalkeeper and more often than not straight off the kitchen table to be carried off by the dog.

But I did like the colours. Kevin, an older boy who lived next door, had a 1960s Subbuteo set, and I would gaze in fascination at the different strips worn by teams with what seemed highly unusual names, such as Notts County, Alloa and Heart of Midlothian. I didn't even own a football, but around this time started collecting

Panini cards, which depicted players such as Wolves' Derek Dougan and Chelsea's Ron 'Chopper' Harris crouched behind a white ball, looking as if being pictured with the hallowed leather orb was the height of pleasurable activity.

But it was music first for me. My early years were lit up by Ed 'Stewpot' Stewart's *Junior Choice*, songs such as 'Puff the Magic Dragon' and 'Albert and the Lion'; it was *Top of the Pops* rather than *Match of the Day*. As soon as I was old enough – seven – to develop anything resembling taste, my first pop hero was Marc Bolan. I longed to have his flowing black 'corkscrew' hair, which is a bit of a problem when you're tiny with ginger hair and your mum takes you every month to Mr Benson on Commercial Street. My strict instructions for 'just a trim, barely anything off at all' would invariably be followed by my mother's whispered but firm correction, 'Usual short back and sides.'

But somehow I must have decided that football colours could make anyone cool. At least, I think that was the logic by which I persuaded my long-suffering mum to buy me the full Wolverhampton Wanderers home kit with her meagre widow's pension. I didn't really support the team – Dougan aside, I don't think I even knew the players – but was mesmerized by the gold and black, which looked fantastic when your hair was what Mum delicately described as 'auburn, not ginger'. I'd turn up on the local field decked out in gold and black top with the 'WW' badge and its little leaping wolf; I had the tracksuit, the shorts, Gola black and gold boots, and even the sock tags. I was seven years old, kicking a ball felt as alien an activity as landing on the moon, but I had the togs.

Dad died when I was six, and I don't remember him ever expressing any interest in footy at all. Mum certainly didn't, which may be why I'd started life estranged from this male bastion. Before long, Kevin and his family moved about three miles away, and in the early 1970s my mum was ill a lot and I found myself being sent to stay at their house, where that old Subbuteo set had been expanded and competed for attention with the Scalextric. Subbuteo invariably won out. The whole family was football mad.

They all supported Leeds, whom I had watched beat Arsenal in the FA Cup Final in 1972 while mimicking the game on my own Subbuteo set on the living-room carpet. In truth, I paid more attention to the tiny plastic players than the real ones, but I remember a faint buzz of pleasure when 'Sniffer' Clarke scored. But Kevin and his dad, 'Uncle' Harry, gradually indoctrinated me. I'd outgrown the Wolves kit, and it felt like a mark of forthcoming manhood when I went out and purchased a Subbuteo team in Leeds United white.

Every Saturday, rain or shine, Kevin and his dad went to Elland Road, and they started to take me with them. My first league game was versus Arsenal on 5 October 1974, which LUFC won 2–0, and after which I was hooked immediately. I remember Kevin proudly informing me that the three huge diamond-shaped floodlights (so powerful they didn't need a fourth – or they'd run out of money) were the tallest in Europe, and another special buzz when I realized I could actually see them from my bedroom window, which must have been a dozen miles away.

According to the programme, which I now notice my eleven-year-old self embellished in Biro with the words 'Supa Leeds', the team that day should have been Harvey, Reaney, Cherry, Bremner, McQueen, Hunter, Lorimer, Clarke, Jordan, Giles, Madeley. However, it was newcomer Duncan McKenzie – whose party-piece before games was leaping over a Mini Cooper in the West Stand car park – who dispatched the two goals.

Revie had gone to manage England and everything was changing: his fabled side was starting to be rebuilt following Brian Clough's disastrous forty-four-day reign at the club. In my fading programme there's a big white empty box where the manager's name should be, and caretaker manager Syd Owen's programme notes suggest that Clough's reign came to a premature end because of training methods, not because of Revie's arch-rival had begun his ill-fated revolution by telling the players that their trophies had been won by cheating and they should throw them in the bin, and then informed mercurial but injury-plagued Eddie Gray, 'If you were a racehorse, you'd have been shot.' 'Over the years, our players have been accustomed to a special-ized type of training at Elland Road,' wrote Owen, his stern words at odds with the smiling picture of him in a Leeds United tie decorated with the famous LUFC 'Smiley' badge. 'It was a totally different procedure that was introduced by Brian Clough and Jimmy Gordon. The training sessions up until a few weeks ago had what I consider to be a free and easy attitude . . . we have taken steps to revert to the tried and tested formula of the last decade.'

But even as the ink dried on his notes, Owen was handing over the reins to Jimmy Armfield, whose first game was that one against Arsenal and whose attempts to build on Revie's decade of success would take Supa Leeds to the dizzy heights of the 1975 European Cup Final, which I watched them lose 2–0 on a black and white telly in Cameron White's house down the road. We were old enough to realize that the referee seemed determined to make sure Bayern Munich won the game.

Otherwise, in almost every aspect supporting Leeds back then was an incredible feeling, a world away from the often stoical, long-suffering, miserable experience it can be now. The players all had long hair and looked every bit as glamorous – from the back of the old Spion Kop, at least – as the glam rock stars on *Top of the Pops*, and it was much easier to wrap a Leeds scarf round a wrist to be part of it than adopt make-up and glitter and try to look like David Bowie.

LUFC seemed invincible and won every game, certainly all the early ones I went to, and crowds were just enormous. I vividly remember a game on Boxing Day, 1975, when everyone had new LUFC hats and scarves and the 45,139 people crammed into Elland Road that day to see Clarke, Lorimer and McKenzie (two) hammer four past Leicester caused such a hazard that I had to be hauled from the Lowfields Road boys pen into the stand above, almost losing a platform shoe in the process.

It wasn't just the action on the muddy pitch that got me. I was a shy, underdeveloped, possibly even mal-nourished child with barely any family who felt a part of something for the first time in my life. I loved the rit-uals – the walk to the ground from where Uncle Harry parked his VW, and the chatter of excitement among blokes much bigger and more knowledgeable than I was. I loved the way the crowd surged forward and I'd be carried along with my feet literally off the ground. And I cherished that incredible feeling when the Whites scored. Harry and Kevin would leap up and hug each other and me and we'd all sing even louder.

It's the songs I remember as vividly as anything. The Glitter Band's 'Let's Get Together Again' was a regular pre-match Tannoy favourite and I naively assumed that it was actually about Leeds, and that glorious feeling of togetherness and invincibility that every Saturday would bring. In those days, the Kop was bursting to the seams every game and the crowd had a repertoire as big and varied as any pop group. The Gelderd End choir would run through songs every bit as heart-stirring as David Bowie's or Noddy Holder's.

'We hate Nottingham Forest, we hate Liverpool too (and Leicester). We hate Man United, but Leeds United we love you.'

'In the Liverpool slums, in the Liverpool slums. They look in the dustbin for something to eat, they find a dead cat and they think it's a treat. In the Liverpool slums.'

Which even then seemed a bit naughty.

'Marching On Together' ('we're gonna see you win,

na na na na na na'), which began life as the B-side to the 1972 squad's top ten FA Cup single 'Leeds United' ('Lasher Lorimer what a shot, then to tie them in a knot, there's Eddie "The Last Waltz" Gray'), had the best tune.

It fascinated me how different songs were wheeled out for different situations in the game. A corner meant a chant of 'Leeds . . . Leeds . . . Leeds' delivered in a gruff tone, like a giant steam train chugging into life. A goal kick to the opposition would see the goalie's run-up serenaded with an enormous howl of anticipation invariably followed by the kiss-off 'You're shit . . . aah!' as the opponent had been intimidated into kicking it into the stand.

One song that particularly affected me was 'You are my sunshine, my only sunshine. You make me happy, when skies are grey. You'll never know just how much I love you. Please don't take my sunshine away.' It was an anthem of pure love with something desperate about it – a default mode I would become wearily accustomed to supporting LUFC. But back then it signified the position football had in the lives of men (and in those days it was always men) who, whatever their problems, poverty or situation, came together as one every week to celebrate their togetherness and unity behind a common goal.

The teamsheet was changing all the time, and I soon found myself forgetting about Joe Jordan and Gordon McQueen, who caused a Cantona-like uproar when they went to Man United, and instead cheering Tony Currie, who was reputed to enjoy a gin and tonic and could swivel his beer belly in the centre circle and unleash a fifty-yard pass of devastating beauty. And still, when Leeds were truly United, it felt like anything was possible. Like Gary Speed when he won the title, I thought it would always be like this.

But with Leeds United, it never is. Within a couple of years Kevin joined the RAF, I was sent away to school because Mum was so often ill, and when I was in Leeds I found myself going to matches on my own, and the magic was fading. I'd got into punk and was listening to politicized bands such as The Clash and Gang Of Four, which sat awkwardly with the hooliganism surrounding 1970s football, the racist chants at black players and National Front leafletters outside the ground. I made a conscious decision to start going to gigs instead of football matches, walked away from the sunshine and didn't attend another match at Elland Road for the best part of a decade.

When I came back, Howard Wilkinson was starting the revolution, and everything had changed.

CHAPTER 4

Vinnie Jones — 'The Enforcer'

This wasn't Wimbledon, where people tread on you like
fackin' beetles. All of a sudden, when you walk through
the jungle, you're this big fackin' white leopard!

I want to know more about how that process happened,
and after speaking to the Sergeant and Speedo I have
been reminded that someone else played such a massive
part in the Wilko revolution, in building the foundations for the 1991/92 success, that I have to try to
interview him, even though he'd been gone for some
eighteen months when Leeds United won the First
Division. The problem is, that person is Vinnie Jones.

It's over a decade since the former midfield enforcer
was in football. These days, LUFC's 1989/90 number
four isn't even in England, having traded kicking people
in the shins and crowd cult hero status for an altogether
more mind-boggling existence. As the star of nearly fifty
films, beginning with a role as the shotgun-toting
enforcer in Guy Ritchie's 1998 hit *Lock, Stock and Two
Smoking Barrels* and blockbuster follow-up *Snatch*, in

which he played the cuddly Bullet-Tooth Tony, he has traded lining up alongside Micky Whitlow and David Batty for Brad Pitt and Burt Reynolds. In 1990 he was holed up in the Leeds suburb of Shadwell, but these days he resides in Hollywood, where he is almost certainly the only superstar actor with 'Leeds United – Champions Div 2 1989/90' tattooed on an ankle.

Even given the luck I had with Gary Speed, securing an interview with a Hollywood actor seems as likely as landing a part in a Guy Ritchie film. Leeds United haven't been in touch for years. Emails to Los Angeles-based film agents inevitably go unanswered. I'm about to give up when I discover that when not portraying a succession of stern-faced hardmen, he's spent the last four years also managing an LA-based 'soccer' team of actors, ex-pats and porn stars, the Hollywood All Stars. A hopeful email to their website produces a reply within the hour: 'Vinnie would love to talk about Leeds United, would you like to do it over the phone or in person?'

Three days and one swiftly drained bank account later, I'm driving a hire car up Mulholland Drive, the famous long and winding residence of the top stars that gave its name to David Lynch's 2001 film noir and a David Hockney painting, and which seems a long way from Beeston Hill, the long and winding path to Elland Road.

Jones's house is easy to find because it's painted in Leeds United white and has a Union Jack outside. I ring the buzzer and suddenly there he is, every bit as stern and menacing as he was in *Lock, Stock* or the infamous

Wimbledon-era photograph of him grabbing Paul Gascoigne by the testicles. Access to the house means walking past a garage containing two Harley Davidsons, a sports car and a gigantic Range Rover, and I'm suddenly in a white open-plan kitchen where Jones is surrounded by guitars signed by Slash and Bryan Adams. Two tiny chihuahuas yap around that tattooed ankle like two miniature David Battys, and on the wall there's a giant poster for the film that changed his life.

'I'd never have thought of anything like it,' Jones admits about his California lifestyle, welcoming his jet-lagged guest with a refreshing cuppa. 'I was assistant manager at QPR. They liked wot I done. Never looked back.'

Until now. In fact, despite being a much bigger – worldwide – star than he was at Elland Road, and his time there being over twenty years ago, it takes less than a minute to get Jones talking about his life and times at Leeds, which he still regards as one of the crucial and most enjoyable experiences of his forty-six years on the planet.

'It was one of the biggest, best and proudest decisions of my life,' he tells me as we leap into the Range Rover to drive to a Beverly Hills golf course, where the inter-view takes place in searing heat with Jones driving a golf buggy like he's in a car chase, me sunburning by the minute and hanging on for dear life. We join his golf pals with names such as Snowy, Bob the Nob and Mikey, similarly big characters who have no idea that their famous movie pal had a previous 'soccer' life at all.

'He's my best friend, you better give him a good

write-up,' urges a man with a sliver of a moustache which makes him a ringer for Lee Van Cleef in *The Good, The Bad and The Ugly*, drily. 'Because if you come to Vegas, son, you might have problems.'

Yikes.

But becoming a Hollywood superstar isn't the first time Vincent Peter Jones underwent an improbable metamorphosis. In 1986 he was a hod carrier turning out for non-league Wealdstone when Wimbledon's manager Dave 'Harry' Bassett took a £10,000 gamble that he could cut it in league football. Wimbledon – the original Plough Lane club, not today's Milton Keynes-based Frankenstein of a franchise that has been renamed MK Dons – were on an adventure of their own, a whirl-wind rise that took them to the First Division just three years after they were in the Fourth and nine after they joined the Football League for the first time since being formed in 1889. In 1988 they pulled off one of the biggest FA Cup shocks ever, triumphing 1–0 at Wembley over a Liverpool team containing the likes of Ian Rush and managed by Kenny Dalglish, whom Jones delighted in informing before the game that he would 'rip his head off and crap in the hole'.

But the following summer he was disillusioned, fed up with life on £500 a week and under Bassett's successor Bobby Gould, with whom he'd had a 'push-ing match' at Luton. So he told owner Sam Hammam he wanted out. He says that Hammam tried everything to dissuade him – 'You're the heart of this club, when you don't play we struggle'. 'He put the tears on. But it was like that for years at Wimbledon, y' know.' Jones suspects this was half-hearted, and says he later found out Gould wanted rid of him as well.

'So Sam says – I'll never forget it – "Things will happen a lot quicker than you think."' As the Welshman tells it, two clubs were interested in his services: Aston Villa (led by future England manager Graham Taylor, who'd been Jones's schoolboy manager at Watford, but released him) and Leeds. He remembers LUFC managing director Bill Fotherby calling him on his phone. 'That was the days of the car phone, with the lead an' all that,' he says, inimitably. 'The walkabout ones were like fackin' breeze blocks.'

Fotherby – as per his reputation – gave him 'the full nine yards. Charlie big bananas. He was more like a market trader than a chairman.' But Jones had heard enough. 'I've 'ad a few punch-ups an' that but when it comes to money and friendships I'm a very honourable bloke,' he explains, over the roar of the golf buggy. 'Fotherby was first on the phone, so Taylor rings up and I tell him I've already spoken to Leeds.'

So you chose Leeds because they phoned first?

'Simple as that,' he insists, stopping the buggy for a moment. 'Weird twist of fate.' And off we roar again.

One of Wilkinson's bigger early buys at £600,000, Jones knew he'd made the right choice before he even made the ground, stepping off the train to glimpse the newspaper headline 'Jones in Leeds Talks' and thinking, 'Wow, this is massive.' At Elland Road, he was impressed that everyone from general manager Alan Roberts to the tea girls seemed to be pulling in the same direction.

When he arrived, another player was due to sign from West Ham but was dragging his feet. 'Alan Roberts was like, "If you're umming and aahing about coming to Elland Road you can fack off." They were on this massive positive thing. No jolly up: a hundred and ten per cent or nothing. I thought, "If you cut these fackers in half they're going to bleed Leeds United."'

Jones instantly felt likewise, but reveals a funny story: at this point he didn't know who the manager was. 'Fotherby – I love Bill – keeps giving me the spiel, "Howard Wilkinson, Howard Wilkinson,"' he says, before confessing that he confused him initially with the then Everton manager Howard Kendall. 'I said, "Howard Wilkinson? He's at Sheffield Wednesday." "No, he's here now!"' he roars. 'Cos apparently he tried to sign me when he was at Wednesday. He was a big fan, apparently.'

Jones was desperate to sign for Leeds, but even then was a good enough actor to keep a poker face during talks, with Fotherby and board member Peter Ridsdale, in the latter's office at club sponsors Top Man. Agents had started to appear in football, but Jones negotiated for himself. He remembers seeing a bottle of champagne on the table – an early glimpse of the largesse Ridsdale notoriously brought to Premiership-era Leeds United as chairman – and thinking, '"I've got him." I was on £500 a week and asked for two and a half grand, plus a BMW. With side skirts. He never even twitched. I remember thinking, "Fack. I could have doubled it."'

But money was a side issue. Jones had arrived at a

club where he knew he could play a major part in something special. 'All right, Leeds were in the Second Division, but now I could really become someone,' he explains. 'This wasn't Wimbledon, where people tread on you like fackin' beetles. All of a sudden, when you walk through the jungle, you're this big fackin' white leopard! Someone that's respected.

'They told me they wanted to stamp out the racism thing,' he continues, unstoppably. 'One of the first things I did was sing from the rooftops that racism was nowhere in my vocabulary. My best mate [Wimbledon's John Fashanu, aka "Fash the Bash"] is one of the biggest fackin' black players in the league and I'd die for him. So I said, "This is not white or black or Asian Leeds United, but Leeds United, and we need all of you to make this town fantastic."

'On the one hand you had Strachan, who was the gentleman, who'd come from Man United. But Wilko brought the Crazy Gang and the Culture Club together,' he says of the unlikely pairing, paraphrasing John 'Motty' Motson's description of the Liverpool–Wimbledon cup final. 'Because, as Gordon will tell you, I was a leader of men, and he was the leader on the training ground and off the pitch. I became a better player because of Gordon. I became a better person because of Gordon.'

Jones had arrived at Leeds more infamous than famous, one of the most controversial characters in the game after much criticized challenges on Tottenham's Gary Stevens and Everton's Kevin Ratcliffe, and the incident with Gazza, which people now think was a bit of fun. 'It wasn't a bit of fun,' Jones insists. 'The boys had come up to Newcastle and said about this wonderkid that fackin' tore teams apart. So I 'ad a job to do, an' Don Howe will tell you to this day that was one of the best man-marking jobs he'd seen. It was my job to man-mark him out of the ground and I was so fired up I got hold of him.'

However, after a ruckus in a pre-season 'friendly' against Anderlecht, during which Noel Blake was sent off, a severe dressing down from Strachan proved crucial to the way Jones performed at Leeds. 'Strach was like, "What the **** are you doing?" At Wimbledon it was, intimidate them. He was saying that we could intimidate them by playing football. Wimbledon were pressure from the top, snap tackles. At Leeds we had a pattern, pass it to Strachan. In that season I forgot about chopping people. He said, "You're not here to kill people, you're here because we know you're a good player and we know you can pass the ball." I thought, "He's right." My reputation was there on the team sheet. People didn't wanna tackle me, so it gave me the space to play.' Jones received just two bookings all season after Strachan's words with him: 'We've got a lot to do this season and we can't have this childish bull-shit. We've got to be this force to be reckoned with.'

'The bond between us . . . what he [Wilkinson] did was a master thing, but fackin' cruel by any standards,' Jones continues, changing tack. 'I thought, "Fackin' hell, that could be me one day."'

His voice falls to a conspiratorial whisper during the golf shots, as he recalls how Leeds struggled in the

Sergeant's first few months, which led to the establishment of 'the leper colony'. 'Vince Hilaire, Brendan Ormsby, John Sheridan, Mark Aizlewood an' all that. Nice fellas.' He chuckles. 'But we'd done the running and that and he said, "Right you lot, over there. Do what you want." Basically, keep yourselves fit an' that, but they were rejects. None of them really did any good. Shez [Sheridan] went to Sheffield Wednesday, dinne?'

Jones then expands on the incident mentioned earlier, the ruckus with Bobby Davison in the players' lounge on his first day at the club. 'Him and Ian Baird,' he begins, naming what were then the two main strikers at Leeds. 'Bairdy was insecure, couldn't carry the line, he didn't know whether he was going to be involved. It was all starting to get a bit them and us, and one of them made this snidey comment like, "We pass the ball here." And I just flew, gave 'em both a smack. That was that. As I went in I saw fackin' Strachan leg it up to Wilko's office. So I've got all my gear. I'm going back to Wimbledon.'

He remembers how coach Mick Hennigan – a 'man's man', whom he loved – came to see that he was all right. 'Next thing – and this is brilliant captaincy for you – Strach tells me to see Wilko. Mick tells me to calm down. So I'm in Wilko's office going, "Fackin' give it to me, you cant. I'm fackin' off down the M1, deal with it." And he's gone, "I'm disappointed in you. I've just been in there, and there's no blood." That's what he said! I'm like, "What do you mean?" And he said, "Why do you think I brought you to this club? To sort those ****ing wankers out."'

Prior to this, Jones admits that he'd been lonely, running up 'ridiculous' bar bills in the Leeds Hilton and even suggesting to Fash the Bash that he may have made a mistake moving north. 'But from that minute I just went whoooooooosh!' he tells me, perfectly mimicking an aeroplane. 'That incident changed everything for me. That was the first time Wilko had said anything like that to me. I realized I was a major part of this thing.'

Why did the fans take to you like they did?

'I started two weeks early. I was the fittest I've ever been in my life. Then I came down on my ankle and it just went bang. Next thing, I'm in fackin' plaster for pre-season. Anyway, we got smashed at Newcastle [5–2, on the opening day of the season] and I'm sitting on the fackin' bench. But we had a midweek game against Middlesbrough and the pot came off. Wilko said, "How are you?" I was chomping at the fackin' bit. I've come roaring on, the crowd has gone fackin' nuts. I went to fackin' head the ball and missed it completely.' He chuckles. 'But then – and bear in mind I've waited eight weeks for this – I picked the ball up and passed it [towards the Boro goal, where the opposition full-back chipped it back to his keeper]. And I remember it just floated over him. That was the end of the game. I've run up to the Kop. "WAAAAAAAAAAAAAAAAH!" And they took to me right away.' The photograph of Jones up on the old railings – installed to keep the fans off the pitch, not the players off the terraces – is among the most iconic of the era, beautiful in its machismo and savagery.

The Cult of Vinnie had begun. Within weeks, Top Man-sponsored Leeds kits with JONES on the back were all over the city. When David Batty gave him a severe crop, 'the Vinnie' became a haircut advertised in every barber's window. 'Then some kid got thrown out of school for having it, so overnight I became a cult hero.'

He threw himself into the role, warming up with the handicapped supporters to make them feel part of the club, buying tellies for kids in a care home and taking coachloads of mates to games. He even had a show on Radio Aire.

Batty was a first-team regular by the age of twenty, and Jones regarded him as a kindred spirit – one of the toughest players in the league. 'Batts loved causing some bollocks,' he says while taking a pee to the side of the hole we're on. 'He was a tough little bastard.' In a pre-season game against 'Colchester or someone' at the training ground, he and Batts had 'buried everyone' so much that the other players had to calm them down. Off the pitch, they became equally inseparable. Jones went to Batty's house for lunch with his parents even when he wasn't there, helped him buy his first house, and joined in more 'causing bollocks'.

One night, when Jones was 'hammered, with some birds', he spun a car round Batty's lawn, wrecking his new fir trees. Then, knowing he kept a key by the back door, he went and crept in wielding a dustbin lid. 'Batts went fackin' nuts. He had a big fackin' Bowie knife in bed with him.' He's shrieking with laughter. 'I said, "Batts, it's me, it's Vinnie!"'

Unlike today, when most clubs' top players avoid city centres, the pair became faces about town. Jones would think nothing of DJing or getting behind the bar, and the southerner made loads of friends among supporters, including one diehard fan called Alex who became a friend for life when Jones dived off a balcony and landed on him in a bar. Jamaican-born centre-half Blake, who now coaches England's Under 19s, introduced him to the black clubs in the notorious Chapeltown district, and after 'Blakey' joined Stoke City in 1990 Jones was 'the only white geezer in there. I used to take my mates. They were terrified. Big geezer with dreadlocks would go, "Boys, you with Vinnie, you safe in Chapeltown." Because at traffic lights they'd mug you, knives and everything. One night they tried to rob me and someone's like, "It's Vinnie Jones! Sorry, Vin!"'

Another time, he went straight from Chapeltown's Silver Tree club into training. 'Wilko never sussed,' he chuckles, lighting up a fag – another blast of football past. Or if he did, he turned a calculated blind eye.

Away from the club, Jones's and Batty's diet was 'fish and chips and lager. He knew we were young blokes and everything.' He shrugs. 'I was having the time of my life.'

When I spoke to Wilko, he'd praised Jones for being 'as good as gold, apart from a couple of incidents'. One of them was what Jones calls a 'right tear-up' in Mr Craig's, a notorious city-centre nightclub at the time. Jones made the front pages. '"Vinnie Jones in Nightclub Brawl",' he recalls with a sigh. 'Wilko went fackin' ballistic. That was the nearest he came to saying, "Fack this, I'm getting rid of him."' Another occurred on a club trip to Magaluf. Jones and Batty had been leading a beach sing-song with some West Ham fans when an argument started with a bloke about some sunbeds and the next thing the 'steamboats' Jones knew he was being carted off to the police station after telling Batty to 'fack off back so he wouldn't get nicked'. The shame-faced number four was escorted back to the club hotel, his on-the-spot fine paid by Chris Kamara.

'I knew I'd let the boys down,' he sighs, the hard features darkening even more. 'We go to this restaurant and I just felt the lads were down on me, so I jump up, smash the fackin' plate, back to the hotel. Same again, Mick Hennigan comes round. "What are you doing, son?" I knew Sheffield United were sniffing around so I said I was going there. He said, "Well, you might wanna read the paper." It turned out Sheffield United, who'd been in Spain as well, had caused a major ruckus and were all over the front pages. So I stayed. And kept Batts out of it.'

Wilko didn't jettison him because it was working on the field. Unlike so many players who've come to Leeds with big reputations over the years and wilted, when Vincent Peter Jones walked out on to the pressure-cooker pitch at Elland Road he felt 'twenty feet tall, invincible'. 'The goal was to get promotion that year,' he explains. 'Looking back, there must have been enormous pressure, but I didn't feel it.'

A core of players – himself, Mel Sterland and Chris Fairclough – had played at the highest level and could protect emerging players, like Mike Whitlow or Gary

Speed, who Jones correctly informed a newspaper would one day play for Wales. He cites the key moment of the 1989/90 season as Wilko's replacing Baird. He was the 1989 player of the year, in his second spell at Leeds after being brought back by Bremner, but his goalscoring record paled in comparison to his successor, Lee Chapman, a proven success in the division above.

Otherwise, Jones's personal highlights include his goals against Ipswich and Hull, when he hit the sweetest volley and Leeds won 4–3.

And the low point?

'Against Wolves, the game when Batts farted and shit himself, and ran straight off. He changed his shorts in the dressing room. I was woeful. Live on TV, and I was brought off.'

He vividly remembers the crucial final day win at Bournemouth, when Leeds needed three points to be champions and Bournemouth needed a victory to stay up, because at half time he'd been under the impression (wrongly) that close rivals Sheffield United were losing and informed the Leeds dressing room, 'Boys, we've ****ing won it.' 'My biggest embarrassment,' he chuckles, patter giving way to candour. 'I got carried away. Imagine if we hadn't won. Batts was laughing. "You complete knob!"'

That night, while Leeds fans took over the town – unfortunately with some incidents of the hooliganism Wilko was trying to eradicate – Jones remembers hanging out of the hotel window with Batty as it felt like the town was being painted white. At Leeds he'd found the approval and adoration he'd wanted all his life, finally banishing the red mist and 'self-destruct button' he says comes from childhood, when his parents divorced and broke up the family. 'My father leaving was a big thing,' he admits quietly. 'Time heals, but I can't blame them, you know.'

However, no sooner did he finally feel settled than his life was wrenched apart again.

A week before the end of the season, when Gary McAllister, the Second Division's most sought-after midfielder, scored a thirty-five-yard equalizer for Leicester in a 2–1 victory for Leeds at Elland Road, Jones says he had a weird premonition that his LUFC career was over. That summer, with Leeds planning for life in a higher division, rumours started to circulate that McAllister was coming in – and when it happened, Jones found his shirt up with the B team. On 28 August 1990, when Leeds faced Manchester United in the first home game of the new season, he wasn't even on the bench, instead having to fend off people coming up and asking, 'Vin, why aren't you playing?'

'I've never told anyone else this before,' he says, in the near-silence of the golf course. 'But I had to walk out of there in tears. I tried hiding my emotions all the way to the car but I was just fackin' gone.' For all the machismo and bravado, Vinnie Jones is clearly a sensitive soul, and the manner of his rejection hurts him even now – his only complaint against Sergeant Wilko.

'How can you go from playing every single game to not being in the squad? Do you know how fackin' hard it is? That's ruthless. He should have said, "Look, you've done a fantastic job. Whichever club you wanna go to,

I'll help you." I could have handled that. But I felt . . . chastised. I was thinking, "Can someone please explain what is happening to me?"'

He made his last appearance for the club a few days later in a 1–0 loss at Luton, and to this day he wonders if things would have been different had they won. But Wilkinson had chosen to sacrifice his brawn for McAllister's guile, and the player took it like a man. 'I felt like Rocky. One day you're champion. The next you're the geezer spitting in the bucket.'

Having been told an offer had been accepted from Sheffield United, he made what his father told him was the biggest mistake of his football career and signed 'in anger', helping them to stave off relegation but returning to his old ways of chopping opponents and disciplinary problems. By the time Leeds won the league he'd enjoyed a more satisfying time at Chelsea, but later drifted back to Wimbledon and played a handful of games for QPR, before the incidents piled up and he felt finished in every way. 'I got in trouble with the booze and let everybody down,' he says. 'Everyone thought I was a scumbag. Even me.'

At his lowest ebb, he even placed a shotgun in his mouth; then his dog appeared at his feet and snapped him out of it. Shortly after that, Guy Ritchie changed his life.

We're just finishing his round of golf when a text arrives on his mobile. 'A hundred thousand for three days' work? Fack 'em!'

On the drive back, he enjoys pointing out his neighbours' houses. 'There's Jack Nicholson's, Kevin

Spacey's . . .' Quentin Tarantino lives next door. He very kindly invites me for dinner back at the house, his mind still on Elland Road. He reveals that he still follows the results and was in touch with the AWOL Batty by email until just a year ago, then the emails stopped. He shows me the tattoo. 'People ask me if I've still got it,' he scolds. 'A tattoo is for life. Leeds is for life, you know.'

Suddenly, he disappears, and when he comes back he's shaved his head, like the midfield hurricane of 1989/90. And he drops a bombshell.

'Daniel Day Lewis took a year out to become a cobbler,' he announces. 'It was a passion in his life, to make shoes. The only thing I've never achieved is to be a manager. I mean, I'm a manager here and we've won the league three times on the trot, and we started with six players. But very honestly, if Batesy [chairman Ken Bates] called me to manage Leeds, I'd take a year out to do it. I'd get a Dirty Dozen of players that know what it takes to play at a higher level and we'd put the town back where it belongs. The crowd are just waiting for that shot. It would be something I'd have to do.'

I fly back reeling from this revelation – and the realization that I've only interviewed three people and already spent well over a thousand pounds. Meeting a football hero and a film star in the same body must be one of life's unique experiences. Still, financially if nothing else, it's probably just as well that my next interviewee is much closer to home.

CHAPTER 5

John McClelland – 'The Terminator'

Kids ask me, 'Have you got a Ferrari?'

The next stop is Billy's Bar at the back of Elland Road, which honours Leeds United's great Revie-era captain by selling beer and pies.

I'm here to meet John McClelland, who isn't one of the household names of Wilkinson's Last Champions but something of a cult hero who earned the nickname 'Arnie' after the Terminator crop he had at Leeds, despite just twenty-six starts for the club. However, this Arnie is unlikely to be making any movies with Vinnie Jones. Having missed out on the wages explosion of the Premiership era and not found a lucrative post-football career, nowadays he gives tours around the stadium he once graced as a player.

'Kids ask me, "Have you got a Ferrari?" No. "Is your wife six foot two and blonde?" No. Cos they've been brought up on the Premiership and they see these average players . . .' He doesn't finish the sentence. What he does have is something even the most highly paid Premiership-era players might consider priceless: a last ever First Division championship medal.

Signed on the same day in 1989 as Vinnie Jones (and Mel Sterland, Jim Beglin, Mickey Thomas, John Hendrie and Chris O'Donnell, the papers optimistically dubbing them 'the Magnificent Seven'), the fifty-three-times-capped Northern Ireland international outlasted them all. His Leeds United career was a strange mixture of being wrecked by injury but then stepping up to the plate in the crucial months.

In the title season, by which time he was a veteran, McClelland made sixteen starts (and two appearances as sub) across the back four, starting the season at right-back and playing in many of the biggest games. His cool head and experience were crucial in the 1–0 home defeat of Liverpool, the 1–1 draw with Man United at Old Trafford, two draws with Arsenal, the 1–0 away win over Chelsea and the 4–1 televised masterclass at Villa Park.

'I wanted to be perfect and had to accept I wasn't perfect,' he says when considering the way he forced himself into Wilko's plans. Like the Sergeant, McClelland set himself little targets. 'Like, no one should have a shot in the game. Occasionally, someone would hit a forty-yarder and you know deep down they have no right to shoot from there, and if they did it in the next ten games they'd be unlikely to score again. At twenty-three, if you have a bad game people say, "Oh, he had a bad game." At thirty-three, if you have a bad game everyone says you're finished.'

So you were fighting against being written off?

'Yeah. But at thirty-three you know by the law of

averages it's not going to happen again for those ten games. You want perfection but you're also mature enough to realize that nobody is ever perfect.'

Two decades on, he hasn't kept in touch with many of his teammates, but says that when they do bump into each other they reminisce like it were yesterday.

'The "football family" . . .' he says, adopting a term much beloved of Sepp Blatter's FIFA. 'You're very tight-knit while you're there, but it's ruthless too. The manager decides which players he wants to keep, and then it's one in, one out. People ask me if I'm in touch with so-and-so.' McClelland has played in every country in the UK and at every level of the game, which he thinks may be unique. 'You'd have no life left if you kept in touch with all these people,' he chuckles.

His features are softer than when he played, but he's still a giant of a man, a genial Irishman with a lovely Belfast burr, like a big friendly bear. 'Arnie' is perhaps more deep-thinking than the average ex-centre-back and is canny, particularly concerning money, a subject that crops up several times in our conversation. We're not talking the telephone number figures of modern players, but the small victories over chairmen in tougher times, when even a proven international was negotiating deals himself, for lesser sums.

'If you get someone on a free transfer, they still want their value, so they get a big signing-on fee and a lower salary, or someone who wants to leave a club will negotiate down. If someone doesn't want to leave they're stubborn in what they want.' He has an intriguing take on how LUFC lured Strachan, asking why a top player like that would drop down a division. 'A player would say it's about money and the manager would say it's about ambition,' he reasons, eerily echoing Wilkinson's words. 'It is about ambition, but if you undersell yourself and say "I'm looking for a challenge" you'll lose out.' Another chuckle. 'If you're going to a bigger club you're generally happy to accept what they give you. It's a bit of a game, I think.'

When McClelland signed for Leeds, he ruffled feathers and broke convention by being honest enough to say he was moving for the money. He wasn't a mercenary – he was a player who knew his worth and that he should be paid to do a job he was very good at, having fought for it every inch of the way via a route that simply does not exist today.

He grew up in Whiteabbey, outside Belfast, living there until the age of seventeen. 'There wasn't even any professional football in Ireland,' he remembers. 'You just watched *Match of the Day*.' However, a guy called Davey Jarvis thought that kids should play football, so he took them to other districts in his van. 'You've got to realize there were no cars,' explains the Irishman. 'You went just where you walked.'

After playing for other villages, when he was sixteen the manager said he was too good for them and put in a call to say 'This lad's worth a look'. McClelland joined Portadown, playing semi-pro while working in a clothing factory. 'One day the manager [Gibby Mackenzie] wanted to see me after training,' he recalls. 'I thought he was going to leave me out of the team. He said, "I've sold you."'

He pauses to rewind, explaining that his mother had owned a newsagent's and brought up three children, getting up at five a.m. seven days a week. His father had died when he was nine, after which he'd visit friends with alcoholic fathers and the like. 'People would say, "Don't you miss having a father?" Well, no. Why would I? I came from a loving family. But sometimes I do think it improves your focus. I've read a lot of books by sportsmen who've had a similar experience – Bjorn Borg and so on – and that experience has proved crucial.'

Because his mother was very busy and he was the youngest of the three, he was given a football to keep him occupied. At this point, his ambitions were to help his mother in the shop. 'I was very good at maths in my head – the twelve times table.' Another learning experience that would serve him well.

Did the Troubles have an impact?

'Well, my mother was a Catholic and my father was a Protestant, so you soon realize life's hard enough in the first place. I wouldn't say it was that bad, but looking back, every pub had to be owned by either Protestant or Catholic and they all had their windows shut in because there were protection rackets. There was a big bookie who lived opposite in the big grounds and he got blown up. Opened his door and boom. Apparently he'd refused to pay anybody, because it would be used to buy weapons and explosives.'

He pauses again, and is momentarily miles away.

'I'd say it never impacted on me, but you think, "That guy over there got blown up at his door." The community, to control an area, was putting up barricades. You're brought up in it without realizing what you're being brought up with. It's like Palestine and Israel. People say, "Why throw rocks at a tank?" Cos rocks are the only thing they've got to throw. Looking back, I don't know if it . . . balanced me a bit. I was considered the strange fellow because I ran about with a football, where there were all these groups and gangs. I was left alone with the football.'

So it was an escape?

'Yeah. You don't realize you're under pressure. When you're in Cardiff you're walking down the street at two a.m. and hear a car coming and you walk into the bushes. And people say, "Why are you doing that?" I hadn't realized. If a car parks in Northern Ireland and the window rolls down you don't hang about, because you'd be shot. You stayed out of certain areas, but someone could be driving through.'

After Gibby Mackenzie did a deal based on appearances, McClelland was off to Cardiff, playing well enough in the reserves to earn a contract. 'Without [my] realizing, it had all been character building. People say I made it to the top because I was single-minded. But if I hadn't made it, they'd say I never listened to advice. I thought if I do things my way and fail, so be it. But if I do it your way and fail, I'll always be bitter.'

Great logic, but at first it didn't work out, and he found himself back in Ireland.

'Somebody once said to me you can have three hundred games and not learn a thing, or have two hundred and it'll all be valuable experience. I didn't drink or smoke, liked training and could read a game. People like Gascoigne, who are very talented, have never had to work hard to get to the top. They get an injury and think they can drink and just recover. But if you've been released, maybe you can analyse things. So when you get somewhere a second time, you dig deep. No distractions.'

He suddenly bursts out laughing. 'Well, that's my amateur psychology anyway!'

When Cardiff let him go he felt he'd let family and country down. He landed back in the village network with a bump, but got a chance to speak to Bangor City in North Wales and start again.

'I'd become independent without realizing it. My son's eighteen and about to go to university, and he and my daughter say, "You left home at seventeen for another country?" But you paid for lodgings and got on with it. That's why football is a community. We're nomads.'

He paints a picture of football in the 1980s as a clandestine world, where clubs would arrange to meet players by a tap on a shoulder at a railway station. 'It was to keep you down. If someone offered Bangor £10,000 for you, you wouldn't hear about the club that offered £8,000. So you're not going to the place that is best for your career.' It was ruthless and unforgiving. 'You might find yourself isolated by the club that wants to sell you.' He accepts that this is where modern agents have been most helpful, although 'It's gone from the clubs completely dominating the players to the players dominating the clubs. And neither way's right.'

By the old system of nods and barter ('Looking back, with experience, you realize managers used to phone each other: "How much is he on?"'), McClelland's nomadic existence continued when he was uprooted from Bangor to spend three years (1978–81) at Mansfield, on £100 a week, before getting a bit more when he moved to Rangers. He found the sectarianism in Scottish football even more intense than in Northern Ireland, but again kept cool under pressure and didn't let it impact on his life. 'If Rafa Nadal walks into a supermarket with six bodyguards, he'll attract attention. He walks in on his own and nobody bats an eyelid. I didn't drive until I was twenty-seven. I walked everywhere in Glasgow. A couple of people had a pop. I turned around and talked to them quietly, it died. They're all right, really.'

Scottish football was a much bigger deal then than it is now. He played against 'Mister Ferguson's' Aberdeen, a team that included future teammate Gordon Strachan. 'He was just the same. Wiry, always busy, a bit cocky. Not arrogant, cocky! Some people don't get booked – Lineker, Charlton, Bobby Moore. They have that presence. Other people have to have a little pop at you, like Ian Wright or Dennis Wise. He'd pull your hair, yap or whatever. It's more psychology. But if it affects you, he's won.'

When his Rangers contract was ending and he was still on £200 a week, he told them to pay a fairer wage or sell him, so he was put in the footballing deep freeze and didn't play. 'That's where agents can protect you now. Now players say, "OK, I won't try. I'll be a disruptive force on £80,000 a week."' He smiles wryly. A different world.

Ferguson's Aberdeen came in for him, but he says Rangers priced him out of their range, and he ended up at Watford under Graham Taylor and chairman Elton John. He remembers players DJing at nights, and Elton in the dressing room. 'Strange times,' he chuckles. 'Having been captain of Glasgow Rangers and played in a World Cup, there should have been a lot of interest in my capabilities.' He sighs. 'But I was told, "Nobody wants you. You're past the sell-by date." That's the club really putting pressure on.'

After years of such shenanigans, he'd finally had enough, and because Watford were bottom of the First Division and needed him, he'd been able to insert a clause in his contract that said they could only sell him for a certain amount of money, and that he would get a cut. At a make-or-break point in his career, Howard Wilkinson came calling.

McClelland had been on international duty with Northern Ireland when he had a whisper from another player that the Sergeant had enquired. So he phoned him up. At this point Wilkinson had been at Leeds eight months, had stopped the rot, and was starting the process of rebuilding around big characters. McClelland certainly fitted the bill.

'I don't suppose every player rings a manager at the other side of the country and says, "Do you want to sign me?"'

The player had an inkling what life under Wilko would be like when the Sarge said he wasn't signing the

Irishman to play in the first team, but to play for Leeds United. 'He decides whether it would be the first team, second team or youth team,' he says with a smile.

He had a bad time to start with, owing to an ankle problem, which he says was misdiagnosed, and was refused a request to do his own training, so as to ease it. 'They'd bought all these new players, and although it was never really said, they obviously thought if they let me do that then Jim Beglin, Mickey Thomas and all the others would be the same. You succumb because you want to be part of it.'

By the summer of 1989 the team, from veteran goalie Mervyn Day to eager ex-non-leaguer Michael Whitlow, was firing on enthusiasm. 'We didn't carry Whits. He was very quick. You had to hold him back. Vinnie was the same.' He reveals that Jones's duties as talisman seemingly required him to turn up in a different outfit every day. 'Cowboy outfits. The lot. And tracksuits! He had a different colour tracksuit every day!'

Everything was set up for a flying start to the 1989/90 campaign . . . then the Terminator damaged his ankle in the very first game of the season, against Newcastle. 'I was hopeless. Mickey Quinn ran past me.' He winces as he recalls the Toon's rather portly goal machine skipping by. 'The next game Howard dropped me. I said, "Listen, I would drop me!"' He laughs. '"But there's something wrong with my ankle. I'm not that bad!" Then it was diagnosed that I needed operations on both ankles.'

He was out of the game for the next two years,

watching forlornly as Leeds got promoted, grew ever stronger and signed ever more players.

Did you think that was it?

'Not really. Sometimes you can have that self-belief. Having diagnosed what was wrong – not an injury, but a condition . . . But it's stupid, belief, sometimes. You wonder where it comes from.'

Maybe it's the inner strength that makes a champion.

In his third year, Chrises Whyte and Fairclough were the first-choice centre-backs, and now the club had signed prospects Jon Newsome and David Wetherall. 'I was so far down the pecking order it was unbelievable.' However, McClelland spent the summer of 1991 doing the heavy fitness work he'd done at Watford.

Leeds were going to Dublin on a pre-season trip, and the Irishman wasn't going, but then Mel Sterland had a hernia op. 'And suddenly a few injuries cropped up and I was going. But I knew I was there as a dogsbody.'

That summer, Wilkinson had also signed pacy striker Rod Wallace from Southampton and his right-back brother Ray, together – 'the rumour was, to keep Rod happy'. But Ray was having a terrible time 'against Shelbourne or somebody', and suddenly Mick Hennigan looked down the dugout. 'Well, it wasn't even a dug-out. It was the side of the pitch. He said, "Can anybody play right-back?"'

A Belfast voice piped up, 'I can play right-back.'

Hennigan laughed. 'You're six foot two and you want to play right-back?'

'I played left-back and right-back for Rangers in two cup finals,' McClelland tells me. 'I played left-back and right-back for Northern Ireland, and I knew I could play. I'd just come to make up the numbers, but Ray was so bad! "Go on then, play right-back," Hennigan said. And I started the season at right-back.'

It was, like Gary Speed glancing up and seeing Bremner at the window, another weird twist of fate. McClelland compares his situation then to former Leeds centre-back Jonathan Woodgate's in recent years – a good player seemingly permanently crocked. 'But he played fifteen games in two years. I played four games in two years and I was thirty-five!'

Big Mac stayed at right-back, keeping Sterland out of the team, until Chris Fairclough got a bang on the head and he switched to his favoured centre-back position. 'So that's how my career at Leeds took off. Four games in two years and then I get a championship medal. People thought I'd conned the medical. I was feeling that pressure. They felt I'd conned them for the money, and was just seeing out my time. So it was nice to get the medal. People say, "Oh, you could play." I could always play. It was just the condition that wasn't right.

'It's funny how football changes.' He sighs, before noting how his luck then changed again. Away on international duty, he won a couple of sprints but then pulled a muscle in his groin. 'I felt like someone had shot me. Then Jon Newsome got in and I never got back in [apart from the 1–1 draw at Arsenal in March 1992; he was sub during the run-in], but that's football.'

Two decades on, McClelland remembers the bad games as well as the good games, like the 3–3 draw at home against Southampton, which Wilko said at the time was the most disappointing result of his time at the club. Leeds were 3–1 up but their opponents managed to scramble a draw courtesy of an eighteen-year-old Alan Shearer and a last-minute equalizer from Iain Dowie. 'I found it hard against big bustling centre-forwards who didn't read the game,' the big Irishman admits. 'If people are clever, you can be clever. The thing with Dowie and Shearer, they were strong boys and sometimes you're not on top of them and they can give you a little . . .'

He doesn't finish the sentence because a fan arrives to ask for a photo with his boy, and Arnie instantly obliges. When he sits back down, he recalls being in the car when Leeds lost 4–0 at City and the title surge seemed over. 'It was bad, so bad. Howard said, "Whether it's 4–0 or 20–0, it's three points. You've got to refocus." Sometimes it's the games you expect to win that you don't. Southampton was like that. But when you have a slip, you fall back on the tried and tested. You think, "That's our standard, and our standard is very high." You have to have that total belief, which maybe isn't . . . credible! You really shouldn't be playing Liverpool, Man United and Arsenal and expect not to lose. But that's how we thought. We stuck together and we believed it.'

Like Wilkinson, he plays down Cantona's contribution, pointing out that the Frenchman was an inside-forward, whereas Lee Chapman led the line. 'He [Cantona] would do things we wouldn't understand. Howard made a jigsaw, and the only people who were allowed to drift from the jigsaw were Strachan and

McAllister. That's where Leeds have struggled lately,' he observes of the current team. 'You look at defenders and you don't know what they're going to do.' He cites Cantona and Harry Kewell from the Premiership era as players for whom, in his opinion, 'when things aren't going well, goals will go in'.

But in 1991/92, things mostly went like clockwork, which he puts down to Sergeant Wilko's meticulous preparation, and partly to a 'false sort of belief, where nobody did believe it, until it came true'.

But when Leeds won the league, McClelland wasn't even on the bench. He was actually out walking the dog. 'It slaughtered me emotionally,' he admits, all these years on, revealing that he hadn't been able to bear listening to Man United's game at Liverpool on the radio in case United scored in the ninety-sixth minute. 'All your life you'd be thinking, "Why did the referee add on so much time?" We'd have still had the chance to win it in the last game [against Norwich] but . . . you're set up mentally to win the league. That was the standard, so you're mentally ready. I was a top player. I expected to play in cup finals. There's a bit of that arrogance – "I'm not out of place in a top team".'

He reveals that he'd approached Wilkinson during the season and said, 'If you're going to give me a free transfer, tell me, so I can get a club. I don't want to cause trouble. I just want to plan.' 'Can't tell you,' Wilkinson had responded. 'Fine, OK. So when he called me in and said he was giving me a free transfer, I remember saying, "Thanks very much for getting me a championship medal."' He was thirty-six.

Within a week of the victory celebrations, which he attended, but at the back ('You don't feel as proud when you're not in the last team, you feel outside'), he was out of the door, thus avoiding the tumble of 1992/93. 'Howard's biggest mistake,' he says with a grin and a twinkle in his eye. 'He probably doesn't say that. How can a team that's won the league almost get relegated, with all the same personnel? Apart from me!' But he isn't bitter. 'If Howard felt I could do better than Jon Newsome he would have picked me. I didn't take it personally, which may be why I had such a long career.'

After Leeds, McClelland tumbled down the divisions, ending up as player-coach at St Johnstone before a double hernia sent him back to Yorkshire, scene of his great triumph. He played at the very top, won the domestic game's top honour and had twenty-three managers but never made enough money to retire, yet he accepts it's just the way it is. For the last seven years, along with the stadium tours, he has made a living as a postman – surely the only postie in Britain with a League Championship medal.

'Thirty-one hours a week, lugging the bag.' He grins. 'People know. They say, "Aren't you . . . ?" I say, "Yes, I was him once."' And he's proud of that fact. 'We did it. We climbed Everest. We were the last team to do it. Now they buy the league.'

He can't stop any longer – there are tours to do, letters to deliver. I walk away wondering what kind of other football project could possibly bring together an international manager, a Hollywood superstar and a postman. This isn't just a sporting story, it's a human one too.

I feel the need to go back. Right back to the beginning.

English Second Division, 9 October 1988

	P	W	D	L	F	A	Pts
Watford	10	7	1	2	19	9	22
Blackburn Rovers	9	6	2	1	18	9	20
Ipswich Town	9	6	2	1	16	8	20
Manchester City	10	5	2	3	16	13	17
Barnsley	10	4	4	2	13	11	16
Bradford City	10	4	4	2	11	9	16
Portsmouth	10	4	3	3	18	15	15
Swindon Town	9	3	5	1	14	10	14
Plymouth Argyle	9	4	2	3	14	12	14
Chelsea	10	3	4	3	12	11	13
Oxford United	10	3	4	3	14	14	13
Hull City	10	3	4	3	12	12	13
Leicester City	10	3	4	3	12	14	13
Oldham Athletic	10	3	3	4	20	17	12
Bournemouth	9	3	3	3	8	9	12
Walsall	9	2	5	2	12	8	11
Crystal Palace	9	2	5	2	14	12	11
West Bromwich Albion	10	2	5	3	9	9	11
Stoke City	10	2	5	3	9	13	11
Sunderland	9	2	4	3	9	12	10
LEEDS UNITED	9	1	3	5	6	13	6
Birmingham City	9	2	0	7	9	24	6
Shrewsbury Town	9	0	4	5	6	17	4
Brighton and Hove Albion	9	1	0	8	7	17	3

AVANTI!

Issue Two   £1

Don't these times fill your eyes...

THE STONE ROSES
The best band on the planet

MOE TUCKER · MUDHONEY
THE BAND OF HOLY JOY
my bloody valentine·dinosaur

THE EDSEL AUCTIONEER   BAZOOKA JOE
plus LIVE - The Stone Roses, Spacemen 3, Birdland and more
ALBUMS - vinyl finals - the year so far

CHAPTER 6

The Only Way Is Up

What *was* it like in the Wilko era?

When I think back, it felt like a time of tremendous positivity. The eighties had been tough for a lot of us, certainly in Leeds and around the north. The Margaret Thatcher era had made millionaires but left millions on the dole, much like how it is today. I graduated in 1984, Mum died soon afterwards and, alone in the house with a puppy, I found it difficult to start a meaningful career, drifting through temporary jobs, and into part-time courses and periods of unemployment. The miners' strike had left deep wounds on the Yorkshire landscape. My uncle was a pit deputy, and hated the divisions that had torn his fellow workers apart and left friendships, families, marriages and once proudly united communities in pieces, and pits facing closure. But as the nineties drew closer there seemed to be a new mood of hope to coincide with the new decade.

Strangely enough, everything seemed to change in 1988, the year Wilkinson joined Leeds. I was finally following my passion and getting regular work as a music journalist. The following year I met the girl with whom I'd spend the next seventeen years and who accompanied me on the 1992 title parade. And in a wider sense, Britain seemed to be in a state of economic and cultural metamorphosis. The onset of acid house was the start of our own Cultural Revolution, as clubs suddenly filled with ravers and smiley badges, and white kids learned to dance and denied they'd ever been into Rick Astley or Simple Minds. Out went shoulder pads and blow-dries and in came flares and floppy bowl-cuts.

On 8 May 1989 I was absolutely blown away by a barely known band called the Stone Roses at Leeds Warehouse and put them on the cover of my *Avanti!* fanzine, which just didn't stop selling. The Roses, Happy Mondays and Inspiral Carpets led a musical sea change that made rock's old guard seem outmoded as effectively as punk had done a generation previously. The following year Thatcher was deposed as Prime Minister, which felt symbolic of the new mood. The records that captured the zeitgeist – Yazz's 'The Only Way Is Up', New Order's 'Technique', Soul II Soul's 'Keep On Moving' and their album '1990: A New Decade', the Shamen's 'Move Any Mountain' and the Mondays' '24-Hour Party People' – were bursting with energy and optimism.

The city of Leeds was being transformed too, as a sudden influx of money brought a wave of construction, from offices to new waterfront developments to reams of often independently owned shops and bars, chic restaurants and shimmering warehouse conversions.

The Leeds of the mid-eighties that I remembered was a grey, intimidating landscape of crumbling buildings, boarded-up shops and Saturday-night violence; suddenly it had turned into an environment where you wanted to go out and eat, go out and dance, go out and celebrate something, anything.

If you wanted to rebuild a football club, you could not have picked a better time.

CHAPTER 7

Leslie Silver – 'The Chair'

There's nobody like Howard. For me, he's better than
Ferguson.

Two decades later, I'm standing outside electric gates in
one of Leeds' leafier suburbs, the entrance to a large
complex of luxury flats.

'Is that you, Dave?' comes a voice over the intercom.
'Where are you? Are you at the gate?'

Moments later I'm met by a gentleman with silver
hair who explains that he's come down because there's
a problem with the lift. This is Leslie Silver, the former
paint magnate and millionaire socialist Leeds fan who
funded Wilkinson's dream.

Now a clearly fairly sprightly eighty-seven years old,
he leads me into a large office with deep-pile carpets
and mementoes of a life well lived. Wooden bookshelves house wartime volumes, the Crossman diaries, a
biography of Karl Marx and books about football. An
award for sixty years' service to the State of Israel sits
alongside a picture of him receiving his OBE from the

Queen. But the walls most capture my imagination: on them hang framed photograph after framed photograph from the title-winning season. There's Strachan with the trophy, and Strachan with directors Silver, Bill Fotherby and Peter Gilman on the pitch at Elland Road. Dotted around are lots of images of Howard Wilkinson – at the Silvers' old house in Scarcroft, wearing a bow tie, and holding up the First Division trophy.

The room is a shrine to everything they achieved.

'I remember it like it was yesterday,' beams Silver, taking his seat behind a desk cluttered with books and papers. 'Sheila [his wife] had just had major surgery. We were at home and Gordon Strachan came round with his wife, a bottle of champagne, and the league trophy.'

He pours us both a whisky. (Later, when Sheila comes back from the hairdressers, he'll suddenly exclaim, 'Quick! Hide the glasses!') I warm to him immediately.

'I'll tell you something,' he continues, leaning forward conspiratorially. 'I'd give a lot to see Howard Wilkinson at Elland Road today. He might not win the championship every week, but I tell you what, he'd make a difference. There's nobody like Howard. For me, he's better than Ferguson. He rebuilt the charisma of Leeds United from a disillusioned point. He built that team from nothing, using the right players at the right time, and in the right manner. And they were a great team then, and Don Revie had a great team before that. But how the hell we're going to get one again I don't know. I still go to games. Not away games. I'm nearly ninety, but I still love football. But it's a different game now.'

His rosy memories and obvious enduring passion

seem a world away from the corporate conglomerates that run football now. But then, Silver's dream was fired a very long time ago – before the Second World War, when the London-born future Leeds United chairman watched Arsenal play in front of crowds of over seventy thousand.

'My uncle took me to my first game at Highbury in 1935/36. I remember Ted Drake, Ted Baxton, Eddie Hackworth.' Arsenal had just won three consecutive league titles, but that 1935/36 side, despite winning the FA Cup, finished sixth in the division Silver would one day help Wilkinson to conquer. 'From that moment, I just fell in love with football.'

Two years later, Silver saw Arsenal win the League Championship for the fifth time in eight years as their manager George Allison carried on the work of the legendary Herbert Chapman – a title-winner in 1930/31 and 1932/33, but who had died midway through another championship-winning season in 1933/34. Ironically, Chapman had managed the old Leeds City before they were disbanded in 1919 amid an illegal payments controversy, after which the Elland Road stadium was taken over by a new club, Leeds United.

In a sense, the story of Wilkinson's triumph begins in 1940, when the fifteen-year-old Silver first arrived in the city.

He'd left school at fourteen in 1939 and was working in a paint factory where his father was a junior manager, but it was bombed out so the Silvers headed north for what they believed would be a short stay. 'We thought the war would be over in six months,' he chuckles. He got a job in one of Leeds' many clothing factories but soon joined the air force to escape it. At seventeen he was told he wasn't educated enough (having failed his eleven-plus exam) to be a pilot or a navigator so he trained as a flight engineer and spent four years in Bomber Command.

'Funnily enough, I was just reading an article in the *Independent* about a woman who's just died. She was dropped into France as a spy. And we were the squadron that dropped her!' He was involved in over forty spy-drops, plus bombing missions in Japan and Sumatra. 'I was lucky to survive that,' he admits.

'As the war was coming to an end my girlfriend wrote to me asking my intentions. If I wanted to marry her she would, and if I didn't, someone else would marry her. See, it was a different generation. In those days, we lived with our parents. Nowadays, people go to university. I thought, "Christ. I've been through a war for four years. I can't go back to my parents. I'd better go back and marry her."'

He nods towards a photo. 'That's us with the Queen there. We had a very good marriage, three lovely children, grandchildren and great-grandchildren. She gave us a good life. Unfortunately she had a bad heart. She died in 1982. I married my present wife in 1984, and her husband had died three or four years before. They were good friends of the Revies. My business had been pretty successful, so I was invited by [chairman] Manny Cussins to join the board of Leeds United.' A sip of whisky. 'I said, "What's it going to cost me?" He said it wouldn't cost me anything. Biggest bloody lie he ever told!' Silver erupts in laughter. 'It cost me £200,000 almost immediately.'

But he didn't baulk. He explains that his interest in Leeds United actually began just after he came back from the war, when he started going to matches at Elland Road and saw one of the greatest players in Leeds United's history make his debut. It was 19 April 1949, and he was at a pre-season friendly against Queen of the South.

'Do you remember Tom Holley?' he asks.

I don't, of course.

'He was a centre-half for Leeds, one of those players who'd kick the ball up the field. He was sick, and they brought a young lad in called John Charles. I said to someone, "Who is he?" A seventeen-year-old kid from Wales. What does he know?'

The opposing centre-forward that day was Billy Houliston, the Scotland striker who just days earlier had run England ragged in a 3–1 win at Wembley, but Charles marked him out of the game.

'I'd never seen anything like it. We were mesmerized. Tom Holley never kicked another ball for Leeds. John Charles became the centre-half and he was magic. A lovely guy. The Gentle Giant.'

Charles, of course, now enjoys legendary status. Regarded as the greatest Welsh all-rounder ever (he could play at centre-half or centre-forward), he was never booked in his entire career, made over three hundred appearances in two spells at Leeds (scoring 153 league goals), and in between joined Juventus for £65,000, doubling the British transfer record at the time.

'He was a great, great man,' Silver says with a smile. 'But the Revie era was a greater period, and that's what we wanted to bring back, with Howard.'

Silver's admittance to the Leeds United boardroom – only a year later, in 1983, he was made chairman – coincided with the failed experiment with Revie-era players as managers. 'Allan Clarke was there when I joined. It didn't work out. We were relegated. We're still very friendly with Allan.' When Eddie Gray and Billy Bremner also failed to get the club back in the First Division, the board were getting desperate. 'I was getting the full boos from the crowd, the works,' Silver recalls, although he can't – or prefers not to – remember stories of bricks flying through the boardroom window.

According to Silver, it was a director called Jack Marjason – a name I remember from my very first programme – who brought up Wilkinson's name.

'Howard Wilkinson? He's the manager of Sheffield Wednesday, and he's third or fourth in the First Division,' Silver remembers saying. 'Why the hell would he come to Leeds?'

Marjason had heard a whisper that Wilko and his chairman weren't getting on, so Silver phoned his Wednesday counterpart ('There was honour between chairmen') and was granted permission to speak to the potential manager.

'We met at my office in Birstall. I'll never forget – I had a new bottle of Scotch. That's why I offered you a whisky.' He smiles, and it's a lovely gesture. 'He said he was interested. I said, "What do you know about my team?" And he went through every bloody player, man and boy, strengths and weaknesses. It was unbelievable. I said, "Have you been angling for this job?" He said, "Mr Silver, you're a paint man. You know the paint trade. I'm a football man."'

According to Silver, Wilko then told him there were two ways to get out of the Second Division: the quick way or the slow way.

'I said, "It's driving me crazy! The quick way!" He told me it would cost half a million pounds. I said, "You've got it." And from that day on, it was a pleasure being a chairman of a football club. Howard was an amazing man, and we made a great team.' He smiles again, adding that he always tried to work well with the people around him, in football and in paint. This was something he carried with him from the war.

'Those are the guys I flew with,' he says, pointing at a photo of a dozen or so grinning airmen, all in uniform, in front of a giant aeroplane, which looks familiar from my childhood Airfix kits. 'That's a Halifax. In the Far East we flew Liberators. You live the life, day by day.' He shrugs. 'I came home from the Far East and my father would ask, "How many shifts have you done?" I was on special duties, and you had to do so many hours.'

As he flicks through an old logbook I tell him my father was on the opposite end of the guns, manning anti-aircraft weapons in the Blitz.

'Two hundred and fifty operational hours,' Silver says, finding the reference, but noting that the strain wasn't on the airmen but their parents. 'Imagine your father being in the war flying planes, and we didn't have television then. So your parents would put on the radio, and they'd say, "Fifteen hundred planes went out, five failed to return." For each crew that's eight people, so there's tens of thousands of mothers and fathers, all waiting.'

I feel a lump form in my throat. My own father never properly recovered from a shell which exploded near him, and after years of illness finally expired in 1969. My mother, who followed in 1984, never got over it and hardly ever spoke about the war, apart from sad little tales like how her mother's favourite pig – so friendly it used to come into the house – had to be killed because of shortages, and how my grandmother refused to eat her share because she'd been too upset.

In 1991/92, Silver was a distant presence, a man whose silver hair I glimpsed from several hundred yards away, and who was hardly ever in the papers. I had no idea the chairman of my football club had such a fascinating history.

'We chased the birds and had a good time,' he continues. 'We got shot at a few times, and a guy got killed on one occasion. It was a direct hit. Fortunately it didn't explode. But it killed a mate of mine.' His voice is faltering. It's almost seventy years later, and he is still visibly emotional.

'It makes you realize what it's all about,' he says. Thus, as he neared the end of his working life, he wanted to do something more, something that would give pleasure to thousands of local people.

After being demobbed in 1947, an uncle who ran a paint factory asked him what he planned to do. 'I said

I'd get a job as a salesman. He said, "How about paint? We make the stuff, you can flog it for us." So he did, manufacturing his own cellulose thinners, then domestic paint, from a little warehouse off Woodhouse Lane, in Upper North Street.

Setting up as the Silver Paint & Lacquer Company, he moved to larger premises in Batley in 1963, and then to Birstall, by which time the company had been renamed Kalon and had taken over Leyland Paints, the name the company goes by today. He remembers how he was on a business trip in Africa – a big export market for them, along with the Middle East – when he realized just how famous Revie had made Leeds. 'My agent said we were going to meet this guy. Charlie drove us up to this most beautiful place. Most traders in Africa, it's all on show. The business is about four times the size of this room, and it's all stacked up. Sun beating down. Charlie said, "I'd like you to meet the chairman of the company." The trader says, "Where are you from?" I said Batley, near Leeds. "Leeds?" he said. "Leeds United!" This is the middle of nowhere in Africa. "Don Revie!"'

We laugh. I want to know how well he knew The Don.

'I didn't know him. I was a fan. But after I met Sheila, we were in a restaurant and she said, "I want you to meet Don Revie." He took my particulars and said, "I wanted to meet you. I just want you to know that the man you're following [Manny Cussins, the chairman in the Glory Years], you're stepping into very important shoes." I thought, "Bloody hell!" But he was a very nice guy. He died tragically young. He was only sixty-one.'

Was it difficult for you when Howard took down the photos?

'I think there's a rule in football that when it comes to the playing area, you respect the manager's decision,' he replies, and I can see why he worked so well with Sergeant Wilko. 'I was absolutely amazed, but what he was trying to do was think about today, not yesterday, and he was a hundred per cent right.'

Silver is adamant. Although they operated in different eras, their different achievements in different circumstances put Revie and Wilkinson on the same level. 'Different styles too,' he concedes. 'Revie did it with love. Howard was a disciplinarian. He did it with quality, experience. According to what I hear, every member of Revie's squad was part of his family. With Howard, they were his team. That's the difference. But he would get involved with the families. He did look after them.'

Manager and chairman mostly sang from the same hymn sheet. Silver says they did disagree occasionally but never argued, offering one example from when they were rebuilding the ground. 'With all respect to Howard, Leeds were employing contractors to put buildings up. One rule of building is you stick to the price.' For the first time he is speaking like a businessman. 'You don't waver when they say, "Would you like me to put a toilet in?" Howard said, "Why not?" I said, "You don't change a contract."'

The builder at the time was Peter Gilman, the lower-profile third party in the LUFC boardroom triumvirate of power with Silver and Bill Fotherby. 'He built the

East Stand, soon after I became chairman. His price was £6 million. It takes in sixteen thousand, and we built some boxes on it for half a million. Arsenal's cost £16 million. Very strange. So we'd discuss these things with Howard.'

He chuckles at Wilkinson's reference to 'posh Yorkshiremen', but both Cussins and Silver hailed from the city's then huge Jewish community, a massive part of Leeds United for some years. 'It was very localized,' he says, remembering a world very different from football's often multinational power structures now. 'When I came to Leeds there were twenty-five thousand Jews in Chapeltown. Now there are about six thousand. They've dispersed. My daughter married an African boy and lives in Africa. None of my children live in Leeds.' He accepts the changes. 'There's a lot of inter-marriage, as you'd expect in this day and age.' Back then, communities were more separate, but he didn't experience much anti-Semitism. 'I had one incident in my commercial life with a company in Bradford who said they wouldn't deal with us because we were a Jewish company,' he reveals. Perhaps the Jewish community's involvement with the football club helped break down some of those barriers. 'The community supported the club, advertised in the programme. It was part of Leeds, part of Leeds United.'

Pulling everyone together, the board also built the banqueting suite on the West Stand, brought in shirt sponsorship for the first time, and worked on Wilkinson's blueprint for a youth academy. They'd already got a friendly neighbourhood landlady to look after young players like Gary Speed, but Fotherby wanted to sell his house so the club bought it – 'facing the big playing field at Roundhay Park, so we had the academy there for a couple of years'. Then money was poured into the high-tech training complex at Thorp Arch, which Leeds still use today.

'In my time you were a director because you were a fan,' Silver explains. 'You never drew a salary, or expenses. If I went to London on behalf of Leeds United, the paint company would pay the bill.' In the pre-Premiership era, few clubs, even the top ones, were wealthy institutions. 'Most are in debt now, but in my day most were family run. I didn't know a chairman who drew a salary. The first director we had who drew a salary was Bill Fotherby, because he'd lost his business and was football mad. He was provincial but ran the world. He knew it all. He came to me one day and we gave him a job as commercial director. A nominal salary, but he got a commission on business and did a very good job.' He's chuckling again. 'He was crazy, Bill!'

His name is on my list.

Silver goes on to tell me how selling the paint firm meant he could put up security for the bank. 'They didn't trust the football club. But as long as I signed they were happy.'

If things hadn't worked, could you have lost everything?

'No, no, it wasn't that bad,' he insists. But it was his name – and his house – underwriting everything. 'I had to either give security or give money. I traded my company in 1982 and held the majority of shares until

1991. If you're sitting there with a company making £10 million a year the bank will trust you. It was more short term in those days. If you wanted a player you put the money up.'

Early on, Wilkinson wheeled and dealed, shipping out players (the most expensive being Sheridan, for £650,000) for a combined £1.5m and spending more than double that bringing others in – a spree rewarded by £820,000 in season ticket sales in the Second Division and returning crowds. Strachan, one of Silver's first investments, was 'the key player. No question about it. He came to us as a successful player, and his personality came through.'

He can recall the day almost three years after that when Wilkinson, whom he regards as a 'fantastic guy to work with, very logical, very sensible', came to him and said, '"There's this guy. Sheffield Wednesday had him on trial, but he's a good player, doesn't want to play trial matches." So we bought Cantona. He was the catalyst.' It's a controversial view. But few would argue that Cantona was, certainly in his first few months, 'a special player'.

Silver remains astonished at the speed of the ascent after Wilkinson arrived. 'I'd been chairman for ten years. I couldn't believe it. I remember going to Rochdale and Oldham, then suddenly it was Liverpool and Man United.'

On the victory parade after Leeds won the league, he remembers Wilkinson telling him, 'You should be at the front.'

'I said, "No, Howard. You should be at the front."'

But within months, the changes started. Sky kicked

off football's financial revolution, and suddenly, almost overnight, the old-school, locally based chairmen were trying to compete in a different world, of high finance, PLCs and astronomically high wages. 'After Sky television started, the first game payoff was half a million quid. It changed football. My predecessor Manny Cussins said, "One word of advice. No footballer in the world is worth £300 a week." Within two years [of the Premiership starting] we were paying £20,000 a week. That didn't work, so we got rid of him. But our initial offer to Howard had been £40,000 a year.'

Forty grand for the man who transformed a struggling club into the Last Champions? The deal securing Wilkinson may have been the best deal of them all.

'But as the wages went up, everyone was on much more. We couldn't expect Howard to manage a player on £2 million a year. I was managing director of a company making £10 million a year when I retired. I got a good dividend, but my salary was £100,000. It was a different world. Another drop?'

He remains bewildered why Wilkinson never got another big job after Leeds, and wonders what would have happened if he'd seen through his ten-year plan, but recalls a poignant conversation. 'He said, "We're bringing on some good lads here, but I won't be here to see them." I said, "What do you mean? We're a team." He said, "No one stays in these jobs more than eight years." Ferguson and Wenger disproved that theory, but basically, he was right.' To the year. But that's another story.

We're getting stuck into the Scotch when a bell rings.

It's Sheila, returning from the hairdressers, so Silver goes down to collect her, leaving me gazing fondly at his photos, then a cry echoes down the hall: 'Where is that young man?' His wife, another great, colourful character, makes us all a cup of tea while Silver disposes of the whisky glasses as skilfully as Cantona. We talk long into the afternoon before I leave him in the shrine, mulling over what are clearly very treasured memories.

One of his favourite stories concerns John Charles, whom he finally got to honour when he hosted a dinner at Leeds Metropolitan University. He'd approached the Gentle Giant to tell him, 'John, you changed the world for Leeds,' and the big Welshman replied, 'Mr Silver, I nearly never came.' It turned out that when the scout came to his mother in Swansea and said, 'I'd like to take John to Leeds, we'll look after him', she said, 'John can't go to Leeds. He's a Welsh boy. John hasn't got a passport – he can't leave Wales!'

Silver shrieked with laughter when he told me this, but his most treasured recollections are from Wilko's golden year. He revealed that when some friends recently came round to watch the 2011 Charity Shield, Man City v. Man United, it brought back fantastic memories of his single most enjoyable day in football, when newly crowned champions Leeds and FA Cup winners Liverpool contested the same competition on 9 August 1992, with Cantona in his pomp. 'David Moores was my opposite number at Liverpool. We won 4–3, and Cantona scored the most beautiful hat-trick. It was a magnificent game of football.'

After the final whistle, they walked out together on

to the balcony at Wembley. 'And Leeds and Liverpool fans were walking up Wembley Way, virtually with their arms around each other, because they both admired each other's teams. It was fantastic. I said, "David, this is what football's all about."'

CHAPTER 8

Chris Kamara – 'Kammy'

I was bombing forward trying to get a goal, and he's shouted, 'Sit in midfield! If you don't I'm going to take you off!'

I'm driving up and down a very long road in Wakefield, trying to find Chris Kamara's house, a converted old farm. Alas, there are several farm buildings on the same road and none of them seem to have names. At the first I'm met by a pack of very loud barking dogs; the second is a huge barn containing nothing but manure. The satnav hasn't a clue where the place is, and I can't get a signal on the mobile. I meet a woman delivering the post, but, typically, she has only been in the job two weeks and still hasn't quite mastered where the house is. 'It's down one of those tracks,' she tells me, pointing over the road, 'but I'm not sure which one.'

After thirty minutes of this wild-goose chase I'm about to give up when a middle-aged couple behind some patio doors spy me looking confused and I tell them what I'm doing. 'Ah, that's Chris's house over there,' says the man, helpfully, gesturing towards a white building behind some houses, which I then can't seem to find by car. I'm just about to start clambering over the fields when a familiar face appears in front of me.

'Are you looking for me?' he asks.

This must be the first time in his entire career that Chris Kamara has been low profile or anonymous.

'Kammy' is, of course, one of the most well-known and busiest figures in the game. I got in touch with him as one of his 415,069 (and rising) followers on Twitter, which leads to the official website www.chriskamara.com, home of the 'Sky Sports presenter, analyst, Saturday-morning entertainer and serial tweeter Chris "Unbelievable Jeff" "Kammy" "Must Have Missed That" Kamara'. Phew.

Barely off the Sky screens as *Soccer Saturday* reporter on Premier League matches and presenter of the self-explanatory *Goals on Sunday*, his inimitable, much-loved style is a million miles away from the typical sit-on-the-fence football analyst. Kamara's catchphrase, 'Unbelievable, Jeff!' (to *Soccer Saturday* host Jeff Stelling), inspired the title of Kammy's inevitably hectic autobiography, *Mr Unbelievable*, and its subtitle, 'Fighting like beavers on the front line of football', is taken from a barmy on-air description of a match between Tottenham and Arsenal. His comical on-air gaffes have become a YouTube phenomenon, especially the time the studio went to him live at a game between Portsmouth and Blackburn and he failed to realize that a player had just been sent off.

If this weren't enough to pack his fifty-four years – he looks ten years younger than he is – he played for nine clubs, making 641 league appearances and scoring seventy-one goals, managed Stoke, and took Bradford City out of Division Two.

Pinning him down for an interview isn't easy. I'm grateful he's taken the time out; he's probably glad of the chance for a sit down.

After Kammy makes the tea, we remove to an adjoining building which contains beautifully framed kits from his time at Leeds United between 1990 and 1992, a time that will always be remembered for his cross to Chapman for the goal at Bournemouth which sealed promotion – one of the most important assists in Leeds United's near hundred-year history.

He'd arrived at Elland Road just four months earlier, after the kind of madcap sequence of events that sounds more like an outtake from one of his TV programmes than the foundation of a league title. He'd been turning out for Second Division Stoke City when on 19 December 1989 they hosted Leeds in the Zenith Data Systems Cup. Mick Hennigan approached him after the game (which Leeds won 5–4 on penalties after a 2–2 draw) and asked if he fancied it 'at our place'. Kammy thought it was a wind-up, but shortly afterwards was telephoned by Wilko's journo pal David Walker, who told him that Leeds had been trying to sign him but were being rebuffed by Stoke manager Alan Ball, whom Kamara suggests liked neither Wilkinson nor Leeds. 'I don't think he liked Howard's style of play,' he says, referring to the England World Cup winner's preference for a silky passing game. 'There was a problem [too] when he first left Blackpool. Revie had spoken to him about signing and ended up getting Johnny Giles, I think.' It's been widely reported that Revie monitored Ball's progress as early as when he was a teenager in Blackpool's reserves, although it was Ball who refused Revie's advances – opting for Everton – when the Leeds boss tried to sign him in 1965, to play alongside Giles. The relationship between the two would not have been helped by Revie, as England manager a decade later, making Ball captain for six games before abruptly ending his international career.

Leeds asked Kamara to let Walker know if he was given permission to speak to any other club, so a week later, when Stoke agreed a fee with Middlesbrough, he phoned the journalist straight away. However, Kamara had already spoken to Middlesbrough's manager Bruce Rioch and chairman Steve Gibson, a childhood friend, and promised them he'd be at their game against Newcastle that evening. On the way up north, when he dropped in at Leeds, he found Bill Fotherby in typically combative form. 'He wouldn't let me out of the office until I'd signed the form!'

Comically, the six-footer found himself in a room with a managing director who thought he was up against a master poker face, stalling for more money. 'But I genuinely wasn't,' he insists. 'It was because of my friendship with Steve. That's the way I am.' Fotherby kept upping his offer, and on the table eventually was £70,000 a year plus a bonus if Leeds won promotion – almost trebling the player's wages.

'Unbelievable! I was quite happy with the first offer, ecstatic with the second, and over the moon with the third. I wasn't that stupid to turn that down,' though he admits dreading the prospect of having to break the news to his childhood friend. 'But I've said it to Steve since . . . Leeds were top of the table. Leeds were like Liverpool or Manchester United when I was growing up. When you get the opportunity to sign for a club of that stature, especially when you've supported them as a boy, you've got to do it.'

Gibson understood. When they played together as children, Kamara would pretend to be his hero, Johnny Giles. In his teens Kamara had watched the great Revie from the windswept terraces at Elland Road, so to help end his boyhood team's Second Division exile and set them on the road to their own Glory Years had a certain ring of destiny to it. 'I just loved it,' he recalls, smiling. 'Every time I stepped on that pitch I felt it was an honour.'

As with most sweet victories, there were one or two hard bumps along the way, but Kamara shrugs them off as character-building experiences, pointing out, not unreasonably, that 'it hasn't done me any harm'.

Born on Christmas Day 1957, Christopher Kamara grew up on the Park End estate in Middlesbrough, a Teesside town that is actually in the ceremonial county of North Yorkshire, so he could equally claim to be a Teessider or a Yorkshireman. His father was from the British colony of Sierra Leone, and obtained citizenship after being recruited by a British ship's engine room during the Second World War – the conflict that had also, of course, fatefully brought Leslie Silver up to Leeds.

'It was very difficult for my dad being the first black man in Middlesbrough,' Kammy tells me. 'It's a very different set of circumstances to this day and age. I think everybody knew racism against black people in those days was rife. He probably had it on the ships. It was never going to be easy for him. He was going to have to fight.'

Like his son on the field, Kamara senior showed no fear. Nor did his mother, a local girl who upon marriage formed half of one of the north-east's first mixed-race couples. 'Mum used to get abuse on regular occasions because she stuck up for Dad, but she was tireless in her support of the family,' remembers Kamara. 'Me? I didn't know any different. It just seemed that people didn't like us for our colour, not who we were because they didn't know us. You end up not trusting anyone, because you're not sure what their motives are. But it makes you stronger.'

He also had some very good friends who 'didn't see my colour', Steve Gibson among them, and the future Middlesbrough chairman and Leeds United midfielder bonded over football. 'It was all we did in those days. We played with a tennis ball under the street lights.' It was a long way from Elland Road and the tallest floodlights in Europe.

Kamara ended up playing for his school and being scouted by Middlesbrough Boys. Since few working-class families had telephones back then, a fellow called David Richardson – now in youth recruitment for the

Premier League – knocked on the door to tell him, 'Middlesbrough Boys have got a game, the coach leaves at nine a.m. . . .' The problem was, the future Leeds United hero didn't have a proper pair of boots. 'I had elastic bands on them,' he grins. 'But he borrowed a pair two sizes too big and gave me those to play in.'

After turning out for the Boys all season, Middlesbrough FC were set to sign him, but Kammy's father thought football was a pipe dream and disapproved. 'He'd made my brother join the army. In those days you virtually had to do what your parents wanted. It's very different now.'

In the 1960s and 1970s the traditional routes out of hardship were boxing, pop music, football or the forces (perhaps it's not so different today). Kammy made what he describes as a calculated gamble and joined the navy, spending six months having orders barked at him on HMS *Vernon*, based in Portsmouth, which ironically brought him back to football. Turning out for the navy youth team against Portsmouth, he scored twice, alerting manager Ray Crawford. 'He said, "How old is he?" I was only sixteen, and they took a chance on me.' Not before Crawford kept the youngster's feet firmly on the ground by informing the local paper, 'His knowledge of the game is scant. His marking is wayward and he hasn't got much positional sense.'

Kamara is grateful for such formative experiences. 'Good stuff, bad stuff.' He smiles. 'I wouldn't change a thing.'

There was plenty of both good and bad stuff in the rough-and-tumble world of football in the 1970s, a bygone era of muddy pitches, dubbined boots and near-the-knuckle banter. Football even looked different then: players and fans alike sported mullets, 'taches and big trousers. I still wince at the memory of going to games *circa* 1975/1976 wearing six-button high-waister keks, a faded Falmers denim jacket, plastic shoes and a silk scarf tied to each wrist, on which were the badly printed heads of players like Brian Flynn and Tony Currie. If you did that now you'd probably be arrested for crimes against fashion. It was a strange era that seems over a hundred years ago, not thirty-five.

Playing for Pompey (1975–77) and Swindon (1977–81), Kammy was part of English football's first generation of black footballers who fought the wars that helped it become the multicultural game it is today, enduring racist chants, monkey noises and even bananas thrown on to the field. There was no Kick It Out or Show Racism the Red Card in those days: racism was part of society as much as football. 'People weren't disgusted by it because it was the norm.' He sighs. '*Love Thy Neighbour* and Alf Garnett were on TV. Black jokes. But you either went along or folded. If you rebelled against it people thought you had a chip on your shoulder.' It's come full circle now; in fact, Kammy argues we've become over-sensitive. 'Carlton Cole was done recently for a joke. He's black and not racist in any way, shape or form. It's so politically correct it's almost embarrassing.'

Back then Kammy would hold his own in banter, unknowingly learning the skills that would serve him so well as a broadcaster, and not flinch in the face of intimidation, racial or otherwise. On the field he reacted just once, as late as 1988, punching an offender so hard he broke his jaw.

Kammy argues that Eric Cantona scored the major blow against racism in football on 25 January 1995 when he confronted that fan at Crystal Palace while playing for Manchester United. 'Once a white man stepped into the crowd and challenged it, it became a big deal. It wasn't a black thing any more, it was where you were from.' But things were already changing by the time Kamara signed for Leeds.

After the eighties, in which mass unemployment had further set people one against the other, the new decade started with hope of change. On the terraces, acid house culture had an impact: young men danced and hugged instead of kicking lumps out of each other. Meanwhile, forward-looking managers such as Howard Wilkinson and, yes, Ron Atkinson assembled multicultural teams that fans adopted as their own.

'I used to get dog's abuse from Leeds fans when I played for Stoke, but from the day I signed, it changed completely,' Kammy remembers. 'When I used to stand on the terraces, it was difficult. Especially if Leeds lost, cos you were the one black face, even though Paul Reaney was playing. They never looked at Paul Reaney as a black man. More character building? I guess so. It didn't put me off.'

Like Vinnie Jones, Kamara regards signing for Leeds as 'one of the best decisions of my career, if not the best. Howard Wilkinson was the best manager I played for, and Gary Speed, Gordon Strachan or Gary McAllister would say the same. He was years ahead of his time, ahead of Arsène Wenger. We had fitness coaches, proper food, everything was laid out for you. It was totally different.'

On 29 January 1990, Kammy arrived at a club 'on the crest of a wave', where the players were confident of winning every game and there was fierce competition for places, because everyone wanted to play their part. He notes that at this point, Bobby Davison, who scored eleven league goals in 1989/90, was still firmly in the camp. 'I had heard that Vinnie and him had had a tussle,' he admits. 'I don't know if that was the turning point, but Bobby was there a long time after that. Bobby was a hard lad as well. Fights are not uncommon in football; you get upset with someone and have a pop. Having the characters we had . . . I always remember Gordon Strachan arguing fiercely with Jim Beglin in the face, at half time. Gordon said, "Thankfully it didn't come to blows, because if it had there would only have been one winner and it wouldn't be me!" But that was the atmosphere then. We all wanted to be winners.

'People said me and Vinnie Jones kicked people,' he continues. 'We could play. Vinnie could be a bit cumbersome at times but technically he was very, very good. The goal he scored against Hull City, a screamer from thirty-five yards, technique-wise was outstanding.'

Kamara and Jones were kindred spirits on and off the field, having bonded over a few beers when Kamara was put up in the same hotel, the day he signed. According to Kammy, Wilko told him he would be replacing a tiring David Batty, but it didn't quite work out like that.

'Howard said, "Batts is coming to the end of his tether, it's his first full season, he's worked really hard." But Batts hung on a bit longer than I wanted him to!' Only at the end of the season did he replace Batty.

Against Oldham, Wilko left out Gary Speed and fielded a formidable midfield of Kamara, Batty, Jones and Strachan. But he began his Leeds career at right-back, in a position he'd never played before in his life. 'I made my debut against Hull City and got the man of the match award, a big Tetley poster,' he reveals, still not quite sure what mysterious trickery or psychology Wilkinson had employed to coax such a performance out of him in an unfamiliar role. 'It was a surprise to me that I did it. He just told you to do it.'

In many ways, Kamara was an archetypal Wilko signing, an all-round player and a big character who could be relied on to – to quote Rudyard Kipling – keep his head while all around were losing theirs.

'I wouldn't say I was the hardest player,' he says. 'People would kick me and I wouldn't react. When I got to Leeds the first thing Howard said to me was, "Stay on your feet. If you mistime a tackle I'm gonna fine you." If you got a yellow card, he'd fine you, because bookings meant missing games. He never tolerated dissent; that was a big fine. Vinnie and me were never sent off, couple of bookings between us. It's an education as you get older – when you're younger you go in for balls you can't possibly win, so instead of doing that, stay on your feet because someone else might win it. Nobody had ever said that to me before.'

Kamara's mental strength proved crucial in the most

unpredictable way possible on the final day of that 1989/90 season. Leeds went into their game, against a Bournemouth team managed by Harry Redknapp fighting against relegation, in indomitable mood. 'You knew we weren't gonna falter. We had a couple of sticky games [losing to Oldham and Barnsley in the run-in]. When we went to that game against Bournemouth, we knew we were going to win, to be fair.' He's chuckling. 'Harry's never forgotten it.'

Nor has Wilko, probably. The Second Division title was sealed when Kamara did something he knew a Leeds United player should never do – disobey the Sergeant.

'We were in touch with the other games around, and I think he was quite happy to settle for a point,' he explains. 'I wasn't. I was bombing forward trying to get a goal, and he's shouted, "Sit in midfield! If you don't I'm going to take you off!"'

Instead, with the score at 0–0, the midfielder kept his nerve and kept on bombing forward.

'Chrissie Fairclough was bombing forward as well, but from the back, and I thought, "Why am I getting all the shit when he's bombing forward from behind me?" So I bombed forward, obviously crossed it and Chappy stuck it away, and of course the rest is history.'

Wilko never pulled him up for the indiscipline. In fact, the team bus stopped at an off-licence on the way home and the manager booked the entire squad and their wives and girlfriends into the Leeds Hilton for mammoth celebrations which took in city-centre night-club Mr Craig's on the Saturday night and ended up at a pub Vinnie Jones knew 'somewhere in north Leeds' the next day. 'Everywhere we went, everyone was treating us as heroes,' Kamara recalls with a smile. 'There's some cities you'd probably get lost in if you won something, but in Leeds the bond between the players and supporters in that era was something special. It was amazing, actually.'

However, as with Jones, it proved bittersweet for Kamara. Just five months later he went from the peak of his career to one of the worst periods of his playing life. That summer he'd been working out in the gym when he saw Gary McAllister and his wife walk through. 'You think, "Oh shit." I knew I had to work harder in pre-season to get a game, and I did. There was Batts, Gary Speed, Macca . . .' McAllister, of course, with Strachan, formed the midfield that would take Wilko towards the title. Kamara ended up playing left-back, but suffered an ankle injury against Coventry in November 1990 which would be the beginning of the end for the promotion hero and see the Sergeant display a different kind of ruthlessness to that experienced by Jones.

As Kammy tells it, the injury was initially mis-diagnosed, and then he tried too hard to get fit, making the problem worse. Meanwhile, the manager suspected he was in a comfort zone, happy not to play. He was banished to the 'leper colony', even sent to see a psychologist who told him, 'You don't want to play for Leeds, Chris, do you?'

'I was out eight months,' he sighs. 'Too long, and it changed Howard's opinion of me. It changed me. I never got to the heights I'd had in terms of fitness after that game. I was going to retire. It hurt me that he thought I was quite happy to sit and earn the money.'

To this day it hurts him that his career at Leeds was cut short like this, and at the time he was furious when the Sergeant left him outside his office for forty-five minutes as he waited to complain. However, at that meeting Wilkinson recommended a specialist in Wakefield who finally diagnosed an Achilles tendon problem.

Kamara made three more appearances in October 1991 when McAllister got injured and he was asked if he was fit enough to go on the bench at Notts County. 'No danger,' he told them, 'knowing I was nowhere near ready'. He came on for twenty minutes and was asked if he could play a full game against Forest in the second round of the Zenith Data Systems Cup on the Tuesday. 'My ankle was fine, but I was twenty-five per cent fit. I managed ninety minutes on adrenalin. He called me on the Thursday saying, "I'm letting you go [to Luton]. But I need you against Oldham on Saturday."' That Friday, Kamara was told that Gary McAllister had passed a fitness test, so he started his last game on the bench. 'I came on for twenty minutes, the fans were all singing "You'll win **** all at Luton" – typical banter – and "There's only one Chris Kamara".' Although the Sergeant's decision to tell him he didn't want him and then play him anyway felt 'strange', he felt the manager did him a favour. 'Without that, the Leeds fans wouldn't have been singing my name. That's one of my great memories.'

Two decades on, Kamara bears no grudges towards a manager who is now more of a friend. 'I didn't really know him then. None of us did. Howard wasn't always great at man management and he knows that, we've spoken about it. He left me outside his office deliberately to wind me up. There's some stuff he regrets and he has apologized to me since, saying, "There were things I did in management which I thought would motivate people to come back at me."

'The perception of him and the real him are two very different things,' he observes, astutely. 'People perceive him as this very boring person, and he's not always the best at communication, but people don't get his irony. He can be one of the funniest guys in the world.'

As can Kammy. He makes his own joke about his contribution to the 1991/92 title: 'I was part of the move that made the goal against Oldham [an own goal], so I guess I played a part!'

Two decades on, the game is unrecognizable in many ways. 'I book the guests for *Goals on Sunday*, and I can ring up Gordon Strachan or Gary McAllister. With many players you speak to their agents. They tell me such stories as "our players won't get out of bed for a thousand pounds". It's a shame, but when I do actually get to speak to the players most of them are happy to do it.' He points out that if you win a championship today you're set up for life, but considers himself among the 'fortunate ones' who are still making a good living from football.

Still, without that fifty-first-minute centre against Bournemouth, Leeds may not have been promoted, the squad may not have been kept together and Wilko may never have won the league. Like Vincent Peter Jones, Christopher Kamara helped lay the foundations for the title and played his way into Leeds United folklore.

Funnily enough, he was recently on a 'homes of the stars' bus tour in Los Angeles . . . and the very first home they stopped at?

'Vinnie Jones's!' he explodes. 'Unbelievable!'

CHAPTER 9

Everything's Gone White

There was a group of five of us in 1990/91 and 1991/92. I remember buying James Brown's *Attack On Bzag* fanzine from him in Dortmund Square outside what used to be Lewis's department store (it's a Sainsbury's now, after a spell as Allders), but by now he was the assistant editor of *NME*, and would go on to set up *Loaded*. Tim Southwell, who would become Brown's co-instigator with the pioneering 'lad mag', was another *NME* hack who had a Richard Hawley quiff and pointed spectacles that made him look like a slightly more rock 'n' roll version of 1980s/1990s trade union leader Rodney Bickerstaffe. Iestyn George – also an *NME* type, and as such should have been the avowed enemy of a *Melody Maker* hack like me, despite the fact that the rival music weeklies' offices were only a floor apart – was a quietly spoken Welshman into Paul Weller. Central to our operations, not least because he had a motor, was Paul Weighell.

'Weighelly' was what record companies call an 'A & R

man' – the talent scouts who, before the onset of the internet and MySpace, used to trawl backstreet pubs up and down the country in the hope of finding the next Beatles. Instead, Weighelly had signed the Levellers, who became enormously popular in the early nineties for a while – but we shouldn't hold that against him. I very much doubt whether Weighelly personally cared for any of the bands he scouted. In fact, he didn't seem to like modern music at all, had something of an obsession with the left-field German 1970s music dubbed 'Krautrock' and would have far preferred to be holed up in his living room with the latest Kraftwerk import or the collected works of Amon Duul II.

I'd met him at a gig in London and we'd bonded over what was happening at Elland Road. Most Saturdays we had a ritual: couple of pints in the Adelphi down near Leeds Bridge and up to the game, either in the motor or on the bus depending on how much Northallerton-born Weighelly had indulged his particular interest in Theakston's Old Peculier.

However, being a roving talent scout gave Weighelly the perfect excuse – and, presumably, an expense account – to travel the country supporting Leeds. It's ancient history now, but I often wonder if it was co-incidence that some of his trips to see obscure reggae bands up north happened to coincide with Leeds games, or how he would have got on if we'd ever been relegated down the divisions and he'd have had to concoct bizarre excuses for journeys to Gillingham and Darlington. He'd also come up for the evening games, and I marvelled at his ability to drive the four hours up from London, cram in the Adelphi, get in at four in the morning and then drive into work next day grimly rueing the fact that the crusty metal band he'd seen in Thirsk the night before hadn't turned out to be the next Beatles after all. Conversely, I used to attempt to schedule attendances at *Melody Maker* meetings around whether LUFC were away at Arsenal or Crystal Palace.

One day, Weighelly was giving me a lift back up north en route to see a management company in Bradford, which meant he could take in an evening game at Elland Road. It was snowing on the M1, and Weighelly was talking on his mobile, or what Vinnie Jones would call a 'breeze block'. The snow was actually quite bad, and as Weighelly was chatting away about the merits of some band or other I felt the car suddenly start to move.

'So how many songs have they got?' asked Weighelly, suddenly breaking off his conversation with a worried, 'Er, hold on, we seem to have a problem.'

While Weighelly had been chatting away, the car had somehow managed to spin 180 degrees round in the snow, so we were staring through the snow-covered windscreen, facing the oncoming traffic. This would be more than a local difficulty at the best of times, but presents a particular hazard when you're in the middle of the M1. I can still picture it now: the snow coming down, the sense of whiteness everywhere, and the approaching headlights in the mist as cars swerved to avoid us.

The weirdest thing about it – which Weighelly reminded me by email recently – was our cartoon 'oooohs' and 'whoooaarghs!' as cars hurtled around us.

Somehow, I suspect far more shaken than he let on, he managed to get the car pointing the right way and we escaped this brush with death with nothing more damaging than a case of the jitters. Like Speedo spying Bremner at the window or Leeds phoning Jones first, it was another of those flukes: a second or so either side and perhaps we wouldn't have seen Leeds United win any titles after all.

I wonder if I'll hear about any more.

CHAPTER 10

Michael Whitlow – 'Whits'

I was a geezer in a Top Man shirt with a Human League wedge haircut.

I'm on the road again, this time to Burton-on-Trent in Staffordshire, headed for the Pirelli stadium, home of Burton Albion FC, now in the Football League thanks to the efforts of Nigel Clough, son of Brian, who decamped for his dad's old club Derby. When Leeds were in the Premiership, Burton was exactly the sort of club our supporters enjoyed making fun of – if such a club registered at all – many of the jokes involving the word 'minnows' and comparisons between their stadium and a coal scullery. But it's not like that any more. Although the Pirelli stadium holds about a quarter of the twenty-or-so thousand LUFC are currently struggling to pull at home, the sponsored new-build stadium is a high-tech palace compared to our increasingly crumbling amphitheatre.

Still, today the Pirelli offers a chance to bask in the days when supporting Leeds United meant following the country's premier club at Fortress Elland Road: Burton Albion is the current home of Mike Whitlow, the man whom Wilko somehow turned from a non-league player into a title-winner and who is now head of youth coaching at Albion's centre of excellence – the same sort of set-up the Sergeant pioneered at Leeds.

'Working with kids now you can see the desire and attitude,' he enthuses, 'and that will take away a lot of the stuff that someone's blessed with. If you don't have that other side and realize it's a job – because it is a job, even though it's enjoyable – someone else will be better than you because they put the work in. I was one of them that had to work at it. I'd love to say I had silky skills, juggled the ball. It's never going to happen. This is me. I'll give it all. If I bodge up I'll hold my hands up, but I'll give you everything I've got.'

Which is probably why Wilko signed him. Over two decades later, he talks exactly like he played: quick, all-action, barely a dull moment, what you see is what you get.

We take a short drive to the pub during which I notice that the only CD in his car is *Now That's What I Call Music Vol. 27*, which appears to suggest that D:Ream's 'Things Can Only Get Better' and M-People's 'Moving On Up' are the football champions' positivity-drenched songs of choice. Then we talk for two hours. Or rather, the solidly built man with 'MW' on his training top talks for two hours while I try to get a word in. Whits's motormouth makes Vinnie Jones seem reserved by comparison; and I soon find out that he can make David Batty's culinary habits seem positively haute cuisine too.

'I had the worst diet ever,' he chortles, ordering a massive pile of fish and chips. 'My favourite meal was chips and egg. Howard didn't know! I used to eat jackie potatoes and all that.' But he never drank, having lost his spleen as a youngster, 'so I was never going to put weight on that way. I was a very good taxi driver, on many occasions!'

He's as untypical a youth coach as he was untypical a player – but I can see why kids can learn from him, because he's impossible to dislike, insightful at times, and very funny.

'We must have been the ugliest football team ever,' he says of Wilko's gallant knights in white shining nylon armour. 'You take Gary Speed out of that and you've got the Addams family.'

David Batty, Leeds' legendary number four, was 'as mad as cheese. He was as hard as nails in training, like he was in games. He couldn't do a twelve-minute run without walking, but give him a football and he'd play all day. He was good at his job, and it was a dirty job. But he went on to play for England.' As for Lee Chapman, 'it would go in off his shin, his shoulder, his back. He wasn't the most attractive footballer but he knew how to score goals.'

Beneath the banter, I can tell, lies genuine admiration.

Whitlow came from nothing and mingled with the stars, but never got ahead of himself amid such exalted company as Chapman, Batts, Speedo, Strachan and others. 'People would come up and talk to you, ask you to sign an autograph. "Why are you signing a piece of paper, Dad?" I was no different from them, but they don't see it like that because you're playing for their club. I was a geezer in a Top Man shirt with a Human League wedge haircut.'

A geezer from little Witton Albion, who picked up the game's top domestic honour. Just how does something like that happen? To find out, we should probably start at the beginning.

Whitlow was born in Northwich, the small Cheshire town that bestowed on him his north-west accent. 'I was a sort of junior blue,' he begins, referring to Manchester City's youth input. But when he left school, it was Bolton Wanderers, not City, that offered an apprenticeship. 'So off I went to sunny Bolton and I was in digs. At that age you don't worry about leaving home. It's a dream. You just wanna play football.' He points out that in the days of black and white televisions 'everything was sport: football in the street, outdoors. This was before PlayStations, Space Invaders, Twitter. Your social network was outside.

'I was a left-winger-cum-centre-forward,' he continues, between mouthfuls of haddock. 'I've always been right-handed and left-footed. My right leg was for standing on. I'm a big daft sod and I love the game. The kids that I coach now think I'm mad. I always wanted to be a goalie like my dad – he played for Northwich Vics. But I was too skinny. They were struggling for outfield players and I was shoved outfield. I played at a decent level, not exceptional – kick it, chase after it, scored some goals. I came through county teams. The best player by a country mile that I played with was Jason Dansky. He signed for Everton as a youngster. Never heard of again.'

Whitlow could easily have finished the same way when, at Bolton, he found himself facing the same make-or-break decision Gary Speed had – but he wasn't as fortunate. He admits that after being released by the north-west club 'I spat my dummy out'. He turned his back on football, aided by the realization that while Bolton were paying him £17 to £20 as an apprentice, cleaning the ammonia tanks out at a chemical firm could pull in £100 a week.

'Football had told me I was rubbish,' he explains. 'I was gutted cos I thought I could have got a pro contract. Now I could afford a pair of trainers. I was a mardy arse, to be truthful. My mum and dad weren't too impressed with me. But I worked. I got a kick up the arse from my dad every couple of months, but I didn't play.'

In fact, as far as he was concerned he was never going to play again. Then his dad and some pals got involved with Lostock Gralam – a small Sunday outfit outside Northwich who, having been established in 1892, are actually one of the oldest clubs in Britain – and he kicked a ball again.

'The one good thing for me about Sunday football was that everyone would go out and get drunk on Saturday nights,' he says of his days with the Grey Lambs, as they are nicknamed. 'Because I never drank, I was sober as a judge and a young whippersnapper. So I'd turn up Sunday mornings – I was a centre-forward then – and I bagged something like sixty-odd goals in twenty games. It was mad!'

By another of those twist of fates experienced by every player I've spoken to so far, two of Whitlow's impressed teammates also turned out for Witton, an even older club (established 1887) that has always played in England's minor leagues. 'They said, "They'll love you at Witton, come play for us." So having been a goalie I went to Witton as a left-winger-cum-centre-forward.' Who went on to sign for Leeds United as a full-back.

'It gets better than that,' chortles Whits, polishing off his chips. 'We weren't originally going to Leeds.'

He reveals that when Mick Hennigan went to Witton to watch right-back Neil Parsley, and spotted Whitlow, he'd been scouting them for Sheffield Wednesday. Hennigan – 'bless him, old school, hard as nails; if you were rubbish he'd tell you, if you were good he'd pat you on the back' – asked Witton if he could take the pair of them to Sheffield for a better look. Whitlow was working in a builder's yard so got the time off work. But by the time he got to Sheffield, both Hennigan and Wilkinson had taken the job at Leeds United. 'I'm thinking, "Oh my God, what do we do now?"' he remembers. 'But Howard, to be fair to him, took us to one side and said, "Listen, I've invited you. [Wednesday coach] Peter Eustace will look after you. See what they say. But I promise you I'll be in touch."'

He had a fabulous week at Wednesday – where Eustace made him feel very welcome despite the men who'd scouted him having gone – playing with the deadly if injury-prone striker David Hirst. That Saturday he turned out for Witton Albion as usual and for Lostock on the Sunday. On Monday morning, Sergeant Wilko called.

Although he hadn't realized it, the Witton experience hadn't just put him in the shop window, it had been a learning curve. Because Whitlow was young and quick and cocky, he provided a target for opposition players. After three or four games, away at Bangor, he nut-megged a defender and was told, 'Son, you won't do that again.' 'Ten minutes later I've tried it again and he's battered me over the touchline,' he recalls. '"Next time, son, you won't get up." For the next thirty minutes he absolutely smashed me. He kicked me twenty-seven thousand times, but I was a wuss. A big girl's blouse. Gimme the ball and I'll pass it. But nobody had ever showed me how to tackle or how physical it was. In that game, I grew up.'

Shortly afterwards, the Witton left-back was hurt and Whitlow filled in. So by the time he arrived at Leeds he'd played eighty games in the position he would play for Sergeant Wilko.

But what is it actually like going from a small club like Witton Albion to the 'famous Leeds United'?

'It was great because you didn't know nowt about it,' he says, a little bit of Yorkshire lingering in his words. 'Turned up on the Monday, all of a sudden I was making my debut in the Simod Cup [the precursor to the equally short-lived Zenith Data Systems Cup] on the Wednesday. Gave away a penalty as I recall, which wasn't a great start.' However, that Saturday – 26 November 1988 – Whitlow made his league debut against Stoke, a home game Leeds won 4–0. He was just twenty years old.

'If it wasn't for Mervyn Day and Noel Blake I'd have

struggled,' he admits. 'A minority of footballers are not very nice and they spoil it for others. But they weren't like that.' Blake didn't survive long under Wilko but passed on his experience to the kid, having played for a string of clubs from Sutton Coldfield to Aston Villa. 'He was like my dad around the changing room. I was young, naive, kicked everyone in training. Everything was a thousand miles an hour. But I'd gone from being a wussy left-winger to "If you try and get past me I'll hit you".'

His determination made him a perfect fit for the Wilko mindset. 'I didn't want anybody to say I was rubbish ever again. In a way, what Bolton did to me was the best thing that could have happened.'

The Sergeant may not have recruited the fanciest player ever, but he had a character he could trust. Overnight, the youngster went from turning out in local parks to playing alongside some of the biggest names in football.

'Until you meet Gordon Strachan and play with him, you don't realize the importance he has in a football team, the presence he has, and the respect players give him,' he says, his tone suddenly serious and respectful. 'He leads by example, and he would tell people.' He cites the incident Jones mentioned, when he was lambasted by the Wee Man. 'You've got to remember that Gordon's this little redheaded bloke; Vinnie's this nutty giant of a lad. But Vinnie didn't say a word, just sat there. He took it all on the chin, and that's why he got booked twice that season.'

Jones had been a bricklayer and FA Cup winner;

Strachan had dropped a league from Man United. In a way, both were rebuilding their careers, when Whitlow's was just building.

The next step was subjecting him to moulding. He was running up hills and around fields until he was fit to drop. 'A lot of us had been discarded, but it was like an athletics club. That's the hardest I've ever worked at any football club, especially in pre-season. The intensity changed, but in terms of wanting to be physically sick, it was up there.

'There was no way I was ever going to get to the front of that group, but I wanted to be,' he continues. 'Gordon took some beating. Chris Kamara was the fittest and hardest player I've ever played with. He'd put a bin liner under his training top because he wanted to sweat. They were like machines. And then Mel . . .' He chuckles. 'But then Mel Sterland could hit the ball harder than anyone I've ever seen, score from thirty-five yards.'

They were a disparate bunch of characters that somehow gelled together on the field. 'Young and old,' Whitlow adds. 'But we all wanted to work hard and succeed.'

He's still not quite sure exactly how Wilko turned him into a double champion (in both Second and First Divisions), but suspects some of it was down to meticulous organization and advanced coaching. He cites another unsung name in the Last Champions story – Dick Bate, a coach who worked alongside Wilkinson from 1988 until 1992 and whose sessions were 'ten years ahead of their time, a different level. Who passes where; which is a player's strongest side, left or right; which way they pull out of tackles. Ultra-fine detail. Twenty years ago, football wasn't ready. But I see him now and he's probably one of the most educated guys within the FA. If you can't learn something from him, there's something wrong with you. The previous generation wouldn't change, but we were the generation who were open and wanted to take it on.'

Similarly, he now recognizes that Wilkinson provided the environment that, for a rookie, made success possible. 'The environment and the way you make them feel is how you get the best of them,' he explains. Contrary to Kamara, he praises Wilko's man management. 'Some you can shout at, they'll go into their shell and you'll lose them. Others need that rocket and you'll get a reaction.'

Egg and chips may have remained on his menu but in every other aspect he is a Wilkinson disciple and praises the Sergeant's dark arts of 'going out of his way to give those players no excuse not to perform'.

For a non-league/Sunday rookie turned Leeds United regular, Whitlow can – and will – trot out the legendary names he played against, especially in the First Division in the early nineties, when Wilko's moulding really kicked in after promotion. There was Man United's 'Captain Marvel', Bryan Robson: 'Every time he tackled me it was like being hit by a car.' Mark Hughes: 'If he got past me I'd kick him. But I never set out to hurt anyone. I wanted to win the ball.' He is honest enough to admit that one player showed him up. 'I had to mark Gascoigne,' he remembers. 'You should have seen him running rings round me. But for me from non-league it was an honour to play against these guys. I knew they were better players than me, but I worked hard because I didn't want that chance taken away from me again.'

Perhaps this mindset helped him play at a level no one would ever have expected, least of all himself. He reveals that Wilko never really told him what he saw in him, but remembers one season's highlights tape during which the Sergeant went through all the players' contributions. 'He talked about my pace and mentioned a game at Villa. Tony Daley was flying then and he said, "Michael gave him three yards and then just went past him."' He's laughing. 'He still calls me Michael.'

He remains proud of having served under the Sarge. 'I like to think I never let him down.'

Whitlow made a total of seventy-seven league appearances for Leeds: twenty in Wilko's transitional season of 1988/89, twenty-nine in the promotion season, eighteen in 1990/91 and ten (three starts, seven as substitute) in 1991/92, scoring the fifth goal in the 6–1 demolition of Sheffield Wednesday. He made his last start in the 4–1 loss to QPR on 11 March 1992, by which time he'd realized that the dream was over.

'I knew when Tony Dorigo came in,' he admits, referring to Wilkinson's £1.3m close-season capture of Chelsea's star left-back. That year, he says, Wilkinson took things to another level. 'I was fortunate enough to see a bit of Cantona, Gary McAllister . . . Football was changing, and the swiney Wilkinson bought the best left-back in the country at the time!' But he's chuckling; he's not bitter. 'He was better than me, simple. He was playing for England. You had Mel Sterland at right-back, who was absolutely flying, and they got Tony Dorigo. Nicest man you'll ever meet. Total respect. Howard wanted to replace a hard-working player with a quality player.'

All these years later, he is philosophical about his career at Elland Road. 'I was given an opportunity, and I like to think I grabbed it.'

He didn't want to hang around and not be playing, waiting for Dorigo to get injured, and Wilkinson understood this and helped him get a move to Second Division Leicester, for £250,000 on 27 March, just before the run-in. He holds a unique but unfortunate position among the Last Champions in that by the time he was a title-winner, he was no longer at the club.

Instead, on the day Leeds United celebrated at home against Norwich, Whitlow was losing at Filbert Street against Newcastle after manager Brian Little had told them not to get booked because of the following week's playoff final against Blackburn Rovers, which they lost as well, although he was chuffed to walk out at Wembley.

But the Whitlow story doesn't end there. After Leicester were promoted, relegated and promoted again, he spent the years between 1997 and 2003 in the Premiership at Bolton, the club that had rejected him as a boy, where he earned more fifteen years into his career than in the entire previous fifteen years, before ending his playing days at the age of thirty-seven after spells at Sheffield United and Notts County.

The Leeds United experience remains special. 'I left

with the fondest memories, and I still sing the daft songs now! Many years later Gordon was manager at Southampton and he invited me in. He was like a father figure. I got so much stick off my teammates, because he was the manager of the opposition. But it never leaves you, the help.' He still sees Wilkinson occasionally on FA business and reveals that 'Fail to prepare and you'll prepare to fail' has become a lifelong motto.

'I grew up at Leeds,' he admits. 'I used to sit in a corner, quiet. Without that chance the journey I'm still going on wouldn't have happened.'

He finally pauses, allowing himself a few seconds, then tells me that when he almost lost a daughter through meningitis, he got involved with a hospice and saw kids dying and it put everything into perspective. 'None of us are here long, you only get one chance,' he says, completing his two-hour transition from joker to philosopher. 'The places I've been, the people I've met . . . I couldn't have dreamed about it really. Howard helped me win two titles. I didn't get a [First Division] medal until someone wrote in and said I'd played so many games, I should have one. I've still got the letter. It was nice. I'd never thought about such things because I'd enjoyed it. I had my Second Division medal, but it's marvellous to have the other one. The last ever First Division medal. We were making history.'

CHAPTER 11

Alan Sutton – 'Sutty'

He grabbed my medical bag, threw it up in the air and
. . . it's come down and he's kicked it . . . And then he
said to me, 'Alan, I think I've broken my toe.'

One of the last things Gary Speed said to me was, 'Have
you talked to Sutty? You should. Sutty knows
everything.'

Shutty?

'No, Sutty! Alan Sutton, the physio.'

So it is that I arrive in Alan Sutton's office, which is
strewn with papers and computers, in Leeds United's
training complex at Thorp Arch. A full-size skeleton of
the human body hangs menacingly by a doorway. The
measurements are too small for it to be the missing
David Batty.

The sixty-five-year-old physiotherapist, who has
spent most of the last four decades at Leeds, is the only
surviving member of the 1991/92 staff and playing
squad still at the club. After being sacked along with
many others in 2007 as United began a three-year spell

in the third-tier League One, Sutton returned as physio within a year. Interviewed in training kit and shorts, the hyperactive backroom staffer is not short of energy and is, as Speedo had suggested, a living LUFC encyclopedia.

'I've got all the stories, but I tend to go off on tangents, so you'll have to guide me,' he says, which proves pretty good advice.

A whirlwind two hours with Sutty careers from tales of Billy Bremner smoking in the treatment room to how Captain Billy enjoyed regaling young players with tales of Revie-era players breaking the legs of opponents who'd hacked down one of their number. He has all manner of Vinnie Jones stories, from how Wilko's enforcer first met Mrs Sutton and promptly crashed out on the sofa (he'd been out until four a.m.) to an incident on the first day of the promotion season, at Newcastle's St James's Park, when the inimitable hard-man was 'fighting with [opposition boss] Jim Smith at the top of the stairs'. David Batty stories come by the sackful, ranging from how the team would be changing and he would be smashing balls around the dressing room, to how his father in the stands would give his opinion on his son's performance with a thumbs-up or thumbs-down – Elland Road's answer to Caligula.

'We were playing Stoke, and Batts came in and said, "I'm injured, me hamstring." Wilko told me to have a look. Batts went back out and kicked the centre-forward up in the air – deliberately gave away a penalty. I said, "What's up with you?" He said, "****in' Dad. He gets into my ****in' head, dunt he."'

But we kick off with a contrast between the mood at Thorp Arch today ('laughter in the morning') with the high-pressure environment of the Sergeant Wilko era. 'He didn't like people to be too happy,' Sutton chuckles. 'He once told me, "Ring Kammy up at Bradford City and tell him he can have [John] Pemberton – he's too ****ing happy!" There's these clubs where they've been pratting about, throwing pillows around, taking the piss. Nobody would ever do that under Howard.

'It was the greatest time, but working for him . . . why my wife never divorced me I don't know. It was seven days a week, twenty-four hours a day, rough mentally and physically.' Nowadays clubs have whole teams of physios, but when Sutton first came to Leeds he was physio and kit man, in charge of fifty players, apprentices to seniors. 'I know people who've had nervous breakdowns about it, and I understand why. I think what saved me is I'd had my own building firm and I'd toiled all the hours in the day. Without that behind me, I wouldn't have survived with Wilko. I would have just collapsed.'

Unexpectedly, he insists that the most stressful period wasn't trying to pip Man United to the title in 1992, but trying to get out of the Second Division in 1989/90. 'Because from day one we were the favourites,' he explains. 'Winning that Second Division championship took me four or five months afterwards to get over. The First Division – we pissed it, comparatively. It was like playing the semi-final of the cup and then the final; all the time there was no pressure. All of a sudden you've won the league.'

Sutty tells all these stories with the breathless, slightly awed air of someone who still can't quite believe he's been in the nerve centre while a piece of history was being made, and to be fair he can't ever have imagined any of it before he came to Elland Road.

Born in Bradford, he was a player for the city's Park Avenue club (in 1965, playing alongside Kevin Hector, who would go on to win the league title under Brian Clough at Derby) before witnessing a car crash gave him a glimpse of his future life. 'Two cars had collided and I just didn't know what to do. I felt useless. A woman arrived who said she was a physio and could deal with it.'

But first there was a spell in Canada, where he spent time in the building trade before the business was hit by hard times and he returned to Britain. 'This was in 1979, 1980,' he explains. 'I actually did the physio for Bradford City reserves at Sunderland one night. I knew nothing, but I really got into it.'

After a year at Lilleshall – the FA's School of Excellence, which is now defunct, and where much later he got an FA Diploma – he got a job at Halifax Town for £50 a week, 'because I was the cheapest. The manager said, "Don't worry, you'll be working with a doctor." The first thing you learn is to ask, "Is it an injury, or a player problem?" It's not common, but you get players, especially younger players, who are fed up, having to compete against other people. Mentally, they cave in. It becomes easier to be injured.' He sounds tailor-made for the Sarge.

It was Bremner who brought him in, on 22 August

1986 (Sutty's elephantine memory stretches to dates and telephone numbers), after the physio had had another glimpse of the future when, while moonlighting with Halifax rugby league club, they won the 1986 championship. He vividly remembers his very first apprentice in the LUFC medical room: 'Gary Speed. He has the same birthday as my son.'

Sutton adored Bremner too, even though 'sometimes you'd say "Morning, gaffer" and he'd just blank you. But on tour with him he was fantastic, laugh a minute: the complete opposite to Howard Wilkinson. He'd be down in the dressing room with all the apprentices – Batts and everyone – playing keepy-uppy. Dave Blakey the chief scout would come in and say "Billy, so-and-so's on the phone" and it could be really important but he'd be there for another five minutes playing piggy in the middle with a hole in his trainers.'

Why didn't it work out for Bremner as manager?

'I think, personally – and this is where it all changed with Wilkinson . . . and this maybe applies to a lot of great players when they become managers. They were such great players, perhaps they needed to be with great players. There aren't so many players who could do what they could do, and I don't think they realized how special they were.'

Sutton regards Leslie Silver as the greatest ever Leeds United chairman, and remains touched that the 'total gentleman' called him into his office to explain why he had taken what must have been a very difficult decision to sack King Billy, one of Leeds United's greatest legends. 'I mean, me, the physio! Billy was passionate, and it was all about the badge. When Wilko came in the attitude was "You think you're fit, you're not. I'll show you what fitness is really about."'

Like Gary Speed, he has plenty of tales about how brutal the training was in Wilko's early days, confirming tales of players vomiting and suggesting that Chris Fairclough, who'd been used to gentle five-a-sides at Tottenham and Forest, was 'almost killed' by the shock to the system. But it wasn't just the team. 'The staff had to be as fit as the players,' he reveals. 'We'd go running together: me, Mick Hennigan and Wilko. We once set off without Howard and he was furious, saying, "Don't you ever go running without me again!"

'Them early days . . .' He chuckles, in a Bradford accent. 'I'm still amazed I survived. I would have thought he must have interviewed every other physio in the country to replace me. Apparently at Sheffield Wednesday he said, "Right, I'm leaving. Anyone who wants to come with me, I'll see you there tomorrow." And there was only Mick Hennigan that went. I think he was really hurt that they allowed him to go, because Wednesday were his team, as a player; they were fifth in the division.'

But from 10/10/88 – the date is carved in Sutton's DNA – Wilko was unquestionably Leeds, and he expected the same 100 per cent commitment from anybody with him. So it was perhaps unfortunate that on Wilkinson's very first day at Leeds United star player John Sheridan didn't bother to turn up.

Sutton explains. 'He had an agreement with Billy that he needn't train on Mondays after going on the lash.'

Apparently this had started one mad weekend when Leeds played Portsmouth at home, and the influential midfielder had gone to see his brother 'Daz' playing in a pub team in Manchester the next morning. 'He rolled up on Tuesday and said he hadn't woken up until three o'clock on Monday afternoon. What had happened . . . on the Sunday morning, Shez has been walking up the street with his brother and this other team come up. "Hey you, you wankers, we're gonna kick your arses today cos we haven't been beaten for two years." That week Shez had just been picked for the Republic of Ireland. So he's, "Right, give me that ****ing number eight shirt and we'll show 'em!" So he only turns out for this pub team on the Sunday morning. They won 6–2. He scored four. So then they've got that ****ing pissed . . .' After the game, the ref apparently called him in and said, 'You're not a bad player. Do you fancy turning out for Manchester FA against Ashton under Lyne next week?' Sutton howls with laughter. '"Oh, sorry, ref, I've got loads of things to do next week"!' If Sheridan had been caught moonlighting, he'd have been in major trouble. 'But you are talking 1988. Nobody recognized him in Manchester. There weren't tellys or internet like there are now. A few years later he scored a goal at Wembley against Man United.' Bremner turned a blind eye to Sheridan's weekend antics 'as long as he did it on the Saturday', but this fantastic story probably explains why he didn't last long under Wilko.

Memory man Sutty can also recall the Sarge's exact first words to his new troops: '"Right, lads, you're third from bottom, which means I'm the third worst manager in this division. So let's do something about it." And it just went from there.'

Remembering that on some days the squad would train in the morning, train in the afternoon and play a game that evening, he uses another funny story to illustrate the manic intensity of this period. It was 21 January 1989 and they'd been playing away at Oxford – 'this is with Noel Blake, Vinnie Hilaire and all of them' – and were losing 2–0 at half time. The Sarge had gone ballistic. 'In them days they always had a big table in the middle of the dressing room, with big square wooden legs. And he's ranting and raving. "You . . . and you!"' Then Sutty bursts out laughing. 'He grabbed my medical bag, threw it up in the air and said "and you ****ing head it" and it's come down and he's kicked it.' There was a moment's silence. 'And then he said to me, "Alan, I think I've broken my toe."' More laughter.

Sutty could – and does – reel off this sort of stuff all day, and his combination of inner-circle but fly-on-the-wall perspective is fascinating for me as a fan. Sutton is full of small but interesting details, like the fact that it was apparently loyal first lieutenant Mick Hennigan who first suggested Wilkinson bring in Vinnie Jones to 'smack a few people who needed to be smacked'. 'But the funny thing is, Gordon Strachan was still the main man in the dressing room,' he says, before unveiling another story that he suggests is 'very telling, about the power of Strachan'.

The Sutton time machine stops at Upton Park, West Ham's ground, on 7 October 1989. A crowd of 23,539 have turned out for one of the biggest Second Division games that season.

'Before we go out, Vinnie's messing round with the crowd. So Wilko says to Gordon, "Take Vinnie out there, let him do his warm-up and then get him back in here." So Gordon's gone, "Vinnie, Vinnie, you're going to do your warm-up with me today." Some lads would have told him to **** off. He's like, "No problem." Who scores that day? Vinnie Jones.'

Fluke, or amazing management?

'You look at those big personalities, and when Wilko walked in a dressing room to deliver an opinion, whether his captain was Gordon Strachan or Gary McAllister, they will have had a meeting beforehand. I am ninety-nine per cent sure that whoever was captain knew what was going to be said. He wouldn't have anyone contradicting him.'

Sutton reveals another of Wilkinson's unusual tricks to relax his players before big games. Prior to the crucial promotion game at Bournemouth, he took them to play the unfamiliar game of baseball. Not that this went entirely to plan. 'Vinnie, who doesn't know the rules of American baseball, hits one and throws the bat. It only hits Andy Williams, fracturing his cheekbone! So I've got to take Andy Williams to the hospital, get him operated on, then back on the coach, boom boom, then get straight down to Bournemouth. It was like something from his movies.'

Again, Sutty recalls Wilko's exact words as the players took the field – with ninety minutes standing between them, the Second Division title and the top division – words that weren't a million miles from the ones he'd use in 1992: 'Listen, lads, imagine you're on the eighteenth tee, and you've got four shots to win the championship. Trust your swing; trust your fellow players.'

Trust your fellow players. It's as beautiful as poetry. How could any player fail to be inspired?

The day's football involved another bizarre twist of fate as inspired as Kamara's ignoring orders to lay on the winning goal.

It's the final day of the 1989/90 campaign, and three teams can mathematically win the title – Leeds, Sheffield United (who win 5–2 away at Leicester) and Newcastle, who face a Middlesbrough side including Ian Baird, the striker Wilko replaced with Lee Chapman. 'If we win,' Sutty explains, 'Bairdy gets a championship medal cos he's already played twenty-five games for Leeds. So Bairdy's winding everybody up, up there, threatening to smash everybody unless Middlesbrough beat Newcastle. As long as Newcastle don't win we get promoted anyway. It worked out, but if Newcastle had won, they had a far better goal difference than Sheff United. Bairdy scored twice that day. They won 4–1, and he got the medal.'

Years later, 'Bairdy' was voted number forty-two in a poll of the greatest ever Leeds United players.

But for Sutton, the unsung hero of 1989/90 was veteran goalie Mervyn Day. 'Because when Wilko came in he wanted £500,000 to get another keeper in and Mervyn proved him wrong.' Day was thirty-five, and would stay on at the club, but after promotion

Wilkinson brought John Lukic back (he'd been at Leeds from schoolboy days until 1983, after which he'd won a League Cup and the 1988/89 title with Arsenal) for the First Division campaign.

By 1990/91, and then in 1991/92, recalls Sutton, the stress was reducing but the mentality was changing. 'Things started to change with television. Gary Speed, Gary McAllister . . . the mental attitude was different.' He reveals that Strachan, 'by his own admission', had only come to get Leeds out of the Second Division, and that when Leeds lost at Anfield on New Year's Day 1991 Hennigan feared they'd been found out. 'But Strachan won Footballer of the Year that season' as they finished fourth.

By this stage, still only Wilko's second full season, David Batty was one of the first names on the team sheet, although Sutton has an intriguing take on why the tough-as-old-boots midfielder never quite took to the manager's technical coaching or Sergeant Wilko routine as readily as the others. 'Billy Bremner was Batts's hero. Howard came in and had this cold person-ality, although he did praise him. But for a young lad . . .' He doesn't need to expand. 'The other thing, everyone has this thing about David Batty, that he's Leeds through and through. He's not, not like Alan Smith or James Milner are. He loved his bike more than football. He loved the fans, less so the club. But once he went out there he'd give everything for the fans, because he knew the fans loved him.'

Sutton's insider knowledge extends to games as well as players. He singles out the match at Villa Park on

24 November 1991 – arguably the most ruthless televised display of Leeds United dominance since their notorious, cocksure 7–0 *Match of the Day* demolition of Southampton in 1972 – as an example of 'Wilkinson at his finest'. 'We were playing on the Sunday,' he begins. On the Saturday afternoon Gary Speed had got the ankle injury he told me about. 'So Gary said to me – and I trusted Gary – "I'll be fine." I said, "Tell you what, have a run around." He got to the other side and just dropped. I thought, "Blimey, I could have dropped a right ****ing bollock there." Cos if there was a three p.m. kick-off we'd be training at ten a.m. on the day of the game. The lads would be bored out of their minds.

'So what happened was, I've said, "Gaffer, Speedo's struggling." So he says, "I'm gonna play ten against ten. I'll bring in John McClelland at centre-half, and Chris Fairclough man-to-man marking against Tony Daley, their top man. Chris, you look after him – he dunt get a ****ing kick."' The conventional decision would have been to replace like with like – play another winger, or perhaps play Whitlow in midfield. 'But he went man-on-man marking, and bear in mind this is twenty years ago. It totally ****ed Villa up. It left Tony Dorigo with a free role to bomb on.'

Sutton remembers that after the game Villa's chief scout Brian Whitehouse asked him and Hennigan, 'What would you have done if Gary Speed hadn't been injured?' It was another twist of fate, coupled with inspirational management. Wilkinson employed man-marking several times again that season, notably away at Everton, when he used Batty to nullify the Toffees' chief threat, Peter Beardsley.

Sutton spent eight years – Wilko's entire reign – in the gaffer's inner circle, but it's perhaps telling that the Sarge remained a detached, almost enigmatic presence, even for his staff. 'He had a brilliant mind,' Sutty tells me. 'You could learn from him about everything from psychology to wines. Everything, really. I'll tell you what: he could drink most people under the table. But he could be the most arrogant and belittling twat as well, and you'd be really unhappy with him, and it might be cos we'd lost a few games and he was being brought back down again. He always said to me, "You, you've underachieved." His communication with people wasn't always brilliant. You had to read the signs. First day of pre-season when we signed Tony Dorigo, he'd had to go for treatment. I'm like, "Hiya, good summer?" And he's, "Why isn't Tony Dorigo here?" That was his first greeting.

'But if you look at all the really top managers, they are successful because they have that arrogance about them. You look at Ferguson, and how he's like that, and has vendettas for years. I don't think Howard had vendettas, but all of them . . . they've got that about them, and that detachment. He wasn't everybody's cup of tea as a person, but only now people recognize what he did achieve. Outside of Revie he was the most successful Leeds United manager.

'I got to know him well enough to ask, "Why didn't you ever get rid of me?" He said, "Have you ever won anything?" I said, "Yeah, I won the championship with Halifax." Whether he believed that I don't know. But he was very loyal, Howard.' And, as Sutton notes, from the Second Division onwards, as well as surrounding himself with troops he could trust, many of them were proven winners. 'Mervyn Day – FA Cup winner's medal [with West Ham, in 1975]. Mel Sterland – top division, a champion with Rangers. Jim Beglin – double winner [with Liverpool in 1985/86]. Chris Fairclough – Tottenham and Forest. Gordon Strachan – two world elevens. Chris Kamara – used to be a marathon runner, even though he was a diabetic. David Batty, Gary Speed – young ones who played with no fear. Vinnie Jones – cup winner's medal. Lee Chapman – Arsenal.' And that's just the Second Division champions.

Sutton recalls the week everything came together in the First Division. Leeds began the weekend of 18 April 1992 two points behind Man United with a game in hand. 'On that Saturday we went to Liverpool and they went to Luton. I remember a guy called Reggie, the groundsman at Liverpool, who said, "I'll tell you what, Alan, I wouldn't be too upset if we got beat today, as long as the trophy doesn't go to that mob up the road!" Anyway, we ended up drawing 0–0. Man U drew at Luton.

'Then on Monday, we're kicking off at Coventry at five p.m. on telly, and they're playing Nottingham Forest at home, and Forest are playing Nigel Clough at centre-half because they had no fit centre-halves. And they beat Man U at Old Trafford, 2–1. We beat Coventry 2–0, which was a game of patience. On the Wednesday they had to go to West Ham, who'd been relegated, and Kenny Brown Jr smashed in a twenty-five-yarder. So all of a sudden we're one point ahead with two games to go. On the Saturday we beat Sheffield, and I think for the first time ever Ian Rush scored against Man United.

'We came back by coach and were drinking champagne, and my nephew picked me up from Elland Road. We got to the roundabout at Calverley and had the rest of the Liverpool–Man U game on the radio. Michael Thomas scored the second goal for Liverpool, with two minutes to go, and my nephew just said, "Uncle Alan, I think you've just won the championship."'

CHAPTER 12

The Missing — and the Mojitos

Soz about that. I wor a bit excited.

I've been surprised how accessible and available people are, with most of the interviews so far clocking in at around two hours. It's not normally like this in football; it was certainly very different when I was interviewing Leeds players in the late nineties and early 2000s. Back then, even the club officials seemed to fear asking anything of the players, so you were generally left to your own devices.

A typical day at Thorp Arch would begin by first attempting to gain access past Mad Jack, the club's eccentric security guard, who greeted visitors from his little wooden hut wielding an air rifle. Once Jack had satisfied himself that you were who you said you were and stopped acting as if he were in *Dad's Army*, you'd be generally left waiting in the car park in the hope of grabbing a three-minute exclusive as the sought-after player made the fifteen-second dash from the training complex to the Porsche.

My worst experience in this respect was trying to interview Harry Kewell for a fashion/culture magazine. The club had arranged everything. A photographer was sent up all the way from London. Not only did the mercurial winger keep us waiting all day, every so often a small window would open, we'd hear sniggers, and then it would close again. It was approaching dusk by the time a club official saw us shivering and asked, 'Hasn't he done it yet?' It turned out the lovable Aussie had done a bunk out of a rear exit. We never got the interview.

Goal machine Jimmy Floyd Hasselbaink could be just as tricky. I remember a similar schlep up and a wait followed by a brief encounter with the star, who was actually very chatty and friendly, although he wasn't in the mood for an interview. 'I'll do it next season,' he said on that balmy May afternoon. Of course, JFH wasn't at Leeds the next season.

However, some players were lovely. Dutch centre-half Robert 'The Mole' Molenaar kindly gave me a huge cake he'd been given for something or other, and I was devastated for him when injury ended his career soon afterwards. Rio Ferdinand was an engaging interviewee, when you got him – but when he famously 'forgot' a drugs test I couldn't help but be reminded of the various occasions on which he 'forgot' an interview, which meant another trek the following day.

Very occasionally you'd be lucky enough to get some-one like Croatian-Australian striker Mark Viduka, who seemed to divide fans at every club he played for but whom I always found to be a fascinating, strong character and a terrific bloke. While other players would mumble clichés taught to them at media training – notably 'the team spirit's great' as they plummeted towards relegation – the skilful colossus nicknamed 'V-bomber' would talk for an hour or more about everything from turning out for LUFC while his father faced a life-threatening operation, to being caught up in war zones and Croatian politics, God, playing guitar along with Metallica songs in his garage, and the type of bones preferred by his two dogs.

The big difference then was that players were supposedly obliged to give interviews, and someone at the club would at least get you access to the building, if nothing more. Now, I'm on my own.

Because Leeds United haven't been in touch with most of Wilko's troops for years, I have to be resourceful in tracking down and contacting players and have no idea of protocol, or how accommodating they might be. Getting such access to the likes of Gary Speed and Vinnie Jones was a dream come true, but I soon discover it won't always be that easy.

After someone gives me his number and I call him at home, goalkeeper John Lukic bites my head off, barking, 'Where did you get this number?' as ferociously as Mick Hennigan. I tell him it came from someone who interviewed him before, but he denies ever giving such an interview, even though I'm staring at it as we speak (it says he has become an avid gardener). Eventually he is pacified, insisting it's not me he's mad at, but the person who passed on a private number, which is fair enough. He says that if I call in a few days we'll sort something out; but calls go unreturned, and then I get a text message saying an interview would 'conflict with my own project', which may or may not mean putting fertilizer on the sprouts. But he says he's looking forward to reading about his teammates.

After upsetting Big John, I decide not to call Chris Fairclough on the number given to me by the same person but drop him a text, which goes unanswered. Then I find out he's patron of the laudable Show Racism the Red Card campaign, and put in a request for an interview, which is 'politely declined'.

Some players are just proving tricky to track down. Finding Fairclough's central defensive partner Chris Whyte involves a succession of emails to everyone from former Arsenal teammate Paul Davis, at the Professional Footballers Association, to the MP for Finchley.

I go on a similar wild-goose chase trying to get to Rod Wallace, who seems to have disappeared into football's own Bermuda Triangle. His Wikipedia entry suggests he's coaching Kingstonian Under 18s, but they say he left some time ago and think he went to assistant-manage Molesey, a lower league team in Surrey, which produces a comical exchange with manager Peter Lelliott.

'You didn't know I was Rod's agent, obviously,' he begins. 'Only joking.'

A while later: 'I see you work for the *Guardian*. I am pleased my "client" has agreed to make contact with your good self. My terms are fifty per cent of the agreed price, haha. Meanwhile, any possibility of doing a piece about Molesey?'

Wallace never calls, although Mr Lelliott does at least give some information about the tiny former forward's mysterious activities. 'Rod has been a big influence on my players, especially the strikers,' he tells me. 'He's a quiet, unassuming fellow who does his conversations with players in a quiet, one-to-one, orderly fashion.'

Within weeks Wallace has left for Epsom, and the trail goes cold again.

Faced with these situations, which cause more than a few sleepless nights, I ask myself, 'What would Sergeant Wilko do?' I start to adopt his maxims – first player, first striker, first midfielder – and fire off an email to Gary McAllister's agent.

One of the more entertaining early encounters is with former goal machine turned successful restaurateur Lee Chapman, whom I find via one of his bars, the swish JuJu in Chelsea. The interview is arranged. I'm just passing Stevenage on the train when I get a call asking, 'Where are you?' Five minutes later, another call – 'Where are you?' – and the interview location changes every time. We finally meet in the street in Earl's Court, where Chappy seems bemused that I'd spotted him from eight hundred yards, but I explain that I watched him play so often I'd know that distinctive gangly gait better than my own girlfriend.

Chappy has another Leeds legend in tow, Paul Hart, whom I saw play in 1978 when he had a gigantic natural afro, and who was a core part of Wilkinson's inner sanctum as the coach of the youngsters who beat a Manchester United team containing the young Beckham, Nevilles et al in the FA Youth Cup in 1993.

Now lifelong friends, they've been catching up and have been on the sauce.

We get a cab to JuJu where more drinks arrive, then even more, followed by a succession of pink and then I think green cocktails, all on our host. After that, the night's a blur, but I remember thinking there are worse places to be than a chic bar in London getting very pleasantly inebriated with two of your football heroes.

It soon becomes apparent that there won't be an interview that day, either because the occasionally tabloid-hounded Chappy is subjecting me to a very complex, Wilko-like vetting process or because he's still just about sober enough to realize that giving any kind of interview after umpteen lagers and Mojitos would be a shpectacuhlarly baad idea. Hic. But we do talk football, and I remember the intriguing revelation that at Leeds he was driven by a restlessness, or unhappiness, which could only be sated by scoring goals. So when he netted a mammoth thirty-one of them in 1990/91, making him one of the top scorers in Europe? 'I wasn't happy. I wanted thirty-two.'

The night ends with hugs and a promise of a proper interview once I've spoken to all the others, and I just make the last train. For some reason I decide that getting off at Doncaster is as close to my home as Leeds, which it isn't. One wallet-slaughtering £65 cab ride later, I realize that a cocktails session with Lee Chapman has cost me a mammoth £200 in transport. Still, they were fantastic cocktails.

Then there's the ongoing conundrum of David Batty. I appreciate that if Speedo or Vinnie haven't seen him in years I've got as much chance of an audience with the now very private midfielder as a confession from Lord Lucan. But we have spoken various times before.

The first time was on his return to Leeds for a second spell in 1999, when I interviewed him in the foyer at Elland Road before he was due to get on the team bus for a reserve game, his first game in a Leeds shirt for six years. We'd only been talking for a few minutes when the bus pulled up, Batts suddenly asked 'Are we off?' and leapt up and away in the middle of the interview, without a word.

'Soz about that,' he explained when I collared him again in the club canteen the following morning. His old grey Volkswagen Golf cut a defiant shape in the car park among the other players' Porsches and Ferraris. 'I wor a bit excited.'

He was – and presumably is – a unique character, and once you realize this is how he is, he's impossible to dislike. During the title season, I remember once glimpsing him – a giant on the pitch, he's all of five foot seven – in the city centre. A ruckus had broken out in the middle of the street, a crowd had gathered, and among them was none other than Batts, in full Leeds United tracksuit, clearly finding the whole rumpus enormously entertaining.

In the canteen he was just as idiosyncratic, revealing that he'd written off £800,000 in signing-on fees by asking for a transfer back home from Newcastle, and admitting that if the deal hadn't gone through football's mystery man would actually have quit the game. He filled in a few details about his Harehills childhood, describing how his father had him doing pull-ups in the garage before school, and after it he'd drag him out for runs and kickabouts.

He spoke very fondly about Billy Bremner, who saw him as the 'blue-eyed boy' despite Batty's embarrassment when he'd be sent over the road to buy the manager's cigarettes. It was Bremner who took the young Batty from right-back and played him in the centre of midfield, which the player credited with 'turning my career around'. Most surprising of all, reading through that old interview, is the admission that he wasn't enjoying life under the new boss, Wilkinson, and in March 1989 had actually asked for a transfer, which the Sergeant refused. Batty knuckled down, and the rest is history.

Our last encounter – in March 2001 – was revealing in a different way. Just weeks earlier, the midfield terrier had made his comeback to a standing ovation from forty thousand people. Behind him lay a two-year injury nightmare that had begun on his first game back at Leeds, against Coventry on 14 December 1998, when he'd broken a rib. That shouldn't have been too complicated. However, shortly afterwards he found he was in terrible trouble. 'Every breath, every heartbeat was excruciating.'

Batty was sent to see a chest specialist, then a cardiologist, who diagnosed pericarditis: inflammation of the skin sack around the heart. The club kept it quiet while Batty, who'd barely even ever had a cold, was put on anti-inflammatories. Rumours circulated about a 'heart problem'.

He made it back for the following season, but in a game against Southampton was forced to leave the field. Soon afterwards he couldn't walk five yards without developing a limp. After innumerable X-rays, scans and injections, an underlying Achilles problem finally became apparent when it ruptured while he was playing in the garden with his kids. Never over-dramatic, Batty compared the pain to 'being invaded by a burning coil', or being shot. Amazingly, surgeons rebuilt the Achilles using tendons from his feet, which left him with a scar on his right leg the length of a bread knife. After months and months of weights, exercise and jogging, he finally made it back to help David O'Leary's ill-fated side to the semi-finals of the 1999/2000 UEFA Cup and the following year's Champions League, both of which saw glorious runs that ended in disappointment.

After falling out of favour with subsequent managers, an injury against former club Newcastle on 4 January 2004 saw the thirty-six-year-old Batty retire from the game. I've now tracked him down to a small village in North Yorkshire, a short drive from the coast, where he reportedly spends his time fishing and ferrying his two boys around to play football, but he clearly relishes his anonymity.

I am left wondering if our paths will ever cross again.

CHAPTER 13

Carl Shutt – 'Shutty'

We were like stormtroopers . . . a relentless machine.

'I'm just in B&Q at the moment,' says Shutty when I call him on the mobile. So the first conversation I have with one of Wilko's greatest goalscorers is about shelving.

Shutty always was one of us. I can still picture his big daft grin as he trotted on to the field. Shutty, like Whitlow, was another non-league player whom Wilkinson turned into a champion, but who never forgot where he came from and seemed to relish every minute. If you'd plucked a fan from the Kop and said, 'Right, get yourself stripped, you're playing for Leeds United,' he would have looked just like Carl Shutt – absolutely thrilled every time he stepped on to a football field. When he scored – which at Leeds was once in every three games he played, whether as starting striker, sub or even playing right midfield – his face would erupt in glee and wonderment. Shutty loved football, loved the fans, and we all absolutely loved Shutty.

Twenty years on, he hasn't changed a bit. We arrange to meet in a hotel just outside Sheffield, but little does either of us know that there are two hotels with the same name, and naturally I go to the wrong one. Shutty doesn't go home in a huff or throw toys out of the pram. He calmly gives me directions to where he is patiently waiting. Then – horror of horrors – about forty-five minutes into the interview my digital recorder runs out of batteries. No problem. Shutty points out that there's a Morrison's about half a mile away, so we head there. He asks an assistant to help locate the batteries and the interview continues, long into the afternoon, in the supermarket's tiny café. The little old ladies clinking cups of coffee seem entirely oblivious to the talk about titles and famous goals at the adjoining table. But this is Shutty all over; on the field, he would always go the extra mile.

Another of the Sheffield Wednesday contingent Wilko took to Leeds, for his first two seasons Shutt was part of a rotating group of partners for Lee Chapman, which also included Bobby Davison and Imre Varadi. Then when Leeds got promoted he was loaned out to Swedish side Malmö, and it could all have been over. But Shutty never would give up. After returning and fighting his way back into the team, he scored a sackful of goals with Chapman in the First Division and then, when the title season saw Rod Wallace make the number eight shirt his own, was still popping up all over, scoring the winner against Chelsea and a goal in the 1–1 draw against Everton.

Shutty was a classic Wilkinson disciple: all-action,

all-effort, run until you drop. Even Cantona's arrival didn't do for Shutty. In fact, in the European campaign after winning the title, Shutty came on for the Frenchman in Barcelona's Nou Camp stadium to score one of the most famous and memorable goals in Leeds United's history.

Leeds had gone down 3–0 to Stuttgart away from home, overturned the deficit to 4–4 with a magnificent fightback at Elland Road, but faced elimination from the competition on the away-goals rule until an eagle-eyed UEFA observer noticed that the Germans had played an ineligible substitute. A playoff was ordered, to take place on neutral territory at the famous Catalan ground.

Moments after Cantona strutted off, Shutty picked the ball up in the opponent's half, ran the entire length of the field and, as the commentator memorably put it, 'had the chance to find Strachan but finds the net!' It was like a dream sequence: the underdog hero scores this belting goal – the sort of goal you dream about when you're a kid, never mind when you are an ageing striker who began his career with Spalding – and runs towards the fans.

'I saw that goal for the first time only recently,' he assures me, explaining that he'd not seen it before because it was shown on Eurosport and not Sky, and he certainly wasn't one to bask in old glories by getting a video, which seems somehow typical of Shutty. As he tells it, he'd gone to Spain in a strange mood because he'd been tapped up by another club that had noticed he was out of the team, but had felt really fit. On the bench he'd been sat with David Wetherall and David

Rocastle (a summer 1992 signing from Arsenal) when he needed to take a pee.

Now, to go to the loo at Barcelona a player has to go down several flights of stairs, and on one of them was a little image of the Virgin Mary and Jesus. Shutty has never been religious – from a mining family, he always thought religion was a tool for the rich – and has never been to church in his life. But at that moment, something struck him.

'I don't know why but I said a little prayer as I went downstairs,' he confesses, revealing that he's never told this aspect of the story publicly before. 'As I've come back, Wilko's said, "Shutty, warm up." I've said to Rocky, "I'm gonna ****in' score here." Wethers told me later that Rocky had said, "Shutty thinks he's gonna score." They must have thought I was mad! I stripped off, but then there was a defensive corner and I'm thinking, "Not now, Wilko, wait." He's like, "You know where your position is."

'Eric came off and he's like that [he throws his head back, as if in a strop], and I'd gone from feeling really confident to thinking, "Don't let the ball come to me." Of course the ball gets kicked and it comes to me. Nightmare. I'm thinking, "Shutt comes on, ****s it up and costs us the game."'

Shutt raced towards it. He was lightning fast, but still struggled to get to the ball, until it hit the opposition defender and came back to him, like a little gift, falling at his feet.

'He's backing off and I'm running through with it. He's trying to force me wide and by the time he's

realized I'm not going to pass it, that's when I've hit it.'
He beams at me.

Alongside him, Strachan's face is a pure picture: annoyance at Shutt not passing turns to bewilderment, amusement, disbelief and finally pure ecstasy as the ball hits the net.

'The funny thing was, I'd pointed to a guy standing on his own and said to Wethers, "If I score I'm gonna run up to him." If you look at the video you'll see this guy standing there. People said I didn't realize where the supporters were. I did, I just went up to this one guy and went "Yeeeeahh!" and all the players start piling on me.'

Apparently, the first thing that flashed through his mind was the thought that he'd messed up any chance of getting a transfer, because the asking price would have rocketed. 'But secondly, it was a religious kind of thing. I've certainly not turned into a Biblebasher, but to come up them stairs and get a feeling, then go out and score . . . it did make me think.' But then again, it could seem like Carl Shutt's entire career was blessed.

He grew up in Sheffield, where most of his family were 'red' (supported Sheffield United). When he first signed for Wednesday they asked who he'd followed as a child. 'I knew footballers were stupid but I'm not that stupid,' he grins. 'I said, "Wednesday!" They asked me about players and I couldn't remember any of the names. I remembered a couple and they asked "Why him?" and I said that he was a good team player. It's not like now where you're overloaded with football. There'd be a couple of games on TV a week and it was the top teams. Leeds were on a lot so you got to watch them. I watched Leeds more than I ever went to Bramall Lane.'

Shutty grew up in the Revie era, and he remembers going on holiday and in every coastal town they visited shops had the Leeds kit. 'With the [post-1973] smiley badge and sock tags. I had Mick Jones's pennant on my wall.'

Nobody at school was too fussed that he supported Leeds, because the rivalry was United versus Wednesday. Starting as he would go on, he played for the school team, Sheffield Boys, and local teams on Saturdays and Sundays. 'I was playing a lot of football.' A pause. 'Probably too much football.'

But his league career started at the late age of twenty-three, first on trial at Rotherham reserves and then banging the goals in for non-league Spalding under Mick Hennigan, who then moved to join Wilkinson at Wednesday. When Shutt refused a new contract after Spalding had scuppered his dream move to Notts County by demanding a bigger fee, Hennigan put in a call.

'He said, "Don't say nowt. Come play for our reserves."'

Shutt scored in the first game but felt out of his depth. 'We were doing crossing and finishing and I was so tense I couldn't cross a road,' he says. 'I felt I'd made a big mistake.' He was working in a factory, but scored a hat-trick against Liverpool reserves. Wilkinson offered him a deal. He describes his first day with the first team as being like a first day at school. 'One of the regulars had been dropped for me so that didn't go down well.'

Wednesday were a top team, and would have been in the UEFA Cup if it hadn't been for the ban on English clubs in Europe following the Heysel Stadium disaster. Hennigan eased him in. 'We'd been mates since Spalding,' Shutty continues. 'The difference between good footballers and not so good footballers is often sacrifices. "Are you coming out tonight?" "No." You were all right with Mick if you respected football. He couldn't stand players who took the piss. We had arguments on the pitch. He gave me a rocket and I couldn't understand why, so I scored two goals. He loved that. He had a coaching effect without me knowing it.'

According to Shutty, Wilkinson and Hennigan both hated footballers who moaned, and would run them so hard they had no energy left to grumble. Then Wilkinson would get rid of them. 'He wanted that team spirit and bond. He had that dressing room so it was closed. Impenetrable. Nothing went out. It was the same at Wednesday. Physically and mentally we were like stormtroopers. We won a lot of games fifteen minutes from the end because people couldn't take us. We were a relentless machine.'

He reveals that at Wednesday, striker David Hirst's pre-match meal was a bacon buttie. But Shutty embraced Wilkinson's nutritional philosophies: 'He had chicken, beans, pasta, all that at Wednesday, and he refined it at Leeds.'

At Hillsborough, the striker also began to develop the understanding with Chapman that would prove even more devastating at Leeds. 'I loved playing with Chappy. Chappy got the goals, I dragged defenders into space so he could move into positions. I knew if I got to the byeline and crossed it towards the penalty spot Chappy had a chance of getting on it.'

He argues that strikers can be over-coached, and that the best have a certain something – almost a sixth sense – which enables them to get into scoring positions where a coach would say they shouldn't be. 'I'm not saying there are natural goalscorers, but people like Chappy, Lineker, they just seemed to be there. The ball ricochets and they're there to knock it in.'

However, despite the partnership's success – Shutty scored nine in nineteen league appearances in 1985/86 and seven in twenty the next year – he was sold in 1987 (he suspects to make way for someone) to Bristol City, where he became a crowd favourite under fearsome, toothless 1970s Leeds striker Joe Jordan. In one game he was clattered from behind – 'that's how it was then' – and within ten minutes the offender was 'sparko, with blood coming from his mouth. Joe's winked at me. It was like having your own minder.'

When he first heard Wilkinson wanted him back he thought they were having him on. 'I said, "Are you taking the piss?" They took a photo as I walked in. The next person I saw was Gordon Strachan.'

Shutty has a bizarre story about the Wee Man's medical, which was conducted jointly with his in March 1989. During the eye test, Strachan covered the same eye twice. 'The doctor never noticed,' he says. 'Strach's pissing himself laughing when I mentioned it. It turns out he had an eye problem from his childhood. I thought, "You're one of the best players in the country. It can't be that dodgy!"'

Even now, Shutt's not quite sure why Wilkinson brought him back. 'Sometimes I wish I'd asked him more things, but you just get on wi' it.' Whatever the reason, it worked. Shutty became an instant crowd hero with a hat-trick on his debut, against Bournemouth on 1 April 1989.

Typically, he'd rather draw attention to one of the forgotten names in the story – Peter 'Fish' Haddock, the Second Division Leeds player of the year, whose career was cut short by injury, and who was last heard of working as a postman. 'He was one of the best centre-halves I ever played with. Would have been a Premier League player. He was just unlucky with what happened to him.' Haddock partnered Chris Fairclough ('quiet lad, did the business') before Wilkinson replaced him with Chris Whyte.

Shutt spent much of the promotion season struggling with a cartilage problem, hence the Malmö loan. But in 1990/91, Shutt and Chapman scored forty-two goals in all competitions; eleven of them were Shutty's, 'and I must have made a lot of Chappy's'.

When Wilkinson signed Rod Wallace at the start of the 1991/92 season and gave him the number eight shirt, Shutt initially thought the new boy would be a 'floating winger', but when the truth dawned he got his head down and worked harder. Of his fourteen appearances that campaign (eight of them as sub), easily the most memorable came on 14 September when he returned from a seven-week injury lay-off, with only forty-five minutes of reserve football behind him, to score the only goal against Chelsea at Stamford Bridge.

Shutty had a habit of scoring against the Blues and reveals he 'hated them with a vengeance'. He'd been on holiday in Cyprus and was playing with his kids when some Chelsea supporters had recognized him and sat behind him. 'After a few beers they started with the songs, "We hate Leeds" and all that. My brother-in-law says, "Walk away." We did, but next time I scored down there I absolutely loved that. Then when I scored against them in the title season I jumped over the dog track, ran halfway to the Leeds fans and thought, "This is further than I expected!" I used to jump over the railings. I came back from one game with nail marks on my hands.'

There's another aspect to this story which is even more bizarre, and not a little comical. Shutty started that game with a bandage on his knee. As he tells it, at a wedding a few weeks earlier, the Shutt entourage had managed to get into a mighty ruckus with another family (of Sheffield United supporters) in an argument over football. 'I punched a lad and I was on top of him and ended up punching the tarmac,' he reveals, making it sound like something out of the Wild West. 'They'd picked on the wrong family. There were broken cheekbones, all sorts. I ended up in hospital for two weeks. It was all kept very quiet. The police came up and we told 'em nowt. If it got out it would have created carnage. Can you imagine? "Leeds United player . . ." So that's why I had the strapping on.' He chuckles.

The wound got infected and left a mark that's still there now. After the next game, against Coventry, he went into the dressing room 'and the bottom part of the skin on my knee had come off. Mick looked at me and said, "Why didn't you say summat?" I was struggling to walk. I should have said something, but you don't want to say anything because you'd be out of the team.'

Shutty's memory produces various other sepia-tinted snapshots of the era. He remembers playing against Nottingham Forest when defender Stuart Pearce scored at a corner and was promptly subbed by a furious Brian Clough. 'He said, "Young man, I pay you to defend, not go up for corners!"' He also recalls Hennigan telling him to ask Eric Cantona to work harder. 'I thought, "Tell me in French and I'll ****in' tell 'im!"' He tells me too about one day when West Ham fans were banging on the Leeds team bus trying to get in.

But most intriguing of all are his revelations of some of the brilliantly underhand methods that were employed to assist success. At Wednesday, a door in the home dressing room led to the laundry room, which meant you could hear what was going on in the opponents' camp – a trick Mick Hennigan utilized to the max. 'We knew who was getting subbed or if they were changing the formation,' chuckles the striker. 'We used to shout, "We know you're here, you bastards!" in case they were doing the same trick. But they never were.'

He's roaring with laughter, and has a similar story about Leeds. Apparently, when visiting teams stayed in the city, the hotel manager would sometimes give the

Leeds contingent their room list, so the staff knew which opposition players had or hadn't travelled. Shutty also noticed that when Leeds stayed anywhere on rival turf, Hennigan would take care to remove the A frame from where the tactical plan had been pinned up in the hotel, in case it fell into opposition hands. The reason for the caution was that Hennigan knew this trick very well and had his own network of friendly hotel managers, who if possible would slip him the opposition's plans. 'So sometimes we knew exactly what corners and free kicks they would be taking, because we'd seen it all written down. We knew what the team was, everything!'

Amazing. But Wilkinson wanted to win – or not lose – every game, and had schooled his players to think the same way. 'He once said, "I hate losing more than I love winning." It's something that stuck in my mind. So we'd play until the end regardless. One of the best games I played in was when we were 4–0 down against Liverpool [on 13 April 1991, during LUFC's first season back in the top flight], and everything they hit went in. It sounds stupid but it wasn't a 4–0 game. Wilko could have laid into us, but he just said, "keep doing what you're doing and you'll be all right". I don't think he could figure out what was happening, but we got one and then another one. As we were going off the fans are singing, "What the **** is going on?" We ended up losing 5–4 and got a standing ovation.'

Shutty's encyclopedic memory dredges up other important details, for instance about the build-up to the 6–1 annihilation of Wednesday in the title season.

The year before, in Mel Sterland's testimonial game, Leeds had fielded veteran Revie-era players such as Eddie Gray against Wednesday's first team. 'Some of the older ones had to be subbed cos they were kicking them up in the air. So when we went to Hillsborough we didn't need psyching up. We thought, "Right, you've done it against the oldies, let's see how you do it against us." We never took our feet off the pedal cos of what happened in the testimonial.'

He remembers that this coincided with the press talking up Wilkinson's chances of winning the league, and that the shrewd manager had told his players to tell them, 'It's Man U's title. It's a competition for second, and we'll be delighted with second.'

'It was a big learning curve for Ferguson that year,' Shutty states. 'Wilkinson was so blasé in public, but in the dressing room he was saying, "We can do this!" When you take your foot off the accelerator it takes a while to get it going again, and by then it was too late. We won it by four points. If you notice, now, Ferguson's learned from that. He always says "Oh, Chelsea's gonna win it" or whoever. It puts all the pressure on the other team.'

Winning the league at Sheffield United's ground was a nice touch for Shutt personally – he played the second half, on for Strachan – although he'd have loved to score. 'You can't take it in,' he admits. 'Away from home, there's no one to celebrate with. I remember it felt surreal. "Have we actually done it?" That's why I look like a duck with a slapped arse in the photos. We were all over the place. Some were celebrating. Some were dead on us feet. Some had tears in their eyes. I look at the medal now and I think, "Is that what it all was about?" But of course what it was about is just immeasurable.'

Which is pretty poetic for a big man with a Sheffield accent. If we weren't in such a public place, with a small Formica table between us, I think I'd have to hug him.

The title and that goal at Barcelona are the stuff of football dreams that barely any player gets to experience, never mind a journeyman striker who started off at Spalding. If there's a bittersweet side to Shutty's glories at Leeds it's the manner of his exit, only a year after receiving the championship medal.

After four years of 'injections, playing through the pain barrier and not letting them down' he was suddenly moved into another dressing room, with the reserves, and given the number twenty-seven shirt. When he got ready for the 1993/94 team photo, he was shocked to be suddenly told, 'You're not in it, Shutty.' 'I was dressed up in the kit and everything. That was the biggest embarrassment of the lot. That's how it was.'

Maybe this was one of those things Chris Kamara mentioned that Wilkinson regretted. Shutty never asked. 'I don't know him any better now than I did then,' he admits. But otherwise, he is a big fan of the Sergeant and still lives by his maxims. '"Success is a matter of luck. Ask any failure." "You can lie to anyone but yourself." "Fail to prepare and you'll prepare to fail." I had that one on a mirror when I was manager at Kettering.'

After Leeds, he played for Birmingham and

Manchester City (on loan), then drifted down the leagues, performing miracles as player-manager of Kettering and Bradford Park Avenue despite crippling financial constraints, and playing until he was forty-one. But despite amassing coaching badges he's been unable to get back into the game – 'It's hard when you feel you've got something to give back to it' – and is currently an assistant manager with Thomas Cook.

He's happy and doesn't do regrets, but Shutty's adventures have had an unexpected twist. Recently he was at the gym when the cross-trainer machine displayed a ridiculously high heartbeat, which he put down to a malfunction. Then a couple of weeks later the doctor found the same thing. 'He said, "You've got a heart problem." It hit me like a bullet to the chest. You think, "You've never smoked, kept yourself fit and never been the biggest drinker." I'm taking warfarin [an anti-coagulant] and beta-blockers. I played after injections and all sorts. You never know what it's done. A specialist said that when you've done that many miles, like a car, eventually you'll have a misfire.'

Sometimes, winning titles has a price. The big grinning man who loved nothing more than playing football literally ran his heart out.

CHAPTER 14

Mel Sterland and Imre Varadi – 'Zico' and 'Imre Banana'

We did what we had to do, and I've got memories. Medals aren't important. Memories are.

I track down Mel Sterland via an internet message board in Sheffield, and a few days later find myself pulling into a housing estate on the outskirts of his hometown, into a street that hosts a police car and a skip, from where Wilkinson's first-choice right-back assists with directions: 'Top of the street, mate. You can't miss me. I'm the fat bloke.'

I glimpse him from all of sixty yards. It's true, he has put on a few pounds – but not perhaps as many as he fears. It must be hard when you've been a supremely fit athlete but are unable to exercise. But his face hasn't changed a bit. I must have spent hours staring at that face over the years – a face which, perhaps more than any other Leeds United player I've ever watched (with the possible exception of Carl Shutt), seemed to explode with joy at the simple pleasure of stepping out on to a football field. Once, I was so close to that face I could see the beads of sweat on his forehead, when Sterland scored against somebody or other and ran towards the corner of the Kop to celebrate, and we all shared in his ecstasy from just feet away.

Twenty years on, he's living in a small but very nicely refurbished semi-detached house, having coped with more than his fair share of ups and downs. A long time ago we dubbed Sterland 'Zico' after the Brazilian World Cup player, a deadly passer of the ball and free-kick specialist who was arguably the best player in the world in the early 1980s. Initially the nickname was ironic, football banter, but as the passes found their target and the free kicks and occasional penalties flew in, it didn't turn out to be so ironic after all. He was a key component of Wilkinson's first eleven, not just as a defender but as a flying full-back whose regular assists for Chapman were such a vital part of the title-winning game plan. That season was arguably the best of his career, certainly at Leeds United; in twenty-nine league appearances (two as sub) he weighed in with no fewer than six goals from full-back until an ankle injury finished his career in the title run-in, and we never saw Mel 'Zico' Sterland fly down the wing or cross those balls again.

'I was one of the unlucky ones. I didn't play in the Premiership, through four operations.' He's propped up on a sofa, in just a pair of shorts. 'I was having painkillers and cortisone jabs through that season, since 1991, but it's a season you don't forget.'

His wife Charmaine brings some tea, and that face is still smiling.

'It was a long, hard season. To win the league . . . most people will never do it. It seems like a year or so ago. You have little flashbacks. The fans were unbelievable. They were like an extra player. People didn't think we'd win it, but we were in front of schedule on everything. We worked hard and had a special bond. Whatever industry you're in – builders, brickies – they've got to bond together. That came early. We had a great bond and some great players, and a great manager: a guy who was very disciplined and knew what he wanted.'

Sterland had played under Wilkinson before, in the latter stages of his eleven seasons at Sheffield Wednesday, when Sergeant Wilko took over from Leeds legend 'Big' Jack Charlton, whose affectionate nickname for 'Zico' was 'The Flying Pig'. 'They were totally different,' he recalls. 'Big Jack was unbelievable. He got names wrong and everything. I always remember a practice match when we had twelve players on the pitch! I said, "Gaffer, you've got an extra man!" He just turned to John Pearson and said, "You're not playing. Get off." It was so funny. Howard was strict. But if you played for him, you got the rewards.

'A lot of players thought it was too hard,' he continues, and I realize that the interview is well under way without me even having asked a question. But that's Mel, always was: couldn't wait to get things going, couldn't wait to run. He's right. It does seem like only yesterday.

'People take their cars in for a service. I used to take

my training shoes in for a service – twenty thousand miles! But it got us results. He got the best out of players. Some liked it and some didn't. Strachan was the best footballer and the best professional I ever played with. I was at Rangers then and had offers from Queens Park Rangers and Sheffield Wednesday. Howard said, "Come to Leeds United. We're gonna win the league." I went "****ing hell, Howard!" He told me the players he was going to bring in and got them all. I'd loved it at Wednesday and I'm a Wednesdayite, but I don't believe in going back. It was another challenge with a manager who trusted me, and I trusted him.'

But Wilkinson had changed his methods. Not so much running – although plenty for Sterland because he had problems keeping the weight off even then. 'He used to fine me, a hundred pounds for every pound I was overweight,' he chuckles. 'One weekend cost me seven hundred. But he was like your dad. My dad died when I was young and he took me under his wing.'

I know that feeling. My own father died when I was six and I was forever grasping at a father figure of my own. Even from five hundred yards away in the Kop I could see there was something fatherly about the Sarge. Like Gary Speed said: authoritarian but somehow, very deep down, you suspected, very caring; awkward, but very wise. As fans, none of us would hear a word against him.

'If you ask him a question it takes him ages to answer,' muses Sterland, leaning back into the sofa, surrounded by white decor. 'He should be a solicitor. He takes everything in and then when he answers, it's spot on. Fantastic guy. He didn't used to tell Carl Shutt he was playing until the Saturday, because he knew he'd shit himself [when I later put this to Shutty, he fires back, 'I knew he'd tell you that! It only 'appened once!']. His man management was superb. Shutty got a lot of bollockings. Then he'd put his arm round him for the next game. Chapman, what a signing. People used to say I made Chapman a millionaire, I made that many goals for him. I'd stay behind in training whipping balls in on the run, putting it in the area where people can't get it. We scored so many goals like that it was frightening.'

Indeed. The Chapman–Sterland partnership was one of the great full-back/centre-forward pairings in English football.

'It's a declining art,' he sighs. 'They earn so much money now they take it in their stride. Speedy used to say to me, "Best full-back in the country. Get me twelve goals a season." We were all in it together, go out with the wives as well. Strachan was a great believer in that.'

I've still barely got a word in.

'Have you spoken to Batty? Amazing kid. He's got twin boys and does everything with them. Nobody can get hold of him. Strange kid, but a lovely kid. Didn't like football. I don't miss it. I miss the banter, the crack with the lads. When my book [*Boozing, Betting and Brawling*] came out [in 2008] I rang Vinnie and he said, "How are you getting on, you fat cant?" He told me to send the book to "Vinnie Jones, fackin' 'Ollywood". A great guy.'

Finally, a pause. The once super-fast sportsman is now unable to walk more than a few yards because of a problem with a lung, as well as the ankle. It must be terrible having so much energy and struggling to channel it.

'I take warfarin every day for my blood, anti-depressants every bloody day,' he reveals, 'but there's people much worse off than me. I've got two kids, fantastic grandkids, lovely wife, nice house.' Then an admission, of sorts. 'People say "You're looking well", but inside I'm rotten. I put on the smile. There's children with leukaemia . . . I wouldn't change a thing.'

At Leeds, he earned £2,000 a week. 'Nobody was on a load. Chappy would have been on double it, I think. Strachan a bit more. But it's scary how quickly it can end.' He cites the example of a centre-half called Tony James, who played in the game against Leicester in 1990 when Strachan scored that famous volley, and had been about to sign for Tottenham for £1.5m when a leg break 'finished him. Just like that.'

In Sterland's case, the tackle from Notts County's Mark Draper on 1 February 1992 didn't finish him immediately, it meant he lasted only forty-six minutes of that 3–0 victory, the scoring having been started by the seventieth goal of Zico's career. He played on for another five weeks, in crippling pain.

'Nightmare. Murder. It's still the same,' he admits. 'That tackle pulled it [the ankle] straight off at the bone. I played on until the Tottenham game [on 7 March, before which he required a painkilling injection] and big Newsome came on and scored. In the same game Chapman had his face all smashed up and had to have plastic surgery. He was pushed into the gravel. Disgrace it was, he was a right mess. I was on big money but I couldn't get myself fit. I still can't run about or owt. I could never have coped with the rotation they have now. If the team wins, the team was kept the same.'

It's another great unknown. If Sterland hadn't played on regardless, would Leeds still have won the league?

'I'd like to know how many goals were made in that time,' he says. 'Have a look at that. Who knows, pal?'

I do look, and while there are no assists, he defensively contributed to two wins and two draws in five games.

He hated being on the sidelines. 'Having to get into training, see Alan Sutton for treatment, get on the weights. What a boring life. But there's no bigger turn-on than a full stadium and seeing the ball in the net. It's true what they say. It's better than sex, Dave! The fans took to me straight away. When the ball went out you'd hear them chant your name. People still recognize me and come up to me. It's fantastic, Dave!'

There's a knock at the door and – of all people – it's Imre Varadi, Sterland's teammate from 1990 to 1993, who acquired the nickname 'Imre Banana' while he was at Manchester City, when fans used to take inflatable bananas to the game (although the chief instigator, City fan Frank Newton, for some reason switched to an inflatable crocodile). 'I don't even know how it started, because Banana and Varadi didn't rhyme,' Varadi said years later, 'and it was certainly nothing to do with what was down my trousers, but soon they were dressing the bananas up in wigs, skirts and all sorts.'

There was none of this at Leeds. After five goals in twenty-six league appearances under Wilkinson, he's now a successful football agent, but has popped in to see Charmaine 'to get his feet done'. That 'special bond' between the two of them has survived for almost thirty years. Varadi, who looks as fit and solid as he did two decades ago, barely played by 1991/92 (two starts and one appearance as sub) but travelled around the country with the squad, and also remembers the 'roller-coaster' like it was yesterday.

'I was going through a divorce at the time,' he sighs. 'But the team spirit. Togetherness. It was an amazing thing to be part of.'

The two great friends met in 1983, on the pitch, when Manchester City – for whom Varadi played in midfield rather than up front as at Leeds – faced Wednesday at Hillsborough. 'It was so funny,' Varadi recalls. 'I found myself defending in the eighteen-yard box, he dived over my leg and got a penalty!'

Sterland chips in: 'He said, "You ****ing . . ."' He leaves the sentence hanging.

Varadi grins. 'My exact words.'

'We've been friends ever since,' Sterland adds.

Like so many of the players I've met so far, they had a common bond in childhood hardship. Sterland, one of nine children, grew up on the struggling Manor estate, and went to the same school as Shutty. 'My mum and dad had **** all, but I loved it,' he insists. 'If you take a kid from a council estate, he will play all day.'

'I was the same,' muses Varadi. 'Humble beginnings.' In his capacity as an agent he says he recently visited some parents whose would-be footballer son had a private gymnasium in the house, but tells me he'd rather have one hungry young player with nothing than a hundred from such comfortable backgrounds.

His mother died in 2001, but before that Varadi grew up in children's homes. 'I don't really wanna talk about that cos it's personal,' he says, reasonably. 'I've got three brothers and don't really know what they're doing. I speak to one. But it was a very dysfunctional family. It rounds you. It gives you a hunger for life. You want to get out there and make it better for yourself.'

Sterland's was a familiar story: good at football at school, supportive teachers, apprenticeship, professional at Wednesday. Varadi grew up in Luton and played in parks, before attending training sessions at Luton Town twice a week. When manager Harry Haslam moved to Sheffield United, he said to Varadi, 'There's nothing down there. Why don't you come up here?' and that's where it started. From Sheffield, Varadi went to Everton and played with Colin Todd, Kevin Ratcliffe, Micky Lyons, Dave Thomas and Mark Wright, then Newcastle, where he lined up alongside Kevin Keegan.

'Playing under Howard was different because we had a different mentality. We had great players in the team like Mel, Gary Speed, Gary McAllister, Cantona, but it was . . .'

'Get it forward!' Sterland offers.

'Exciting!' Varadi says. 'Howard Wilkinson was the first manager to use wing-backs, when he had Mel and Nigel Worthington at Wednesday, and three centre-halves. Howard bollocked me or ignored me' – he chuckles at this – 'but he bought me three times, from Newcastle to Sheffield, Man City back to Sheffield, and then at Leeds.'

Sterland won the Scottish title during a four-month spell at Rangers before Wilkinson came calling. 'I met Howard on the motorway. It's crackers really, but that's how it was in those days.'

'It's different now,' says Varadi, with his agent's head on. 'Back then business was conducted at motorway services. Nowadays it's mainly meetings at the clubs, sometimes hotels . . . or Abramovich's boat!' He doesn't remember any meetings with Leslie Silver or Bill Fotherby, just Wilkinson and Hennigan. 'I was on my way up to Celtic and Howard's said, "You're not signing for them, you're coming here."'

'I didn't know that,' admits Sterland.

'I was on my way up to sign for Celtic, Mel! I said to Howard, "But we've agreed terms." He offered me more than Celtic. I had to ring the manager, Billy McNeill, but he was all right about it.'

Because the pair knew each other, they helped each other settle in.

'It was fun,' says Varadi. 'That was the main thing. We got away with murder in those days. Racing cars away from the ground or training ground. You couldn't do it now. After a game on a Saturday we'd go out drinking. We'd go out on a Wednesday drinking. Not various groups – the entire squad. I think that's changed now.

'Testimonials were a big deal in our days. It's not like that now. Money has changed. Foreign investment, Sky TV. If players don't get it, their chairmen will. In our day, the power was with the club. If they didn't want you, you were gone. Now it's all about the players. Clubs can't bully individual players like they could.

'I don't know if the game's faster because I don't play. The pitches are better. We used to play in winter, muddy pitches with a tiny bit of grass left. We had to get the ball into wide areas because we couldn't get it down and play. They're like bowling greens now. But if you want to create space you go wide and long. If you've got more space you've got more time on the ball, so it worked.

'We had a competitive edge whether we were playing football or table tennis.'

Where does that come from? I ask Varadi.

'We're like horses, just trained and trained to win.'

'There weren't many easy games,' says Sterland. 'You could play the bottom team and they'd give you the hardest game ever. We lost to Oldham and Crystal Palace. Everyone remembers our 6–1 against Sheffield Wednesday but that was a hard game.'

Varadi remembers Wilkinson jumping on the table with delight after the Wednesday game – another uncharacteristic show of unbridled emotion. 'On that day, being his old club, we suddenly knew how much it meant to him. When he went to Wednesday he left me behind! He signed me, and seven days later went to Leeds. But he came back [for me], yeah. He's never got the credit he deserved, because the game changed. But he will probably be the last English manager to win the league for a long time. He left no stone unturned. Seaweed tablets! Everything. If there was an issue in your life, he'd get involved. He'd get these two [Mel and Charmaine Sterland] in all the time.'

Sterland has had a lot of problems in his life, even when he was playing. At Wednesday he became so anxious he was convinced he was dying of cancer until Wilkinson arranged for tests, which gave him the all clear. Wilkinson also campaigned for Sterland's England appearance (against Saudi Arabia in 1988, which added to his tally of three England 'B' caps and seven outings for the Under 21s). Like so many players from George Best to Paul Gascoigne, Sterland was happiest when playing but struggled to experience the same pleasure between games. Alan Sutton mentioned that Zico could either be 'a hundred miles high or six foot underground', the sort of mood swings that make me wonder if he should have been looked at for depression. But you don't talk about that sort of thing in football even now, and certainly not in 1992.

His escape route was the well-worn one of drink and gambling. 'Howard wasn't daft. He knew.' Again, it was Wilkinson who became a counter-signatory on his cheques to try to control his spending. 'On a night game, the lads would be in the hotel. I'd be in the bookie's. I won a few. I won £5,750 once on football. I had five draws at a tenner and was waiting for West Ham v. Liverpool. Julian Dicks got sent off and I thought I'd had it. But at full time it was 0–0.' He soon lost the lot. 'I walked out with fifty quid.' His face bursts into that familiar smile. 'I'd still made forty quid! I was crackers about gambling.'

The big problems came following the injury, when he

couldn't play at all. 'It happened to a lot of people,' he argues. 'I don't think anyone realized how bad it was. I just wanted to play football. I had cortisone, painkillers. I had to say, "Hold on. I just can't continue." Howard played Jon Newsome at right-back, Gary Speed.' He made a return in 1992/93 against Blackburn but lasted only twenty-five minutes.

'Four operations on the same ankle,' sighs Varadi. 'Incredible.'

'And you start pulling a hamstring somewhere else,' says Sterland.

'I've had a few cortisones in my time,' admits Varadi. 'They used to throw it at you then. Now you're only allowed to have two or three. It's an anti-inflammatory which works quicker because they can get it right on the spot.'

But it doesn't solve the problem, just papers over the cracks.

'I remember playing at Newcastle,' Varadi continues. 'I had a dislocated shoulder, got fit and needed cortisone at half time to get me on the pitch. In those days squads were smaller and you had to play. But we wanted to. Nowadays players are paid so much they can afford to say no.'

Sterland tried everything to get back before conceding that the injury had won, which was when he spiralled into a drink-fuelled depression. He'd lost £90,000 on the house they'd owned in Glasgow; now the family home with its pool and games room was up for sale as well. One day it just got too much, and he headed out to rural Hathersage, near Sheffield.

'I'd been to meet Imre at the airport.'

'Was it that day?' Varadi asks.

'I'd come home with my gear. Training kit. What brought it on? You just think everything's gonna end, don't you? So I went up there, put the exhaust into the car, and I heard the voice of my [deceased] mum saying, "What are you doing, you daft bugger?"'

The car had filled with fumes?

'Yeah, and—'

'He ran out of petrol!' hoots Varadi, prompting much laughter. 'He couldn't even get that right!'

It's dressing-room banter, and it pulls Sterland out of a difficult moment as effectively as when they were together on the field. But even his closest friend didn't know how close Sterland came to the edge.

'He kept it quiet for a long time,' Varadi tells me, serious once more. 'When you do things like that, you keep it in, don't you? I'm lucky he's here to talk about it, to be honest.'

'I look back now and think, "What the hell was I doing?"' Sterland says. 'Especially when I look at my kids, my granddaughter. But at the time you think everyone's against you. I couldn't see a way out, but there is a way out. I talked to people, went to see a few people. You go through a lot in football and you don't realize how many friends you've got, through football. Cos when you're injured or finished, there's no one there. Cos they've got their own things to get on with.'

As Varadi goes on to emphasize, there was no after-care then for players who had problems, especially after leaving football. 'At the end of the day, you're just a number. None of us got calls from our various clubs saying "How are you?" You go through the system and that's it. Current players maximize their career and look after themselves, because once you stop playing, that's it.'

Varadi still gets to Leeds but says it doesn't tug his heartstrings, because he's there all the time. He enjoys dealing with the players and executives. Sterland had a spell as an agent too, but it didn't last. The pair managed Wilkinson's old club Boston for a while but wouldn't do it again. 'It was good,' Varadi says, 'but we had players who had jobs turning up late in midweek. We were used to being professional.'

In recent years, Sterland has tried everything from delivering fish to opening a pub, until the finances fell through. In 1995, Wilkinson helped him out of another awkward spot when he was charged with handling stolen property; he was later acquitted after protesting his innocence throughout. He still sees his former manager quite a lot. Only recently the Sarge took him for a curry, picking up the tab.

Ironically, what they achieved in 1992 has proved Sterland's salvation. After selling his championship medal for enough money to pay off the mortgage and take Charmaine on a cruise, he's still a regular at the Hallamshire hospital (where he bumps into Shutty), but for the first time in a long time is financially stable.

'I don't regret anything,' he insists. 'Everything I've done, I've loved. Yeah I could have more money, but some players can't work. Imre can. We did what we had to do, and I've got memories. Medals aren't important. Memories are.'

More and more, I'm struck by the enormous sacrifices made by some of these guys to climb football's Everest. I have to ask the obvious question. If he'd known the injury would cause him problems for the rest of his life, would he have played those last few weeks to help his teammates win the league?

His reply is as predictable as it is both heartwarming and inspiring: 'One hundred per cent. Definitely.'

CHAPTER 15

Mick Hennigan – 'The Right Hand Man'

The game's about crosses and skirmishes in the box, not this keep-ball nonsense we get now!

I've heard a lot about Howard Wilkinson, but not much about the man behind the Sergeant Wilko image. I decide that if anyone can peer behind the inscrutable façade it will be Michael Hennigan, Wilkinson's assistant manager throughout his time at Leeds. In games at Elland Road, Hennigan was as distinctive a presence as the Sarge, pacing the touchline, conferring, and barking out the Sarge's orders to Mel and Shutty. With Wilkinson's assistance, I track him down to a small house in Sheffield's High Green, an area that has recently become better known as the birthplace of various members of the pop band Arctic Monkeys.

The house is small and immaculate, not a single piece of paper out of place and with scant clutter beyond a few family photographs and a couple of African ornaments. The man propped up on the sofa isn't quite the fearsome Arthur Scargill-voiced sergeant major I'd expected. He's seventy now, has had a few back problems, and his speech is a slow and steady stream of South Yorkshire rather than a Scargill bark, but he has a wonderfully mischievous grin which reminds me a bit of Albert Steptoe.

'I watched Manchester City versus Sunderland last night on the telly,' he begins, pointing at the small screen with palpable disgust. 'I had to turn it off. Watching Man City pass the ball about does my 'ead in. They're keeping it for the sake of it. They had all the game and they weren't having any strikes on goal. The game's about crosses and skirmishes in the box, not this keep-ball nonsense we get now! At Leeds it was about creating chaos, especially in the penalty box. That was the theory underpinning it all.'

He settles back into the sofa, and looks thoroughly content. 'Later on I put the telly back on and I noticed they'd lost 1–0.' He grins, and it's not too hard to imagine how his straight talk and bone-dry humour must have clicked with Sergeant Wilko. His favourite mantra is the Wilko-like 'Footballers should earn their keep'. He thinks modern young players are given 'meaningless praise, all the way' and then are devastated when they're told they won't make it; and he really hates players, such as a recently departed Leeds centre-forward, whose 'body language says everybody else is shit or crap'. After all these years, Hennigan is very much a Wilkinson disciple.

'I loved it at Leeds, and I loved Wilkinson,' he admits.

'Cos he brought me into football when I was forty-two. Nearly forty-three. And I was football daft at the time. So anybody who does you a favour like that, or gives you an opportunity of fulfilling a dream, you're forever gonna like 'em. And you're never going to forget 'em.'

Perhaps they were destined to end up together. Wilkinson and Hennigan were both miner's sons who grew up just thirteen miles apart – Hennigan in Thrybergh, Wilkinson in Nether Edge. Although their paths didn't cross until much later, both were united – as almost everyone was in those areas – by poverty and football.

'Poverty was more out there because people talked and we all knew each other was poor,' says Sonia, Mrs Hennigan, who doesn't just sit in on the interview but joins in with what will prove to be some rather telling asides. 'Not like now where people are very isolated. You don't know them.'

Hennigan was particularly 'football daft'. He supported Rotherham United but remembers queuing up for Ivor Allchurch's autograph, even though he played for Swansea. 'He was the Welsh wizard,' explains Hennigan, 'the golden boy of football before John Charles.' All Hennigan wanted to be was a footballer. He never dreamed he'd be good enough, but after spells with the juniors at Huddersfield Town, Rotherham United and Sheffield Wednesday, he played briefly for Southampton and then Brighton – oddly enough the same club on the south coast where Wilkinson turned out, a couple of years later.

At Southampton, Hennigan's manager, Ted Bates, had

given him some very distinct advice: 'You want to be the best footballer, best trainer, best fighter, best drinker, best, er, ****er.' And Hennigan took it to heart. 'I said, "Well, boss, you've got to have ambition."' He grins. 'I was daft! Nobody trained harder, but between football matches I used to go out.'

When his father was killed down the pit ('He was forty-five. It does stay with you, aye. I go every fortnight to me dad and me mam. They're in the same grave') he took this advice extremely literally.

'His friend who died last year said that had his dad not got killed, Michael was good enough to play for England,' insists Sonia, to Hennigan's visible embarrassment, but he doesn't argue with her assertion that his father's death made him 'lose the plot – he went off the rails'.

'I had a theory at the time that when you're younger, your capacity for enjoyment is greater,' adds Hennigan, naughtily, with a shrug and a glint in his eye that makes Sonia mock a frown. 'So I gave the ball a kick.'

As a single man looking for adventure, when the opportunity came up to play in South Africa, he was off. But he turned up having no idea about apartheid, and while playing for Durban and Bloemfontein lost his (Catholic) religion after walking into a cathedral and seeing blacks and whites sat on opposite sides. 'I remember sitting at the back of the bus cos all the blacks sat there. They'd say to me, "You shouldn't sit with them." It just didn't seem right.' His off-the-field shenanigans made him 'come home a bit quick', and he made a similarly mysterious exit under a cloud after playing in Australia. 'Oh aye, you don't want to dig up too much,' he chuckles.

By the time he'd been kicked out of Irish club Sligo Rovers for fighting, and was turning out for Silverwood Miners Welfare Club back home in Sheffield, he'd 'run out of clubs'.

At this point – 1973, the year he met Sonia – he was treated to an extraordinary preview of his future, but years before it happened. He was invited to Leeds United, with the prospect of signing for Don Revie at Elland Road.

'I didn't have any stars in my eyes,' he insists, explaining that one of the local scouts took him up. 'It was a hope and a prayer and nothing happened. I didn't have a trial. He looked at me and talked to me and was nice to me and said, "I can't sign you, kid." It was all over in five minutes. It seemed a bit of a waste. But when you're talking to someone like Revie . . . Christ Almighty.'

Instead, Hennigan got a job working for the Central Electricity Generating Board, and although he kept his hand in by studying for coaching badges and playing local football, he was out of any professional involvement for over a decade.

But during this time he was starting to cross paths with Howard Wilkinson. The future Sergeant Wilko was one of the 'big three' coaches in the area (along with Jack Detchon and Dick Bate, who joined Wilkinson at Leeds), and he seemed to run all the courses in the area. Hennigan coached at Matlock Town and Sutton ('Did I? Oh aye. Christ! You know more than me!'). When he became coach, then manager, of Spalding (where his leading goalscorer was none other than Carl Shutt), Wilkinson was the opposing manager when Spalding played Sheffield Wednesday in a friendly. 'So I'm coming across him. And I was a bit of a lad at Brighton, and when he went there after I left there would have been a few tales flying around. I used to like a fight.' He sniggers. 'Especially amongst players.'

Sonia remembers how one day Hennigan came home from working on the pylons to say, '"Howard Wilkinson wants to see me." He went in, in all his muck! Unshaven – cos you get dirty on these pylons – but he came home and said, "He's offered me a job!"'

When Wilkinson made Hennigan his youth coach, he was so excited that he forgot to tell the boss how much he was earning, just telling him about the CEGB wage, not the coaching, which gave Wilko a Christmas party piece for years: 'This is the only bloke in football I know who took a pay cut.'

But the money was irrelevant: Hennigan had found not only his calling, but also a mentor. When Wilkinson passed him in the Hillsborough tunnel and said, 'I'm thinking of going to Leeds United, do you wanna come?' he didn't need to think.

Hennigan has his own ideas about why none of the other Wednesday coaches went along. 'I was too embarrassed to ask, but I imagine one or two thought they might take his place at Wednesday. Me? It sounds daft, but [in my forties], I'm his lad now. He gave me the chance. I'm on his side until he wants to kick me out.' It was the beginning of an eight-year reign at Elland Road.

Sonia, with a forensic woman's eye, has a particularly revealing anecdote about the state of the club they walked into, making Elland Road sound almost Dickensian. 'There was this grubby carpet on the floor; the offices were wood panelling. Everywhere you touched was full of dust. It looked old and dowdy and tattered. You'd think, "How can anybody do anything with this?"'

But they did. Hennigan points out that at this stage Wilkinson was very ambitious and had been a success everywhere he'd been, and that at Wednesday his activities included putting a roof on the old Kop. 'He doesn't just build football teams, he builds clubs,' Hennigan says. 'Thorp Arch was all Howard. If he made a mistake it's that he should have gone abroad and really developed his football education. He was one of the best in England. But he knew what he wanted and made it happen. He controlled the club to the smallest detail.'

Sonia Hennigan observed this herself, pointing out small but revealing and previously unknown details like the fact that Wilkinson apparently redesigned the badge the players wore on their blazers and had a sub-stantial input into the rebuilding of the stadium and the giant East Stand Upper. An email to the Sarge confirms this: 'The badge – I decided we needed a new one and redesigned it. The Euro shield [still worn by Leeds players today] was my design, inspired by Spanish and Italian club badges. The stadium was me on technical, Bill [Fotherby], the Chair [Silver] and Peter [Gilman] on detail and commercial.'

I'd had no idea about any of this before.

'He was very talented – drawings and designs – but keeps quiet about it,' explains Mrs Hennigan, intriguingly. When I came to interview the assistant manager, I never suspected that his 'other half' would prove such a fount of information. She remembers Wilkinson as a very quiet person socially who, while everyone else was dancing and laughing, would sit in his chair at parties with a glass of wine and just observe. 'He wasn't a loud person but very knowledgeable. He knew all the birds in the garden and what food they needed. There's all these private things about him that people never knew. He'd visit poorly kids until they died, but nobody saw that. A very caring, dependable person. If anyone needed anything he'd sort it out. I didn't like football, but I was intrigued by the organization side of it, so I observed a lot of backroom stuff. If he rings up he chats to me more than him. If Michael became ill I know I could ring him.'

'His chief scout at Wednesday is poorly now, and Howard's been over and sorted out Sky television and all sorts,' reveals Hennigan.

Gradually, and without Hennigan breaking any loyalties, I'm getting a tantalizing glimpse of the unseen Sgt Wilko. It even turns out that the house we're talking in used to be Wilkinson's: in 1987, when the Hennigans were living in a huge Victorian house that swallowed money and wanted a smaller more compact home, the Sergeant sold them his. Pointing at another semi through the window, Sonia reveals that Lee Chapman lived there when he started dating actress

Leslie Ash, whom of course he married, much to the tabloids' delight when they became an early nineties Posh and Becks. 'They were denying it to the press, but I could see her putting stuff in the bin,' she chuckles.

But, typically, Hennigan isn't so presumptuous as to claim any great insight into the inscrutable manager. 'I loved working for him,' he explains. 'I'll leave people alone. If I were as clever as him, I'd need two heads. He helps people out money-wise, his ex-players and so on. He doesn't shout that from the rooftops either. He leads from the front.'

Sonia reveals that it wasn't just Wilkinson who worked all hours. Hennigan, too, was at the training ground by 8.30 a.m. and often not back until midnight. 'With the kids at Wednesday he did the canoeing and rock climbing with them, and that was the mentality that went to Leeds. He had them running up and down the Kop and everything.' It's a wonderfully romantic image. 'Relentless. But most of the kids he had are still in football, and it moved to Leeds with a bigger design.'

Her husband then notes that on their Friday nights off, he and the gaffer would watch the Bundesliga – which led to the signing, in 1994, of Ghanaian goal machine Tony Yeboah.

I wanted to know how involved Hennigan was in identifying players.

'I weren't bad at having an opinion, I weren't one for sittin' on t' fence,' he replies, suggesting that he would have 'held my hand up' to suggest Carl Shutt's move from Spalding to Wednesday, and then again at Leeds.

There's something else I've just got to ask him. Is

Shutty's story true, about filching the other team's tactics boards from hotels? He doesn't say a word, and then the broadest schoolboy grin spreads across his septuagenarian features. 'If you come across something like that, you have to take advantage. Nothing was left to chance, and he loved the challenge of all that, Wilkinson. He'd find out what end a team preferred to play to. His planning and preparation was something else. He knew every player's weakness. One that springs to mind: [Phil] Babb at Liverpool. Let him have the ball.'

Why?

'Cos he'll give you it back,' he responds with a snigger.

I'm starting to understand why Vinnie and Shutty loved Hennigan. His sly humour is most endearing, his passion for football unstinting. He tells me that something which fascinated me in 1991/92 – the way Leeds would steamroller teams in the first fifteen minutes – was design, not accident. 'Zoom . . . and the crowd backed them up. All part of Howard's planning.'

Of course. Did he hate losing?

'He got better . . . Well, his body language was more subdued. At Sheffield Wednesday I was only the youth coach but I was there, and he would really show his dislike of it. There were less histrionics at Leeds.'

How important was Dick Bate? He seems a lost figure in the story. He was head coach during the championship season but seemed to depart the picture around 1993.

'You do come up with some bouncers! He was a teacher with Howard at Abbeydale. I love him to death.

I wish I could see Dick Bate every day to talk football. That's now! Then . . . Howard brings him in. Howard and Dick are like that [Hennigan entwines his fingers] at Boston. Howard brings him back in. The youth set-up at Leeds is good – Peter Gunby. Dick brings organization, scouting, really makes the set-up stronger. Brings in kids from all over. In terms of knowledge, he must be among the best in the world. Then Dick left [Wilkinson tells me he got a job with the Malaysian FA]. For whatever reason, football has never had the best of Dick Bate. If I owned a club I would bring in Dick Bate and Howard Wilkinson, two wise men. I get on with him [Bate] better now than I ever did at Leeds United.'

Intriguing. I ask about some other unknowns, players I haven't yet managed to speak to. What was John Lukic like?

'His own man,' he begins, which reflects my experience. 'Players like to get in a group and act daft. That's not Lukic. Footballers are self-employed; John was certainly self-employed. But no trouble, a good worker and a good goalkeeper. I think he realized this career wouldn't last for ever, so he was sensible with money. He wasn't queuing up to open this shop or that fete. I think he wanted to get back and be with the kids and his missus.'

Chris Fairclough was a 'giant for Wilkinson – and Wilkinson was a giant for him. Another one, more than earned his keep. Good around the place. We had some good people, players, at Leeds.'

Sonia's favourite was, inevitably, Gary Speed. She

remembers the time he modelled for Top Man and 'the full window was just him. I'd go in and think, "By God, you're a handsome boy!"'

I ask her husband about the incident in La Manga, when he'd covered for Gary Speed and not told Wilkinson after the midfielder crashed a car. Do you think if you had come clean about that to Howard the fallout could have cost him the title?

'Howard's not there,' he explains. 'Sometimes he came [abroad], sometimes he didn't. As I remember, Batty's tried to take the blame for Speedo. Cos me and Batty were never lovey-dovey. Batty would have took us on, whereas Speedo would have been more civilized. If Batty had three wishes, five minutes with Hennigan would be one of them! But he could play. I thought Batty had kind of taken responsibility for Speed, but I never mentioned it to the boss, no. I don't like telling tales. Sometimes it's your duty. But if I can I'd rather not. Not behind your back anyway.

'I first saw Batty in the youth team [when Hennigan was at Wednesday], and Batty scared all our kids,' he continues. 'I remember putting Dean Barwick on him, saying, "You sort Batty out," and Barwick's held his hands up. He never saw him, because Batty ran the show. So while we never saw eye to eye, he was price-less. You talk about enforcers. Batty was a top enforcer.'

Was he a big character in the dressing room?

'Not really. Strachan was the man. He could cut you down with his tongue, which can be good and bad. But he was a very good captain. McAllister got stronger as time went on. He'd want Wetherall to bring it down and pass it, and I'd say, "He int that type of player. You want your centre-halves to whack it and hack it!"'

He says Wilkinson was a magician at playing to players' strengths and hiding their weaknesses. On Chapman: 'He got the best out of him. He knew how to talk to him and treat him and it wasn't all lovey-dovey. But you can get on in different ways. Some need shaking. Some might even need bullying. Some needed stroking. I think Chappy had a bit of everything. If he basked in his own glory, Howard would snap him out of it and tell him a few home truths. You're dealing with egos. But certainly when they ran together they were good for each other.'

We talk about the one area in which players have been critical of Wilkinson – the timing and especially manner of their exits. Hennigan, perhaps unsurprisingly, backs the manager. Kamara was let go because of his injuries. 'If he'd stayed injury free Kamara could have been in the team. He could play in several positions and was good to have around the place, but he was always with the physios.' He thinks Vinnie Jones was let go at the right time – 'Howard did him a favour, because he couldn't guarantee a place' – but concedes the player, any player, will never see it that way. 'A player will always disagree with the ending, but a player has to think about himself. The manager has to keep the unit ticking over.'

Which leads me straight on to the topic of how the South Yorkshireman got on with Eric Cantona.

'Left him alone. Cantona was his own man. I don't think Cantona was looking for me . . . and I wasn't exactly looking for Cantona. Admire him as a player? I admired him more as a player at Man United than Leeds United. I remember one game where he should shoot, but instead he passes it to Chapman, and Chapman looks so surprised he nearly tripped over the ball! Chappy scored, but Cantona would surprise them, especially in training. He was the first player I noticed where you could give him the ball and he'd give it you back, what I used to call the double pass, which they all do now. I think Cantona was probably two or three moves ahead of everyone else.'

We'll talk more about Wilkinson's and Hennigan's own departure from Leeds, which proved so painful for the assistant manager that he has never watched a Leeds United first team in the flesh since. After Elland Road, he went to Bury, helped Bill Fotherby at Harrogate Town, and renewed his global adventures coaching in Turkey, Trinidad, and even Malawi's national team for a while.

And now?

'Michael doesn't do computers,' sighs Sonia, launching into another unexpectedly enlightening aside. 'He started a course and came home and said, "That's me done." The FA rang him up and asked "Are you ill?" because they couldn't imagine him not wanting to do it. I used to have to answer his emails. Some people are so single-minded they have a form of autism. He knew every player in the country – what injuries they'd had, everything – then come home and couldn't switch the heating on. He'd say, "I'm thick." He's not thick. He's just very focused in one area of his life. In our relationship I manage the money. If we go to America, I book the hotel, the flight, pack the cases, and Michael comes with me. It was the same with Wilkinson. Every away match, the entire time he was with him, Howard chose his meal. If he put a can of beans and a spoon in front of him, he would have eaten it. But Howard knew what he would and wouldn't eat. In that sense they were a very close pair . . .but weren't. But they did know how each other worked.'

'I could only ever pay Wilkinson back by working my bollocks off for him, and I tried to,' says Hennigan.

We've talked for hours, but Sonia has one more thing to tell me: Wilkinson and Hennigan almost worked together again in 2004, when the boss briefly took a job at Chinese club Shanghai Shenhua. But Hennigan was working as a kit man, and his back was so bad that he was bent double. He needed surgery urgently, but insisted 'Kit men can't have a day off' and refused to let anyone down by having his back seen to during the season, so he missed out on an emotional reunion with the gaffer.

'This is Michael!' sighs Sonia, with a mixture of love and exasperation.

Hennigan smiles doggedly. His devotion to his duty, and the Sergeant's principles, is humbling.

'As Howard used to say, "loyalty to task"!'

CHAPTER 16

For the Love of Money

Football was affordable back then.

When I first started going, and paying for myself, it was a pound for an Under 16 like myself to stand in the 'adult' Spion Kop. I remember being irked when it went up to £1.25. To get this into some perspective, a pound in 1975 (using the Retail Price Index) equates to £6.54 at today's prices. But in 1975, watching Leeds United was affordable enough for a child like me to be able to pay using pocket money. Even then I had to make sacrifices, walking a mile or two to Ireland Wood in north Leeds to catch the number 4 bus to Beeston, which stopped within another long walk to Elland Road. By the time I reached the top of Beeston Hill I was nearly there. Other fans remember paying around fifteen shillings (75p) in the Kop earlier in the seventies, and 50p in the boys' pen around 1980.

Once, I'd got all the way to the ground and realized I'd forgotten my money. I rang my mum, the idea being that Cameron White down the road could ferry my one-pound note to me on his motor scooter. Instead, Mum said she knew someone on the ticket office, and I was to go up and say 'I'm Olive's son'. The kind man there gave me something called a complimentary ticket. I stared at it for ages and it seemed so precious I didn't want to hand it over. It's hard to imagine something like that happening now.

As for season tickets, in the old Second Division in 1983/84 a season ticket in the Kop cost £34 (equal to £89.50 in 2012, using the RPI). In the title season of 1991/92, an adult Kop season ticket to see Wilkinson's team become the best team in the land would set you back just £130 (£208 today). Ironically, one of the tunes regularly blasting over the Tannoy in 1991/92 was the O'Jays' 1973 hit 'For the Love of Money', a soul/funk stomper which detailed all the things people would do for money over Anthony Jackson's wah-wah treated Fender bass. Sometimes, it seems a million years ago.

Back then, none of us could have possibly guessed how much the line 'Don't let money change you' would come to apply to football. If I want to buy a Kop (cheapest adult) season ticket to watch Leeds in the second tier in 2012/13 it will cost me £582, payable before the end of March 2012; the seemingly pie-in-the-sky promotion to the Premiership would significantly increase the cost. Comparatively, the cheapest season ticket at Man United in 2011/12 was £526, while Blackburn's supporters paid as little as £225. It doesn't seem fair compared to them, never mind what we were paying in 1992, which may be one reason Sports Minister Hugh Robertson recently stated, 'Football is the worst governed sport in this country, without a shadow of a doubt.'

And it's why a lot of people like me are feeling very disaffected. After something like twenty years as a season ticket holder, I'd seen the number of my friends attending games dwindling, one by one. Eventually I realized that I too could no longer justify the expense – especially when none of the money seemed to be making its way into investment on the pitch. These days, like a lot of fans, I don't go as often, and I pick my games, more often than not returning home disgruntled, with a feeling that I just don't enjoy the football fan experience any more. That old song from 1975 seems more apt now than ever: 'You are my sunshine, my only sunshine. You make me happy, when skies are grey. You'll never know just how much I love you. Please don't take my sunshine away.'

These days, my sunshine fix is arriving via time machine from 1991/92, when football really was something anyone could enjoy, anyone could play, and almost anyone could afford. And I still have players from that era to track down, to tell me what it was like for them, for my heroes of that time twenty years ago.

I get home to an answerphone message from Chris Whyte.

CHAPTER 17

Chris Whyte — 'Huggy Bear'

I said, 'Is this a wind-up?' I put the phone down!

'Soooorry, Dave, I hardly ever read my emails,' explains Chris Whyte down the phone, his sleepy voice suggesting exactly the laid-back character Wilkinson and others had depicted.

When we meet in a London pub a stone's throw from Tottenham's ground, I tell 'Huggy' Whyte a story that Vinnie Jones told me, from when the players lived together when Whyte first arrived at Leeds, which somehow seemed to sum up the 'cool customer' Wilkinson had described.

Jones had two sponsored cars, including the BMW he'd asked for in the transfer deal (later at Sheffield United, he even had a Vauxhall, which everyone knew was Jones's because it had 'Vinnie's Vauxhall' painted on the side). One day, when they went out for fish and chips, Jones parked his car while Whyte stayed in his own vehicle, watching telly (even in 1990 footballers enjoyed special perks). 'And when I came back these young lads had got the car, nicked all the stuff out of it and everything,' the enforcer remembered. 'I chased after 'em, came back covered in shit and everything. I was gone an hour, or two, more! I came back and I said to Huggy, "Didn't you see those ****in' pricks doing over my car?" And he says [and he perfectly mimicked Whyte's sleepy, dulcet tones], "No. I thought you were gone a long time. I was getting really hungry."'

Whyte shrieks with laughter. 'I can't remember the specific incident, but that does sound likely.'

Not for nothing, then, did Wilkinson call Whyte 'the cool customer' whose casual demeanour – once the Sergeant had ironed out mistakes by 'keeping him on his toes' – made him one of his two 'unsung heroes' of 1991/92. Arriving in the summer of 1990 as Wilkinson also recruited McAllister to tackle life in the top division, Whyte formed half of a formidable central defensive partnership, with the similarly under-heralded Chris Fairclough, which conceded just thirty-seven goals in forty-two games in 1991/92. But it was the way he did it that made him as well loved as Mel or Shutty.

Nicknamed after the similarly laid-back character in *Starsky and Hutch*, 'Huggy' had one of the most unusual playing styles I've ever seen, stroking the ball so casually it looked like he could fall asleep at any moment. His legs always looked a foot longer than anyone else's ('I was always told that,' he hoots) but then a foot would come out in a sort of pincer movement and he'd seize the ball as effortlessly as if he was flicking up a piece of litter.

'It was just the way I might have come across,' he

chuckles. 'With my style, I wasn't casual, I was just very comfortable on the ball. Never frightened to receive it off the keeper. Like a lot of foreign teams, very confident receiving the ball in tight areas; confident with running with it; and even if the player was in a tight situation, Gary Speed or Gordon Strachan, Gary McAllister, I had the confidence to give them it and they could deal with it.'

In 1991/92 alopecia had his hair falling out in chunks (which Vinnie Jones said hadn't bothered him at all) and this gave his head a distinct, rather fetching appearance which one wag compared to the Jules Rimet World Cup trophy. Twenty years on and in his fifties, his head is now shaved to reveal a striking mark, like a little crown or halo. Otherwise he looks eerily the same, with the same mixture of affability and calmness that proved so deceptively effective on the field.

Whytey was one of those much-mythologized but actually quite rare footballers who always played with a smile on his face. 'I appreciated every minute, Dave,' he explains. 'I was very confident. When your own fans are singing your praises and you see the supporters that everyone knows are some of the best in the country, you just want to go out and perform to a standard that you know true football people would appreciate. There was an unbelievable togetherness between all of us: team morale, spirit, characters, all the elements that make up a winning formula. I honestly believed that we weren't going to get beat on a Saturday. Even if we went a goal behind, which didn't happen a lot, I believed that we would pull back and win the game. Good players, performing at the top of their game, got the best out of each other, and it was an absolute joy to play in. Personally, I could not wait for three o'clock on a Saturday afternoon.'

Thus, from such an awkward, gangly, large frame, emerged one of Wilkinson's key players.

Brought up four hundred yards from Highbury, Whyte's childhood was dominated by the almost mythical experience of playing football in parks and cobbled streets. 'Two jumpers down for goals,' he says, smiling at the memory, 'pick your sides and play.'

With Arsenal literally on his doorstep, he became a ball boy and watched them from the terraces, while playing for his school, a Sunday team, as well as at one time a midweek team. Then there was the district side – he played for London. 'I was football crazy,' he remembers. 'My mum was forever having to call me in to get my dinner.'

His mother was from Jamaica, his father from Barbados. They'd met here after arriving in the 1950s but never married. His father lived in Edmonton, which meant Mrs Whyte raised six children on her own. 'Four boys, two girls. It can't have been easy for her.' Mrs Whyte instilled strict discipline, something he learned the value of at a very early age.

When he was playing for Islington Boys, his future life came calling. 'Picture this,' he grins. 'We're gonna go and play Bristol Boys at Ashton Gate in a final – they were a talked-about team. After the game my coach introduces me to a man called Ernie Collett, who was the chief scout at Arsenal. He said he was impressed, asked me if I was interested in evening training two nights at Arsenal.'

Whyte was fifteen years old and admits that he would have been bowled over if a Third Division side had come calling, never mind his boyhood favourites, 'one of the biggest clubs in the world'.

Whyte progressed rapidly: two years each in the Arsenal youth team and reserves, then making his first-team debut aged twenty in 1981. He started all but one match that season – alongside a future Leeds manager, David O'Leary – but gradually faded from first-team action in the mid-1980s with the emergence of the England centre-half pairing of Martin Keown and Tony Adams. 'There was a lot of competition,' he admits. 'It was difficult. You think, "Crikey, I'm not as good as them." It can knock your confidence.'

Looking at his options at the end of the 1985/86 season, he did something that could be seen as bold or reckless but was a leap of faith that seems typical of his attitude to life: he decamped to America. Not the North American Soccer League, which in the late seventies and eighties hosted the fading talents of Pelé and Franz Beckenbauer, but the lesser-known Major Indoor Soccer League. The move came about after Arsenal played an exhibition match against start-up franchise New York Express in 1985, and one of the American team's coaches expressed an interest in the defender, who wasn't the Gunners' first choice.

'I enjoyed the trip, the game,' says Huggy, remembering how he didn't even think about whether there might be interest in him back in England. 'I just thought, "I'm gonna go for it!"'

In a similar cultural upheaval to that experienced by his parents on their adventure halfway across the world, he immersed himself in a totally new lifestyle and a very different 'soccer' game.

What was it actually like playing football indoors, under a roof?

'Weird at first!' He grins. 'But all the American sports were indoors, so I accepted it. Like basketball, it was fast, entertaining, high scoring. I enjoyed it. Soccer, as they call it, was growing and trying to get on a level with the other sports.'

Like many Premiership clubs today, the Express had a new owner who'd arrived with big ambitions but found them dented by the somewhat cruel financial and sporting realities of trying to win a league. 'He probably thought he was gonna go and walk it,' admits Whyte. Instead, rumours started to spread that the owner might walk away. 'Other American players were saying, "Yeah, Chris, that's what happens here. Clubs fold and all sorts."'

In fact, with only three wins in twenty-three games, the club lasted just one season. Like with the draft system in American football, when this happens, the team with the worst record gets first choice of two of the dissolving team's players. Thus, over a decade before Vinnie Jones, Whyte found himself headed for Hollywood, where he played for LA Lazers.

He lived in Long Beach, 'in the land of films and stars, and it was a nice lifestyle'. But despite the attractions of sunshine and palm trees, he still harboured thoughts of English football. 'I'd still think, "How did Arsenal get on? Who's top of the league?"'

When the Lazers looked like folding too (they did, within a year), Whyte realized he didn't want to be thrown around the States again and that he was missing the great outdoors. 'Something pulled me back,' he tells me. 'Deep down, I felt my time wasn't done in England. I thought I had a lot to offer. I'd got my confidence back. Out there, San Diego were the biggest side and they got eight to ten thousand indoors. But even the American players knew how big English football was. I kept saying to myself, "I have a lot to offer. I could play at the top level." There was talk of other teams not lasting the season. I put the feelers out that I wanted to come back to England, and I did.'

Initially he joined Ron Atkinson's West Bromwich Albion. He was voted player of the year in his first season and enjoyed it immensely. 'Like me, [Atkinson] was very laid back, very bubbly. He loved his players to express themselves.' But after two seasons he was told that another club was interested in his services, though he wasn't told which club.

Shortly afterwards, his roommate, striker Don Goodman, passed him the phone, telling him it was someone claiming to be the assistant manager of Leeds United.

'I said, "Is this a wind-up?" I put the phone down!'

A couple of seconds later, the telephone rang again.

'He says, "Chris, don't put the phone down again! This is serious. I'm Mick Hennigan, Howard Wilkinson's assistant. Howard's asked me to find out if you'd be interested in joining the club . . ."'

A few days later, in a Yorkshire hotel, Whytey warmed to Hennigan just as much as I had. 'When I think of Mick, I think of people like Don Howe,' he declares. 'Someone who eats, thinks and sleeps football. Very Yorkshire. I could see how much they wanted me.'

Who knows? Had Whyte not answered the phone that second time, perhaps one of the greatest modern Elland Road defenders would never have signed for Leeds.

Whyte was placed on £1,500 a week – good, if not enormous, wages, but he knew he was joining a newly promoted club who were 'on the march'. He didn't have any idea of the extraordinary impact Leeds would make on Division One, but recognized a kindred spirit in his manager: 'Very laid back, very calm . . . confident. Very comfortable to be around.'

When it comes to specifics, Whyte's powers of recall fail him several times during our two-hour encounter. Unlike Carl Shutt, the finer details of his time at Leeds have been lost in a fog of two decades' passing. Much of our meeting is taken up with me reminding him of things to try to jog his memory. But I do notice that he's an avid listener. Whether I'm mentioning specific games or telling him about Leeds before he came, he listens intently and soaks it in as if it were a Wilko team talk. I suspect that this is what he was like in 1991/92.

'As a youngster I felt I could eat anything, just go out on the pitch and play. All of a sudden I'm finding out you've got to eat chicken or whatever, and you can't eat two hours before a game because you'll feel better. I always took for granted that managers and ex-players were passing on the knowledge, but with someone like that you'd be wise to take it on board.' The listener in him is speaking. 'You don't buy into it at first, but then you realize it's good for you.'

He pays close attention when I describe the Leeds United of the days before he joined, with its National Front pamphlets and violence in and especially outside the stadium. He knew Leeds was a big club ('I remembered the seventies – aggression, toughness, big support') and that it had had a bad image in the past, but none of this deterred him from signing. 'I remember violence was pretty bad all over the country at a lot of clubs,' he reasons. 'Coming from London, I'd experienced it. I hated playing at Millwall, but once I was on the pitch, especially if we won . . . But the abuse we used to get there. I just wanted to play football and express myself. You've got to be mentally strong, Dave. You're playing something that you've been lucky to have the ability and the talent to do. You'd like to think people enjoy watching. The odd comment of course is sad. But you have to focus.'

Thus, Whyte had the perfect psychological make-up for the cauldron of Elland Road.

'As good a side as we were, it wasn't easy. You have to earn the right to play – you've heard that so often, but it's true. We had the kind of side that obviously when you're at home you've got to take the game to them, and we had a side that dripped confidence from Lukic up to Lee. Everyone mucked in. Players would come into the side and obviously felt as important as if they started the game. Howard's got to take massive credit for bringing these players together.'

Great centre-back pairings have been rare at Leeds over the years: Ferdinand/Radebe and Woodgate, Hunter and Charlton/ Madeley. Whyte seemed to have an almost telepathic understanding with Chris Fairclough. How does such a thing come about?

'Simply by taking in what we were being given on the training pitch,' Whyte replies. 'Howard's ideas, and having that team in a shape, and getting the best out of each other. We knew each other's strengths and weaknesses. I got to know him, but no more than anyone else. I roomed with Gary McAllister.'

I encountered Fairclough once myself. It was the title season, and he was in Boots, looking at electrical products. He had his head down, and looked as if he'd rather be invisible.

'He probably was a low-profile, shy character. Don't get me wrong. He was all in amongst the players, but he was a bit like that. We were a mixture.'

Was the man who brought you together more inspiring to play for than other managers?

'Good question. For me, I just became used to Howard's way,' Whyte says, pun intended. 'He was very . . . not overly engaging, it's just who he was. Everyone has their own character. When Howard would speak to me, I knew that was his way. I wouldn't say he bollocked me a lot, but if he had to he would. Because if you imagine: those two seasons, very gruelling. Of course there were times when he didn't think we were playing anywhere near our capacity, and his voice would . . .' Whyte is laughing as he tries to tell a similar tale to Shutty. 'You think, "Is he gonna lose it and lay into us?" But he didn't. He did it in a way that was calm. You wouldn't want to get on the wrong side of him, definitely. But I didn't see it a lot.'

He doesn't recall how the Sarge ironed errors out of his game by somehow keeping the laid-back character 'on his toes'. 'This is the first I've heard of any of this!' he remonstrates, then ponders it for what seems like an age. 'He may well have done . . . but it was without me catching on.'

Whyte rewarded his manager's faith and methods with forty-one league appearances in 1991/92 and a goal in the 4–2 away win over Notts County. The one time he may have got on the wrong side of Wilkinson came in March when Leeds crashed 4–1 at QPR. With the game already slipping away at 3–1, Whyte conceded a penalty near the end of the match and was sent off for a so-called 'professional foul' on tricky winger Andy Sinton. Whyte's memory of the game is hazy, and he was anything but a dirty player; he suggests he will have made a genuine attempt to get the ball 'and I've obviously taken him first'. It was a rare mistake and a unique sending off, but he doesn't recall incurring the Sarge's wrath. 'I'm sure I'd remember if he went mad, but remember, we'd won the rest of the games. His way with words would be: "You lot are better than this." Because of how he was, he didn't panic the players. We hadn't instantly become a bad team.'

Whyte does have very strong memories of what it felt

like to win the league: 'An absolute buzz. Joy. Delight. Indescribable.' It's as if time has airbrushed any negative details and left a golden seam of good ones.

'I played for eighteen years and it was the highlight of my career,' he beams. 'I played with some very respected players when I was coming through at Arsenal, but we never won anything. Years later, you're winning the last ever First Division title. It's one hell of an achievement. I get flashbacks of individual events. But the feeling . . . the feeling never goes. Winning the top honour in the domestic game is everything you dream of when you start playing football. You're never going to forget that. If you can't get happiness out of doing something like that, you never will. I was on a different planet.'

He was particularly touched when his ageing mum, who hadn't previously been to Elland Road, made a special journey up to see him celebrate the championship. 'I could see how proud she was.' He smiles, then tells me that sadly she's no longer with us.

Whyte has one difficult memory of his time at Leeds – his exit, at the end of the following season. But even that tale is rendered with his trademark positivity. 'Sometimes you're pushed into a corner,' he says with a shrug. 'It's out of your hands. Personally, I was disappointed on my side, but in the end it wasn't difficult. As a player, you've been around football long enough to know all good things come to an end.'

Wilkinson had been bringing through Jon Newsome and David Wetherall more and more, and the penny dropped after one particular game. 'I got the feeling that they were the future, that was the way it was going. I believed I still deserved the number one spot, but it wasn't working any more. He's got in his mind what way it's going to go now.' Again, Whyte doesn't remember the specifics, he simply says, 'Knowing how I got on with Howard, he will have wished me well.'

After Leeds, he drifted down the divisions, to Birmingham, Coventry and Charlton, and even back to indoor football in the US with Detroit Safari. Leeds supporters saw him again – and gave him a hero's reception – in 1999 when David O'Leary's big-spending LUFC came up against him playing for Rushden & Diamonds in the FA Cup, and they held the supposedly far superior Whites to a replay. In recent years Whyte has done a bit of chauffeuring, but now isn't doing much at all, apart from a bit of after-school coaching. But, as ever, he has plans. 'I'm trying to get a business up and running, to help youngsters – if they're good enough – to get them looked at, because I've got so many contacts in the game.'

Typically, he doesn't do regrets.

'Of course I'd have loved to play for England at the top level and played as many games as Tony Adams or Rio, but it never worked like that.' He shrugs. 'I'm just lucky to be able to have my health, play in the odd charity game. My legs feel fine. Of course, my bones creak now and then when I wake up. I don't regret missing out on the money. Of course it would be nice. But my time's gone.'

As is mine. We shake hands in the street and go our separate ways. He's a lovely, lovely man. I hope everything works out for him.

Chris Whyte was one of the thrifty acquisitions in Wilkinson's complex jigsaw puzzle of team-building that made the Last Champions. My next appointment is with the wheeler and dealer who helped that happen: Bill Fotherby, aka 'The Godfather'.

Transfer Fees of Players Featuring in the Two League Fixtures between Leeds United and Manchester United in the 1991/92 Season

Leeds United		Manchester United	
John Lukic	£1m	Peter Schmeichel	£505,000
Mel Sterland	£600,000	Paul Parker	£2m
Tony Dorigo	£1.3m	Denis Irwin	£625,000
David Batty	£0	Neil Webb	£1.5m
John McClelland	£100,000	Steve Bruce	£825,000
Chris Whyte	£400,000	Gary Pallister	£2.3m
Gordon Strachan	£300,000	Bryan Robson	£1.5m
Rod Wallace	£1.6m	Paul Ince	£1m
Lee Chapman	£400,000	Mark Hughes	£1.8m
Gary McAllister	£1m	Brian McClair	£850,000
Gary Speed	£0	Clayton Blackmore	£0
Chris Fairclough	£500,000	Andrei Kanchelskis	£650,000

(subs)

Steve Hodge	£900,000	Ryan Giggs	£0
		Mike Phelan	£750,000
		Lee Sharpe	£200,000
		Mal Donaghy	£650,000

Total	£8,100,000		£15,155,000

The Godfather

"QUITE SIMPLY THE FINEST GANGSTER EVER MADE."

STARRING
WILLIAM J FOTHERBY

CHAPTER 18

Bill Fotherby – 'The Godfather'

I went over to have a word. I said, 'I want to sign Maradona.'

A quiet, leafy street on the outskirts of Harrogate isn't the kind of place you'd expect to find a Godfather. There are no black cars outside; no shifty-looking suited henchmen clutching violin cases; no disembodied heads mounted on the gateposts. What there is is a large house containing a poster of the house's male occupant mocked up in the style of Marlon Brando as Don Corleone in Francis Ford Coppola's 1972 masterpiece. *The Godfather*, starring William J. Fotherby, reads the poster – 'Quite simply the finest gangster ever made'.

Of course Bill Fotherby isn't really a gangster, but he certainly presided over the Elland Road empire as efficiently as a footballing Corleone.

I'm greeted at the doorway by a very friendly lady called Josie (Mrs Fotherby, not some gangster's moll). I walk in and plonk myself on a giant sofa next to a large stuffed bulldog in front of the largest television I have ever seen. In an armchair opposite me is the Leeds United Godfather himself. Now in his eighties, and until recently chairman of Harrogate Town, Fotherby is wearing beige trousers, sparkling fawn shoes and braces, and looks every bit as dapper as when he was a young tailor making his own suits in the 1950s. The years have not dulled his trademark chutzpah.

'There's only one person who can tell you everything about Leeds United,' he begins, brightly. 'And that's me!'

This is the mentality Fotherby brought to Leeds United – an effortless mixture of charm and sheer Yorkshire brass neck; Wilkinson would remark that he 'could sell sand to Arabs'. But it is buying, not selling, for which Fotherby is remembered. Leslie Silver's money may have bankrolled the Wilkinson revolution, but it was Fotherby's wining and dining and wheeling and dealing that made the dream possible.

Fotherby is more Arthur Daley than Don Corleone. For Vinnie Jones, he was 'Charlie Big Bananas'. For Leslie Silver, he was 'a provincial man who ran the world'. When Leeds United needed new sponsors, Fotherby went out and did a deal with Top Man. When Wilkinson wanted to sign Eric Cantona, Gordon Strachan, Jones or Gary McAllister, Fotherby pulled the strings – and offered the sweeteners – that made it happen.

But we begin with an earlier deal that got away and is a perfect example of the needle-sharp and often very funny way in which the Godfather operated: the time he tried to sign Diego Maradona, who had just held aloft the World Cup and was unquestionably the greatest, most sought-after player in the world. For lowly Second Division Leeds.

'I'll tell you the story from the start,' Fotherby says, and for the next hour or two I will get barely more than a word in. As he tells this extraordinary tale – which I'm led to believe has never been divulged in full in public before – he explains that he'd not been managing director for long and was looking to make a mark. 'I kept saying to them all, "We've got to build Leeds United up. We've got to get the public believing that we're really going to town."'

Thus, in 1987, just months after Argentina won the 1986 World Cup, the Godfather was at a dinner and spied John Smith, acting agent for Maradona in the whole of Europe at the time. 'I went over to have a word. I said, "I want to sign Maradona." He said, "You must be joking! You couldn't afford Maradona!"'

Fotherby told the agent that he had sponsors lined up who were putting in millions of pounds, and when Smith challenged him to name one, he instantly fired back, 'Montague Burton's want him [Maradona] to be walking on the beach in their jeans, with two girls.'

As Fotherby tells it, discussions progressed as far as a 'nice lunch' in one of the executive boxes at Elland Road, after which the Leeds supremo and Josie drove the Maradona entourage back to the airport. Later that evening, the Godfather was at popular Roundhay restaurant the Flying Pizza when two diners told him they'd seen him at the airport, and asked him who he was trying to sign. 'I said, "No comment. I'm sorry, I can't say anything."' He says this in a voice that would be loud enough to sell newspapers, even in his comfy living room.

Shortly afterwards, when Fotherby came out of the toilet, they pestered him again, and this time the Godfather just couldn't help himself. 'I said, "All right, I'll give you a clue. Think of Evita."' He sniggers. 'They're like, "Evita? What's he mean?" I sit down. This goes on for twenty minutes. All of a sudden, "Not Maradona?" I didn't say a word. The funny thing is, that went round like wildfire. I'd told the agent I'd arranged to have a reception at the Civic Hall and we'd have an England eleven versus a World eleven to play at Elland Road. It had gone that far that I couldn't stop it! I thought it would be four million but they were looking for eight.

'They rang me to tell me they couldn't get hold of Maradona for the England game, he was somewhere in Montevideo. I thought, "Thank God!" I had to cancel all the arrangements with the Civic Hall, everything. But the publicity we got from that, fantastic! The difference that made to me as a commercial director and to Leeds United I can't tell you. I got phone calls from all over the world. Everybody laughed at me, and it was a gamble. Nobody realized how close we were to being embarrassed, but I tell you, that was the foundation.'

He flexes his braces, and somehow seems to swell in his chair like a giant bird.

'After that, we started thinking, "What can we actually achieve?"'

It's hard not to be charmed by the Godfather, who

has perfected this patter over many, many years. In his office there's a wonderful framed letter from Gordon Strachan, which reads:

> My new contract is designed to keep me at Elland Road until 1993, and I shall look forward to completing that contract, which was only achieved after some hard bargaining. I had a meeting with Bill Fotherby. I say meeting because you don't really have a chat with Bill, you listen while he talks and before you know it you end up paying him money to stay with the club. I went in with Bill for contract talks and came out with three season tickets and owing the club money!

'See, you've got to convince them and you've got to believe it yourself,' says the Godfather, in a rare and I suspect rather revealing moment of humility and vulnerability. 'It's important to be liked, and be honest about it. Convince them all. Howard was right to say I'd sell sand to Arabs, but it was for the benefit of Leeds United.'

In those hazy, glorious days of the Wilko era, Fotherby's was a name in the programme and occasionally you'd glimpse him in the local paper, more often than not wearing a fedora, or pictured with his expensive shoe on a ball. A bridge on Gelderd Road still bears some unflattering graffiti about him which has been there for as long as I can remember – 'Fotherby: liar, cheat, crook' – presumably in response to some failed signing or other, which misunderstands how he operates.

Yes, Fotherby may have promised and failed to land the likes of Tomas Skuhravy and Ruben Sosa, but so many times he delivered. Some fifteen years after he left, the message boards are still full of people who'd have him back in an instant, and with him deals somewhat more adventurous than shelling out a reported £500,000 on utility player Danny Pugh, the sort of deal that was small potatoes to LUFC even in 1989.

What I didn't know until I met the Godfather was that, like Leslie Silver, his association with Leeds United goes back years.

In the late 1940s and early 1950s, Hunslet-born William James Fotherby was a 'Buckley boy' – a young Leeds United player under 'Major' Frank Buckley, a soldier turned manager whose own radical (if, inevitably, unsuccessful) ideas to transform the club included playing dancing songs over the PA during training, and firing footballs at players from a wooden contraption called a 'shooting box'.

After three years of his madness, young Fotherby was told he wasn't good enough, and joined the army, while remaining a regular spectator at Elland Road. Many years later, by which time he had established (and would lose) a clothing company, he saw the names of the Leeds shareholders printed in the *Yorkshire Evening Post*, and urged his secretary to write to every one of them to make an offer for their shares. 'They were penny shares,' he explains. 'This must have been 1976, 1977. But Manny Cussins was the chairman and thought I'd be a trouble causer. He'd always wanted to buy my company and didn't like the price.' Thus, despite the support of Tom Holley – the post-war centre-half Silver had seen displaced by John Charles – the Godfather was turned down.

Fotherby has a fabulous turn of phrase, and goes on to recall how Holley then tried to get him in at Halifax Town with a description of then chairman Percy Albon as looking like 'he'd come straight out of Montague Burton's window with his flat cap'.

'I watched a match as his guest, against Southend,' he explains. 'I was supposed to put £10,000 in, and he said it had to come to him. I said, "If I put £10,000 in that's to build the club, starting with players." I wanted to take someone like Norman Hunter as manager. Or Peter Lorimer.'

Fotherby has always thought big. But it didn't happen. He turned his sights back on Leeds, and after joining the 100 Club, an exclusive club at Leeds United in the 1970s, he met another new member, Silver. When the latter was invited to join the board, he persuaded Cussins to let Fotherby join too. 'The story was "Fotherby's all right but he'll want to pick the team",' recalls the Godfather. He's smiling. 'Which wasn't far wrong! It didn't happen, but I knew a good player . . .'

This was 1981. Seven years after that, the Silver–Fotherby partnership began to transform Leeds. But when he was just a director, Fotherby had very little influence, which must have been frustrating when things weren't working out with the Revie players as managers. He loved Allan Clarke – still sees him to this day – but says that the FA Cup winner turned manager did a 'very silly thing' when he went on holiday after relegation in 1982, and so was absent when the club faced crucial meetings with the bank about the future. 'The manager was vital, because he had to put values on the players. Manny had to say, "I'm sorry, the manager will not be coming, he's on holiday."' According to Fotherby, he and Silver were the only directors who voted for Clarke to remain manager. Then, after Eddie Gray 'didn't work out' either, he remembers Billy Bremner as 'magnificent' but not necessarily suited to managing the club through changing times. 'There was a party for the new sponsors. Billy got up and said, "I'm looking forward to the day when we don't need sponsors," and everybody cringed.

'I have to admit I didn't think these managers would have taken us where we wanted to go. We needed someone a bit different.' And by this time Fotherby was having more influence.

Thus, he was entrusted with the task of finding a new manager. Amazingly, he reveals that Sergeant Wilko wasn't the first choice. After initially approaching Everton's Howard Kendall, Oldham's Joe Royle and Liverpool/Wales legend John Toshack, Fotherby – not content with having pursued the world's best player – then attempted to bring the most unavailable manager in the country to Second Division Leeds.

In his thirteen years at Ipswich, Bobby Robson had won the FA Cup and UEFA Cup and helped a small provincial club stay in the top six of the First Division using mainly homegrown youth players. In 1988 he was the manager of England, about to embark on the famous World Cup campaign that led to Gascoigne's tears and semi-final penalty shootout heartbreak. For anyone else, he would have been absurdly unattainable. But Fotherby is not just anyone.

'I went to see Bobby Robson. He said, "Look, Bill, I'd love to come to Leeds, it's a very good club, but I'm on the verge of something with England and I'd like to see my contract out." I said, "Right, I'm going to ask you something. If not you, who? Because it's essential we get out of the Second Division." He said, "If I were you, I'd go for Howard Wilkinson at Sheffield Wednesday. He's one of the best managers in the Football League."'

So Sir Bobby Robson recommended Wilkinson to Leeds. Who would have thought that?

Fotherby is in his element now, holding court and spilling precious beans about a halcyon era of football, when deals were done in restaurants and caffs, not by international get-togethers and video conferencing. He revels in introducing his story of how he sealed the deal for Wilkinson – 'This is pure nectar juice!' As he tells it, the Sarge had agreed in principle to join but said Fotherby would have to meet him 'after Wednesday's game at Blackpool'.

'So we meet in some car park on the motorway. They were having an annual general meeting on the Friday. So I knew what would happen at the AGM: the Wednesday board would say "We don't want you to go", and persuade him to stay. So I took along a contract on the Saturday we were playing at home. Billy had gone. Peter Gumby was the caretaker manager, we'd lost three games and there were semi-riots, police on horseback. My car was damaged, same as the chairman's

Rolls-Royce. I couldn't get my car out to meet Howard – the police have to get me out. But I meet him on the motorway and I ask about the AGM. He says, "I have to tell you, Bill, they asked me to stay." Of course they would!'

Leeds had agreed a salary for the new boss but hadn't written it in the contract. Fotherby took out his pen and wrote in a figure, right there in the middle of the car park. 'I said, "Howard, I want you to consider that." He looked at it, he says "Give us your pen" and he signed the contract there and then.'

Later that evening, Fotherby knocked on Leslie Silver's door and used words similar to those uttered by British Prime Minister Neville Chamberlain when he thought he had appeased Hitler in 1938: '"Peace in our time, Leslie; he's signed!" And that was the beginning.'

However, he admits that there were some teething problems. Wilkinson, who was used to dealing directly with his chairman, was uneasy about having a managing director doing all the deals until Fotherby assured him, '"I know you've always dealt with the chairman, but in this case the chairman is not a social type. If it doesn't work after a month, I'll step back, but you won't regret working with me." From that day until the day he left we had a relationship that was second to none. I worked and dreamt football with him. Never missed an away game, whether it was Malaysia, Japan, reserves. Me and Howard were – if you'll pardon the expression – like shit stuck to a blanket.'

According to Fotherby, their relationship was based on a mutual awareness that each could do things the other couldn't, and was almost telepathic. And Wilkinson benefited from Fotherby's chutzpah. Very early on, the Godfather found his Sergeant and assistant manager feeling low after a defeat. 'I went into his office with Mike Hennigan and said, "What's wrong with you?" We'd got beat. "It's depressing when you're down." I said, "Get out of that tracksuit, get your jacket on, let's go for lunch." I took them to the Flying Pizza and they felt a million dollars, and from that day everything changed.'

All these years on he recalls his deals like an old general talking about wartime manoeuvres.

On building the stadium: 'My vision, I sketched it, and the architects did it. The family stand, seventeen thousand seats, it cost £6.5 million. I had to get the businessmen of Leeds interested. Our crowds were eleven thousand, thirteen thousand tops, and you couldn't get a cup of coffee outside of the 100 Club. We had to make hospitality suites because the businessmen would pay a thousand pound for it, that's like a thousand people.'

It may surprise many Leeds supporters to hear that the blueprint for much of the rebuilt Elland Road was across the Pennines. 'I did the Goal Line restaurant. I went to Manchester United and copied everything they had,' Fotherby reveals. 'They don't want to stand in the rain and have pea and pies, they want nice carpets and somewhere comfortable to sit.'

Meanwhile, in the initial period £3m was splashed on players – quite an investment at the time. Top of the outlay list was the Vinnie Jones deal, costing £650,000;

John Hendrie came for £500,000 from Newcastle, and Chris Fairclough was coaxed to drop a division in a £500,000 deal from Spurs, on transfer deadline day. 'I knew Terry Venables and I spoke to the Spurs secretary. The deadline was five p.m. but they didn't know where Terry was. He finds out that he's in the Bamboo Bar at the Royal Gardens Hotel, which was like his office. I said I wanted to do a deal for Fairclough. He gave me his number. We were racing against time.'

During the conversation, Fairclough insisted that he couldn't come to Leeds at that time because his wife was about to have a baby. 'I said, "Chris, they have babies in Leeds, you know. We have some of the top maternity units in the country!"' The deal was sealed. 'I got his signature on a fax and we signed him – one of the best centre-halves in the country.'

On the same day he pulled off arguably the most important transfer in Leeds United's history. As the Godfather tells it, Wilkinson knew that Fotherby was acquainted with Manchester United chairman Martin Edwards and manager Alex Ferguson ('I knew everyone in football'), and he asked about a deal for Strachan. 'I rang them up. They said, "He's going to Sheffield Wednesday, he's meeting Ron Atkinson."' 'Big Ron' had been appointed following Wilko's departure from Hillsborough.

Fotherby did his stuff.

'I said, "Please, help me out here. Would he give me half an hour with Howard Wilkinson?" They put it to Gordon and he said he'd call in.'

According to Fotherby, many of the signings were done

at his house in Park Lane, Roundhay, so as not to alert the press. During such negotiations Wilkinson would not get involved in any talk of money, just football. Mrs Fotherby played a very special role in the deals. 'Josie used to come in, say, "Howard, you're wanted on the phone," and he would get up and go out,' reveals Fotherby, wonderfully. Wilkinson would then come back and say, 'It's vital I get back to Elland Road,' leaving the Godfather to wheel and deal.

However, on this occasion, things didn't run like clockwork.

'We're sat there and Gordon says, "Well, I've got to go, I've got to see Ron Atkinson." Now, my fear was that if he did . . . I wanted to be the last to see him. I didn't want him to go, but he says, "I have to, that's the kind of man I am."'

This incident says everything about Strachan. He kept his word, and went to Sheffield Wednesday.

'Most footballers don't even ring you,' continues the Godfather. 'Anyway, at seven p.m. he walks into my office at Elland Road, where I'd told him I would be. I couldn't believe it: he said he'd been to see Ron, had a very good chat, and said, "I'm coming to join Leeds. You've sold me it so much I want in." I knew Ron very well, and he said, "I can't believe it. I had him there and he went to Leeds! You bastard!"' He's smiling. 'But that's how it is in football.'

Indeed. And when it comes to signing players, Fotherby suggests he had a 'gift'. He remembers signing Eric Cantona when nobody wanted him (and the Frenchman was using the players' union boss to do the deal), and convincing Atkinson to sell him David Wetherall and Jon Newsome for a knockdown price. One of his favourite stories concerns Gary McAllister, signed from Leicester City for £1m in the summer of 1990 to replace Jones (whom he thinks should have been retained, because 'It wasn't just his football, it was his whole personality') as Wilkinson prepared for the First Division, and ultimately the title.

'Howard said, "Top priority, midfield. Get me Gary McAllister. I need him."'

Fotherby went to an FA dinner, sat next to Leicester manager David Pleat, and did the deal. 'But he said, "I don't know if you'll be able to sign him, Bill, he's going to the World Cup." His agent was a man called Jon Holmes. Gary Lineker's agent. So I said to Allan Roberts, "Get me a contract, drive me down to Leicester!"'

This was the Friday. Within twenty-four hours, McAllister was due in Glasgow to board a flight with the Scotland squad for Italia 90.

'They said, "We can't get hold of him, he must be playing golf somewhere." I said I was desperate, that I'd done a deal but it was up to Gary. They said, "You've no chance." Anyway, I get to Leicester, they've left messages all over. He turned up at about seven o'clock. I was a great one for sponsorships and selling, I'd gone down in a virtually brand-new, big Mercedes, and he'd obviously seen it in the car park. So we're negotiating, and we break for ten minutes to consider, it's about eleven thirty p.m., and he says, "I'll sign when I come back." I said, "No, no. I'll tell you what will happen:

you'll have such a magnificent World Cup that you'll probably want to sign for Real Madrid or Barcelona. Listen, we need you to help us win the championship." It got to about a quarter to twelve, when he said, "If I can have your Mercedes, I'll sign." I said, "You can have it.'"

He hoots with laughter. 'The only problem was, it wasn't my car! It was a sponsored car, but I knew it would make no difference. I had to get him to sign. I could always get him a Mercedes.'

At 11.50 Fotherby rang Wilkinson, who was on holiday in Ibiza, to deliver the good news. 'He said, "**** off!" I said, "It's true, he's signed!" He couldn't believe it.'

Minutes later, Fotherby was on the phone to *Yorkshire Evening Post* sports reporter Don Warters to announce the key signing to an expectant public.

'Of all the signings, that was an achievement,' he beams. Fotherby had indeed signed one of the most sought-after players in the country for a club that had only just joined the top division.

What the supporters didn't know was that while all these signings were happening, the finances were being stretched. 'The bank demanded guarantees,' explains Fotherby. 'My house was a guarantee. I daren't tell my wife. You pay it off. I was doing deals like Wigfalls [a popular Leeds television rental company in the 1980s]; I was paying monthly! I let people think we had money at Leeds. We didn't have two ha'pennies to rub together, but I would do it. I would go to a sponsor and say, "Look, we're going to win the championship, we're going to get promotion." You don't throw money, but you gamble. Borrow money from next year's commercial deals, everything. I did some impossible deals! Got away with murder.'

For the time being at least. A decade later, borrowing on a more extreme and ultimately ruinous scale would be part of Leeds' downfall. Fotherby and I will talk more about the aftermath of winning the title, and the complex set of circumstances that led to Wilkinson's demise, but for now we'll leave the Godfather and Josie in their private office, surrounded by their scrapbooks and their memories.

'They were the best years of our lives,' muses a smiling Josie Fotherby over a desk littered with clippings about Wilkinson, Strachan, Gary Mac and El Diego.

It's quiet and intimate in here. Even the Godfather allows himself to drop the chutzpah.

'I wish they could have gone on for ever,' he says.

CHAPTER 19

Steve Hodge – 'Hodgey'

I suppose it's like being in the army, or acting: you're in the public eye, your highs are massive, you're slagged off, but it's all part of the package.

I meet Steve Hodge – ex-England international, title-winner of 1991/92 – in a motorway services near Nottingham, where the much-travelled trophy winner sits unrecognized among tea-supping travellers going about their business. Which is probably just how 'Hodgey' likes it. Currently coaching back at his first club, Nottingham Forest, the quietly but determinedly spoken forty-nine-year-old has been part of or around some of the most historic moments in 1980s and early 1990s football but never really hogged the spotlight or, perhaps, received the credit he deserves. In this sense, he is a microcosm of Wilko's unsung heroes.

As a Forest apprentice who joined the club straight from school, he enjoyed two separate spells at his hometown club under Brian Clough. In between, in the mid-eighties, there was a period at Aston Villa and then

Spurs, where he played on the left side of David Pleat's sublime midfield alongside Glenn Hoddle, Chris Waddle and Osvaldo 'Ossie' Ardiles, three of the most gifted players ever to light up English football. However, that Spurs side often fell at the final hurdle, including losing in the FA Cup Final in 1987, whereas in a second spell at Forest Hodge won the Simod Cup and League Cup – his first domestic honours.

Along the way he chalked up twenty-four England caps and is perhaps best remembered for trading shirts with Bill Fotherby's mate Diego Maradona at the end of the infamous 1986 'Hand of God' game, when Hodge's inadvertent slice to goalie Peter Shilton was mischievously, indeed illegally, handled by the Argentinian superstar into the net.

None other than Gary McAllister has said that, as a technically excellent goalscoring midfielder, in today's game Hodgey would be the equivalent of a Frank Lampard, able to command over £100,000 a week. Yet, almost two decades after he held up the First Division trophy, our interview takes place at an outside table in a motorway service station, litter blowing around us, and continues in Hodgey's old BMW, which is filled with sand. 'I've been doing the house up,' he chuckles – another job he is no doubt conducting with quiet application.

Everyone remembers Wilkinson's favoured midfield four, but this left-footed midfielder (who could play left or central) made twelve starts (and eleven appearances from the bench) in the title season, and weighed in with seven goals, which have certainly been remembered –

and credited – by almost everyone I've talked to. Given that Hodgey's tally included the match winner and crucial equalizer in the home games against Liverpool and Sheffield Wednesday respectively, those goals alone earned four points – the gap by which Leeds United won the title. Add to that crucial braces in the 4–3 home win over Sheffield United and the 3–3 draw at Elland Road against Southampton, and without Steve Hodge perhaps Wilkinson's team may not have won the title at all.

'I think because I was older, I really appreciated the achievement,' he tells me as the wind blows dust off distant memories. 'I'd been – not near it, but I'd finished third a few times, so I knew how hard it was to win the league, in terms of performance, and having a squad that fused together. So to win it was a real surprise. But I felt I'd paid my dues to earn it over the years. I'd played in that team with Hoddle and Waddle and Ardiles, which finished third, but we got beaten in the cup final by Coventry and we lost to Arsenal in the semi-final of the League Cup that year. It was as good a team as I played in, in terms of flair and technical ability, but with a soft centre. We weren't defensively strong enough, as a unit, to win the league.

'Leeds were a bit more conservative, a bit more pragmatic, more structured at set pieces. We were regimented in what we did, in terms of how we played against certain teams, getting results, whether it was against Wimbledon [0–0 away, 5–1 at home] or Arsenal [2–2 at home, 1–1 away], the big teams. We were very much a really organized unit of players, in every individual game, against different teams, which seems to be the key to winning the league. It's to Howard's credit that he realized how to win it. We weren't the best group of players in the world at that time, or in England, probably, but he managed to get us organized and motivated, and pick the right team enough times to win the championship. We lost four times in forty-two games, and weren't beaten by any of the top teams. We stayed in there the whole course of the season and eventually outlasted Man United, which was satisfying to say the least.'

A £900,000 capture from Forest in the summer of 1991, Hodge was one of the later pieces in the jigsaw, along with fellow summer 1991 recruits Rod Wallace, Tony Dorigo, David Wetherall and Jon Newsome. Gary Speed recalled their arrival, which coincided with a pre-season 'friendly' against Botafogo of Brazil in Tokyo, which turned out to be rather unfriendly. Typically eccentrically – or brilliantly – Wilkinson kept his players on English time, as Speed told me. 'So we were getting up at four p.m., having breakfast, going training about seven p.m. and then wide awake for the rest of the night. We were like that all week, and you'd have four hours' sleep. It all kicked off on the pitch and we were all fighting, but it was a good week. The team spirit really kicked in with the new signings Tony Dorigo, Hodgey, Rod – everybody bonded.'

Hodge arrived at Leeds just weeks after he'd been involved in a more famous confrontation of the period – the 1991 FA Cup Final, in which his old team Spurs triumphed 2–1 despite Paul Gascoigne being so pumped up he ended his own involvement after just minutes, damaging cruciate ligaments while scything down Forest's Gary Charles. It proved to be Hodge's last game under Cloughie; after meeting Wilkinson and Hennigan at the latter's house, the deal was sealed with Bill Fotherby in a nearby Holiday Inn.

Hodge knew Lee Chapman from his Forest days and Mel Sterland from England, and also knew that he faced a battle breaking into the formidable Leeds midfield, but he wasn't fazed. 'I'd been at Forest where they had Neil Webb, Roy Keane and myself, and at Tottenham I'd been with Hoddle, Waddle and Ardiles, so I'd been in good midfields.' And, of course, he'd played for England against the likes of Johan Cruyff and Maradona. 'I knew what midfield play was all about. I knew it was competitive. In those situations you back yourself to get in the team and stay in.'

Hodge had played against Gary McAllister at Leicester, knew all about Gordon Strachan from when he was at Man United, and had faced a young David Batty in the FA Cup when he was 'snapping at your heels and very competitive. Quiet on the pitch, didn't say a lot, just got on with his job.' If there was a weakness, and a way in, he suspected it might be Gary Speed, who was young and up-and-coming. It didn't happen. 'Howard thought he was a quality player, which he turned out to be,' admits Hodgey, who with the benefit of hindsight realizes he was probably signed as an experienced, versatile 'safe pair of hands' to cover for injuries and suspensions. He sighs wistfully. 'I just had to take it on the chin.'

So Hodge became the fifth midfielder. He had a taste

of what was coming when he started the season on the bench – at home, ironically against Nottingham Forest – and didn't feature. 'Gary Speed was great in the air, a good athlete,' he recalls. 'I knew pretty quickly that whenever I got in I had to do well to stay in the team.'

It may not have been the role he'd envisaged when he signed, but he took to it with gusto. Hodge made his mark in the very next game, against Sheffield Wednesday on 24 August. David Hirst, whom Wilkinson had signed for his old club for a bargain £250,000 from Barnsley, was giving the defence a torrid time and the South Yorkshire club were 1–0 up. On came Hodge and Sterland, the double substitution paying valuable dividends when the left-footer stabbed home the equalizer from twelve yards in the final minutes. 'I scored on my debuts for Villa and Tottenham,' a delighted Hodge told the *Yorkshire Post* after the game. 'This one fell nicely to me to give me a hundred per cent on debut goals away from Forest. It's unusual but it's a nice feeling.'

The following month, on 21 September, he got his first start at home, against Liverpool, when Carl Shutt was rested and Gary Speed selected up front, and kick-started his Leeds career by hooking a Dorigo cross into the top corner. It was a perfect strike. For the next few weeks he was installed in the Sergeant's team, until a failed fitness test against Oldham left him kicking his heels, and the frustrations started to creep in.

'I was in in spurts,' he tells me. 'Four or five games and then out again, which is obviously frustrating for a player. A manager in his mind has his best eleven, which he'll play in the majority of games when he can. But if someone like me is in decent form, plays when you beat Sheff Wednesday 6–1 and gets dropped, you're not going to be happy with that. So it was never going to be sweetness and roses between Howard and me. But as I've got older, and as a coach myself, I've grown to see the bigger picture.' Which is that however frustrating it was at times, Wilkinson managed him to something Cloughie never did: a league title.

Perhaps the shrewd Sergeant even realized that an impatient Hodge could benefit the team. As the player himself suggests, when he did step up, he was hungry to succeed.

Did he feel he had a point to prove?

'I had no point to prove as a footballer. I had a point to prove to the manager. But he knew me anyway. He knew I could play. I got seven goals. It wasn't enough.'

As Hodge ruefully points out, he grew to feel that whatever he did wouldn't be enough to keep him in the first eleven. Even the brace against Southampton didn't cement him in the starting line-up. 'Wilko went bananas at the team,' he recalls of this match in which a 3–1 lead was let slip. 'I remember Shearer getting them back in the game. But they weren't a bad team then. They had Shearer, Mickey Adams, Jimmy Case, Iain Dowie. They were no mugs.'

Were things more evenly matched back then? That season Leeds lost to Oldham and Crystal Palace. 'I wouldn't say it was more even then, but nowadays I could tell you the top two or three without having to think. In those days it was supposed to be Man United and Arsenal because Liverpool had just gone past their best, and we came in out of the blue. A dark horse, to be fair, and you can't take that away from Howard.'

In a sense, the precedents for Wilkinson's surge from Division Two to the Division One title were Clough's own championships with unfashionable, regional Derby (Second Division champions 1968/69, First Division champions 1971/72) and Forest (promoted 1976/77, champions 1977/78), which formed part of Ol' Big Head's array of honours, including two European Cups (1979 and 1980), the trophy that eluded Revie. And Hodge wasn't the only player the Sergeant recruited who'd had a football education under the legendary if controversial manager. As well as Chapman, Chris Fairclough played for Clough from 1981 to 1987, and I'm intrigued to find out how the two disciplinarian managers compare.

Hodge insists that apart from finding Clough as frustrating as he did Wilkinson, they were 'chalk and cheese'. 'The majority of managers I didn't really get on with as people, but as a manager you're looking for that player to go over the white line and put his lot in for you. They were different, but their careers were excellent. With Cloughie it could be difficult, but I think as players got older, or retired, they probably realized that they'd been lucky to be around him. Not all got on with him, but they benefited from being under him, in the long term. The hardships, the verbal blasts, often being dropped without a reason – it was done for a reason, which will have been three points on Saturday. I liked his sharp wit and humour. Sometimes it wasn't a nice humour – when it was your turn – but he could bring a team together to laugh at each other and they got used to guys laughing at each other.'

Except at Leeds, where Clough went down like a whoopee cushion at a funeral. Intriguingly, he never talked to his long-serving midfielder about his forty-four days at Elland Road in 1974, even when Hodge was about to embark on the same journey. 'Nobody will ever know the inner workings of what went on,' Hodge says. 'He'd been at Derby, then the stint at Brighton. He was a manager trying to get back in football and probably felt vulnerable, I think.' It's a perceptive suggestion. 'And he was facing a lot of superstars at the time. So either you go in there and tiptoe around quietly or you set your stall out, and knowing him it will have been a bit of bravado and he probably didn't realize the depth of loyalty towards Don Revie. They'd won everything and been in all these finals, and he was still their master. It was a family, and with hindsight he went in too strong, to change it, and it backfired in his face. He'll have wanted to make the point that there were these big lads and he wasn't scared of them and he could put them in their place. And all he could do really was go in there and try to win the league again, but in a different manner. That was his Holy Grail – to win the championship, but with style.'

And Wilkinson? 'More pragmatic. No grey areas. A facts and figures man. Being an ex-schoolteacher, he'd have the information in front of him – long ball, short passing – and would work out mathematically the best way to get results. He realized that there were certain ways to beat teams and certain ways to beat individuals. He's got a trained eye, and would see things on a football field nobody else did. Howard Wilkinson's way would work a long time in football.'

Intriguingly, Hodge remembers Wilkinson when he was at Notts County, and he reveals that back then he employed the unusual tactic of sitting at the top of the stand, on the gantry next to the TV cameras, which must have been precarious. 'But from up there he could gaze down and see the formation of the teams a lot easier than at ground level, so he could see the game plan of the opposition and how to beat them. Extremely clever.

'He was revered at Notts County, still is. With Jimmy Sirrel he basically took them from the doldrums into the top division, kept them in there before he left. He was innovative, very intelligent, certainly one of the brightest coaches. It was like a chess game to him. He's got a trained eye, and could see things on the pitch nobody else did.'

Hodge also reveals that at Leeds, Wilkinson placed motivational slogans around the training ground. Revie did something similar (the words 'Keep fighting' were pinned up in the dressing room), but generally it's associated with the current game, and modern psychological techniques. Similarly, for all Wilko's dismissal of team talks, Hodge remembers 'heart-stirring' speeches, especially towards the season's end, when all the planning had been done. '"You've done it for yourself and your family, and the fans are happy, but don't cave in now." He was mentally very strong.'

Hodgey remembers his Liverpool goal – 'bobbled on the six-yard box and whack. It was a huge thing. I hadn't realized that Leeds hadn't beaten Liverpool for years. No one mentioned it before the game, because it would have become a mental block. Sheff Wednesday was another big moment. They were a top team – Chris Waddle and all the rest. So to win 6–1, you think, "We've got a chance here." Up until April we were happy to be in the race, making Man U at least sweat for it. They were always favourites, but they lost to Forest at home – Scot Gemmill scored the winner – and it began to dawn that they might crumble. The rest is history.'

He's smiling, and for all his frustrations in 1991/92 Hodge always looked happy on the pitch. 'Happy? God, I was pleased to be on the pitch! It's the only place to be.'

As it was for other players, Hodge's triumph was bittersweet. The following season, he was out in the cold. He'd had a lot of calf problems. He shows me two scars, which look like something left behind by Jack the Ripper. 'As I got older, my gait was changing, and I was getting cramping in my calves. Mick Hennigan gave me these [he produces two special insoles, which he still wears] and within three weeks I was fine. I had it when I joined Leeds. But Howard and I had got off on the wrong foot with injuries; he was obviously frustrated that he'd paid a million pounds for me and I wasn't fit. I couldn't prove to him that I had a problem with my calves. Hence the first season I was injured a bit, then I'd be fit, then injured again. Eventually I had an exploratory operation and they sliced them open. It was to do with the way I landed on my feet. I remember one day saying to him, "I can't explain to you but it hurts when I run. I can't show you a bruise or a cut." I'd hardly missed a game in my career. But to be fair, this was the days before informed medical stuff. When I look back now, I became stressed out and fed up cos I couldn't get myself fit. Mentally I stopped training. I fell out with the manager. I wasn't in the team. I was on the motorway every day. It wasn't great.'

In his book, *The Man With Maradona's Shirt*, Hodge reveals how he ended up training with the kids, with Wilko making wisecracks about 'the misfit'. Horrendous – or just Yorkshire banter? Players today don't get that kind of treatment, but Hodge insists that as an older player he was used to it.

'My main concern was that I wasn't fit, and nobody understood the injury that I'd got. The worst thing for me was when I played well [the following season] – there was a run of games and we beat Arsenal at home 3–0 on telly. I got left out again. I just thought, "It doesn't matter what I do. I'll always be a bit-part player." I was thirty-two, and needed to be playing.'

Two decades later, Hodge regrets what happened but doesn't regret going to Leeds, and is sanguine about his time at Elland Road. 'I learned another way of playing, very simple, scientific. It was an eye opener really. I think Howard would probably think I was a bit of a misfit and moaned too much, but he was in his shoes and I was in mine. We had great times, and some not so great. Twenty years on, we did win the league together and I'm happy we did. And it was nice to play for Leeds United, because they were a big club then.'

Hodge made sixty-six appearances for Leeds, scoring ten goals, before spells at QPR, Watford and a final game for Leyton Orient convinced him it was over.

'It was difficult because it's been a way of life. That's why footballers associate together because they understand those highs, which are so high no one can explain it, and the problems they have along the way. I suppose it's like being in the army, or acting: you're in the public eye, your highs are massive, you're slagged off, but it's all part of the package. You get used to it, but you never quite replace it.'

And at the end, all that's left are medals, and memories. But what memories! That 'Hand of God' game – it must be surreal, thinking that you were on the pitch that day.

'It doesn't feel surreal because I remember being there, but as I've got older it's got more infamous. He's probably the best player that ever played the game and that goal is probably the most infamous, and in the same game he scored probably the best goal I've ever seen at a World Cup. So it's not surreal; it reminds people I went to a World Cup. Being a lower-profile player, I did come into two World Cups and England did quite well in them, so it probably reminds people I wasn't half bad as a player. I did my best.'

He's not bitter about missing out on the really big money of the last few years because, as he points out, as an apprentice he cleaned the boots of Forest's European champions but made more money than them from the game. He still sees Chris Fairclough – whom he suspects won't speak to me because he's even more low profile.

And Howard Wilkinson?

'We say hello. He managed a team in Bobby Robson's memorial match a couple of years ago.' He laughs. 'I was sub that day as well. He put me on for twenty minutes.'

CHAPTER 20

Tony Dorigo – 'Aussie'

You're coming in here asking me whether to play at Old Trafford or Fiji?

The Old Peacock pub has been opposite Elland Road for as long as I can remember. Now owned by the Leeds United Supporters Club – in quiet but determined opposition to the club's Billy's Bar opposite – it is, like Leslie Silver's office, a shrine to Leeds United. To walk in is to experience a paradise of memorabilia: the place is decked from walls to ceiling (literally) with posters, banners and pennants from LUFC's glory days.

However, when I walk in with Tony Dorigo, the place is almost empty, and none of the bar staff seem to recognize the greatest Leeds United left-back of the last forty years, in a black suit and white shirt rather than the all-white kit he sported when he graced the hallowed turf. Earlier we'd arranged to meet in the Elland Road foyer, where the championship-winning number three was confronted by a security guard who wouldn't let him into the building and all but turfed him off the premises.

While many of the Revie-era players are still involved in or around the club, it often feels as if Wilko's heroes have been all but airbrushed from history. 'I get invites from my old club Aston Villa all the time,' Dorigo tells me with a shrug that's more bemused than bitter or angry. 'Chelsea less so. Leeds? Absolutely nothing.

'I don't think that team got the credit it deserved,' he continues over a drink, a tiny insult perhaps having been added to injury when the Peacock turned out not to stock the sparkling water favoured by Wilkinson's sports science devotee. 'Now the game's all media driven, and we won it the last year before Sky took over. So you'll hear about Blackburn's title, and Jack Walker's money, and Alan Shearer and all the rest of it, but you won't hear about us. But I accept that. That's just the way it is.'

Dorigo doesn't like to grumble, which made him a perfect fit for Sergeant Wilko. Arriving in the summer of 1991, the wonderfully assured left-back was one of the last pieces of a team he compares favourably to Bobby Robson's 1990 World Cup side. 'I played with Lineker, Gascoigne, Chris Waddle, Beardsley. Great players who could turn a game. But it was the same with Leeds. Great balance, great strikers; that midfield had a bit of everything. Speed, Batty, Strachan, McAllister: air, wind, trickery, passing. Whatever the situation was, we had something to deal with it.'

Beautifully put, but just how does an Australian end up playing for England? Dorigo's father is Italian, which meant his son could work in England on a six-month resident's permit, and after five years of renewals could become a 'good old pom'. In Dorigo's early days at Villa, Australia asked him to play in the World Cup qualifiers, which meant being away for weeks; it also meant the perhaps less-than-tantalizing prospect of facing Tonga, Western Samoa, New Zealand and Fiji when Villa were due to play Man United and Liverpool. 'Not to play those countries down,' he says, 'but to a kid who's never played at Old Trafford or Anfield and you've got a long flight and all the rest of it for a 10–0 at half time job . . .' He doesn't need to explain further.

He sought advice from his manager, the 1982 European Cup-winning Tony Barton. 'He said "You're coming in here asking me whether to play at Old Trafford or Fiji?" and just erupted,' roars Dorigo. 'I said, "Thanks very much, boss!" and just ran out.'

His laughter fills the room. A genial, gregarious Aussie, Dorigo is terrific company, and between the laughter come insights quite unlike those I've had from any other player, which perhaps reflect one of the more unusual paths to Elland Road.

When Dorigo was at school, the headmaster asked the class to write down the three things they wanted to be. He put down 'professional soccer player' three times. 'He said, "Tony, what are you doing?" I told him it was all I wanted to be.' He was just nine years old.

Growing up with a 'football crazy' Italian father and becoming 'hooked' on imported BBC highlights of the English game, Dorigo was turning out for clubs in Australia by his teens, and was subsequently picked for specialist training at the National Athletic Institute in Canberra. But Aussie 'soccer' was in an embryonic stage organizationally and he arrived to find just five other players. 'I thought, "Hang on, it's eleven v. eleven."' So he decided to try his luck in England. Aged just fifteen, he took the extraordinary step of writing to the top dozen clubs in a country literally on the other side of the world, offering his services.

'I'll never forget, I got this letter through the post with the claret and blue badge on the front and nearly jumped out of my skin,' he tells me, recalling the reply he received from Aston Villa. 'They said if I could get over there myself, I could have a four-day trial.' He'd already said yes when another letter arrived, from Man United. 'I'd love to say I told them where to stick it but it was "thanks for your letter, but no".' He grins, although ironically Leeds' big rivals would actually attempt to buy him from the Midlanders.

On his first day at Villa Park, Dorigo was so nervous he couldn't touch the ball, but subsequently impressed enough to be taken on as an apprentice, then a professional. Six months after his arrival he was in the first team of a club that had just won the European Cup. It was a 'dream come true', for the price of a stamp.

He doubts whether such a miracle could happen in the modern game, where even English, Irish and Scottish players aren't getting a chance. 'You look at Ian Rush going from Chester to Liverpool, or the Ian Wrights of this world, who came from non-league. Clubs think, "Shall we give the guy from down there a chance, or spend ten million on a Spanish international?"'

Dorigo arrived in England to play a sport that was already changing. He was the first of a new breed of silkier, pacier full-back that would transform the way the game was played. 'Nowadays, someone like Ashley Cole is the mould of a technical, speedy player who can pass and shoot,' he explains. 'When I came over they were big old-fashioned cloggers who didn't overlap, they just sorted you out.' Thus, the 'young whipper-snapper whizzing up and down the line' became accustomed to shouts of, 'Oi! You don't do that at full-back!' 'Half the games I played, I could have played with a cigar,' he insists, more matter-of-fact than immodest. 'Because the guys I played against just weren't quick. They'd threaten to chop my legs off but they'd never catch me. Vroom! Nowadays, everyone's an athlete.'

Like others I've met, Dorigo remembers football in the eighties as a much more tense, violent activity, on and off the field. On landing in Britain, his father took him to a Spurs game at White Hart Lane. 'And then suddenly the police horses are everywhere and they're charging the crowd. I'm like, "Dad, what's going on?" It was like a war zone. Then it dawned on me: there was an edge to this.' And he found that, on the field, he actually thrived upon that edge. 'If someone wanted to rip my head off, I loved it.'

The atmosphere fuelled adrenalin. He describes playing at West Ham's Upton Park as like a 'chicken run', although admits to being 'a bit frightened' on a cup visit to Millwall, the so-called Lions whose old Den ground was 'in the middle of nowhere, so everything was pitch black, apart from the floodlights'. Before the game, Dorigo noticed that his teammates were warming up in the centre circle, but began his own sprints up and down the touchline, as is normal. 'This guy goes, "Doreeeeeeego!" I turn round and he looks at me with this vicious face on him and he says, "Your mother does – a very rude thing! – with kangaroos!" And spits! It just misses me. Everyone's going, "Grrrrrrrrrrrrrrrrrr!" Oh my God! So I ran straight to the middle of the pitch and warmed up there as well. At least he knew I was Australian. He'd done his research. But it was nasty. At West Ham the players would want to kill you, but you'd wink at them and they'd go doolally.' Which Dorigo loved.

As he racked up eleven England Under 21 caps and a player of the year award, life in Birmingham couldn't have been much better for a man who admits he would have been happy to sign for twenty years. However, after four years the flying full-back was brought down to earth with a bump.

By 1987, the club was struggling to score goals and needed a striker urgently, identifying Chelsea's David Speedie as the man. However, on transfer deadline day, Blues chairman Ken Bates would only let Speedie go if he got Dorigo in return.

Dorigo was astonished to get a call from Villa chairman Doug Ellis telling him, '"Tony, I'm picking you up in one hour. You're driving down with me to London to talk to Chelsea Football Club." This was the first I'd heard of it. I was devastated. I thought it had been going really well.'

For the young international, this was an early lesson in how football was starting to become a very big business. On what he describes as a 'surreal' day, he found himself in a Heathrow hotel room with 'Batesy', with Speedie in the adjoining room. When he suddenly heard Speedie howling with laughter, 'Batesy, quick as a flash, says, "They must have made him their first offer." He was a very clever man. I loved him for that, but I remember thinking, "Football's not as straightforward as I thought."'

Neither player would sanction the deal and Villa were relegated, although Chelsea still kept trying to acquire the full-back given that Dorigo's international ambitions wouldn't be helped by playing in the Second Division. When Villa unveiled their new manager in future 'Do I Not Like That' England boss Graham Taylor, he sat the players down and insisted he only wanted men who were committed to the club, 'prepared to fall on their sword'. '"And you, Dorigo,"' the Aussie remembers him saying, '"you decide whether you're going to Chelsea or staying with us." Unfortunately he pointed at Gary Williams, who looked a bit like me. Gary's like, "No, boss, Tony's over there!" But that broke the ice and it was easier for me to leave. It wasn't down to my making. I'd worked out what it all meant. It was a business.'

Dorigo spent four years at Chelsea under Bates, now the Leeds United owner, but says he knew very early on that 'issues behind the scenes' would cause problems. 'I wanted to win things,' he explains. 'Being seventh or ninth didn't do it for me. OK, maybe I was over ambitious, but I wanted to go to a place where we had a chance. At Chelsea we could win ten games or lose ten games. We had some ridiculous things there. We were relegated [in 1988] and the next year in the Second Division didn't lose for thirty-six games, because we had some terrific players – Gordon Durie, Kerry Dixon, proven internationals. But there was a lot of meddling outside the team. You'd train for six weeks with the intention of being ready for the start of the season and a spanner would be thrown in the works, totally under-mining the manager's good work.

'It happened so often. Silly things, like charging us for the drinks when we were away in a hotel. You were allowed one soft drink, then would have to pay for yourself. Mind-bogglingly stupid things! So you upset the team spirit for a quid. Someone from the club tried to get us to sign a document to agree to have a deduction from our wages on the season tickets we were due for the whole year, for a tax thing, an hour before the first game. Half an hour before kick-off, I was still sitting in my suit. Whoever was doing that didn't understand the influence it had.'

Dorigo wanted out, but Chelsea refused to sell, so he ran down his four-year contract. 'They offered me new terms and I can honestly say I never looked at them. I handed the letter back. The fans were tremendous, but if you can't win anything, what are you there for?' When Wilkinson offered Chelsea £1.3m – and 'really wanted me, which was fantastic' – it was a no-brainer.

However, when they first met, Sergeant Wilkinson surprised him by talking about golf, not football. 'It was the most bizarre conversation. I think we played about two or three holes, verbally. He took about half an hour to say something he could have said in two minutes, but I listened, and it made a lot of sense.' He can virtually recite Wilkinson's epic even now: '"It's like playing a par four, OK, and you can hit the ball three hundred yards down the fairway. However, at two ninety there's a lake, and you're against the wind, so play clever. You don't need to hit a fancy shot high into the air. Play under the wind, and knock it on to the green." He was basically telling me to play to my strengths, trying to get across that even if your ideal is the Barcelona way, don't try it if you can't do it.' He's smiling. 'Anyway, despite all that I signed.'

For all the Sarge's beloved golfing maxims, Dorigo reveals that when they played together in a charity tournament the first thing Wilkinson did on teeing off was wallop his ball into the woods. 'I wouldn't trust his swing for love nor money,' he guffaws. 'Everyone was asking, "Where's the boss?" I'm saying, "I dunno, he's in the friggin' woods somewhere." And he came out with all these balls.'

Another anecdote is more revealing about the Sarge's controversial man management style, which some seem to have responded to better than others. Dorigo began the 1991/92 pre-season with a double hernia injury, for which he underwent an operation. He arrived back in Leeds to be told 'The boss wants to see you', and found himself in a room with a stern-faced Wilkinson and Hennigan. 'No welcome "hi", no talk about the golf holes, just "How did the operation go?"

'Then he says, "You're an Aussie,"' at which point Dorigo admits he was starting to wonder where this was leading. '"Do you know who else had this operation?"' Wilkinson continued. '"Nigel Worthington. The doctor says you'll be back in six weeks. Nigel was back in five. Northern Irish, you see, but you Aussies are as soft as—"'

Dorigo still can't quite work out what Wilkinson was up to, talking about the Sheffield Wednesday left-back. 'I thought, "Jesus, is he really having a go or is he testing me?"' He opted for the latter, replying, '"If you're used to Nigel Worthington, wait until I get fit, cos you're gonna love me!" And he was, "Right, let's have a laugh!" They were wetting themselves. But he always drove you on to the next thing. He was constantly moulding you, to see how you'd react.' Dorigo was fit just four weeks later, for the start of the season, and received the man of the match award on his debut, the 1–0 home win against Nottingham Forest.

Dorigo loved playing for Wilkinson. Yes, training could be boring and some players, notably Batty, grew to dread the Thursday sessions on set pieces – but it was effective. Dorigo reveals the full extent of Wilko's meticulous preparation.

As the left-back, he would be required first to practise throw-ins in his half, then on the halfway line, then in the opponents' half. 'Then free kicks in my half, then I'd be the free-kick taker on the right side of the pitch with my left foot. Macca [McAllister] would do it the other way. We'd do the same thing week in week out – throw, throw, cross, cross. Then we'd do the same thing defending.

'It was boring, but say Manchester United have got ten minutes to go. The pressure's really on and they're piling forward to get an equalizer or nick a win or whatever. We never panicked, because we went into our positions without even thinking about it, and it was all put there by him. We scored from a lot of set pieces, a lot of late goals. But there was a side to him that no one saw. He was funny, Howard.'

A drawback, Dorigo adds, of Wilkinson's painstaking Sergeant persona was that it then became problematic for him to alternate with his more humane real self, which became an issue when things weren't going as well. 'The first time I tell you the golf story, you might listen for half an hour,' he explains. 'But you think, for years and years, the same message . . . that's when it got more difficult. David Batty – it would have driven him mad.'

But in 1991/92, it worked beautifully. Dorigo tells me that anyone could be on the end of one of the Sergeant's military-style dressing-downs, even Strachan, albeit 'in different ways'. Dorigo may have been the man of the match against Forest, but this didn't stop Wilko tearing him off a strip at half time. 'I tried to explain why I wasn't closer to the winger. I'd tucked in because the centre-half had slipped, and the danger was towards the goal. I still think I was right, but it doesn't matter because he was the manager. And he told me that! Two or three games later, I got another rocket. Der der der, like a machine gun. This time I got it. I said, "You're right, boss!"'

What was crucial was the respect, and each player's

understanding of his role in the team and others' weaknesses, and their willingness to help each other out. Dorigo remembers some 'amazing' performances, especially that 6–1 at Sheffield Wednesday, where he scored past England teammate Chris Woods, and like Shutty has an interesting tale to tell about the 1–0 win at Chelsea in September. As a returning player, Dorigo was given dog's abuse. Every time the ball went to him in the warm-up he was roundly booed. 'My teammates cottoned on to this, so every second pass was to me . . . booo, boooo! The Chelsea fans thought it was getting to us, but we thought it was hysterical. We went and beat them.'

He loved Elland Road – much noisier and more enclosed than the spacious, quieter Chelsea – and loved living in Leeds. His home was in leafy Scarcroft, after originally trying to find a house in Seacroft. 'They gave me the wrong address,' he grins. '"Round here, honey, what do you think?"' He remembers too the special bond between the players, and the warm welcome he received from none other than Mike Whitlow, whom he replaced. 'Whits was great. He loved me and he hated me. He hated me because he couldn't get past me but he loved me because he was a great guy, and an excellent player.'

Dorigo has a mound of David Batty stories, like the time they were away with England and roommate Batts went fishing and came back with his England tracksuit covered in guts and scales. 'I said, "Batts, friggin' hell, your tracksuit!" He said, "What are you talking about? It's your tracksuit!" He took it off and gave it to me. His was neatly folded.'

And the time Batts suddenly left an important meeting because he had to pay his 'leccy bill' at the post office. 'He wasn't taking the piss. That's how he is.'

The holidays in Filey. The hatred of travelling and the circus around football. The time he broke Keith Curle's jaw in England training and walked off without a word. 'Keith had to be taken to hospital, have his jaw wired up. The next day he had to eat soup. There was no "sorry" from Batts or anything, and that's the bit people found odd. It is odd . . . but you have to know him. He's his own man and I'd have him in midfield any day.'

They'd been due to fly off together to Moscow for an England friendly against the CIS (as modern-day Russia were then briefly known), after Leeds United won the league. 'I didn't want to go, to be frank,' admits Dorigo. 'I'd just won the title.' In the end he phoned Wilkinson, hours after the stunned manager had been confronted by the media over his Sunday lunch. 'He was half cut. I'd had a couple too. I can't remember what was said, but something was sorted and we didn't go.'

He remembers the following week's game against Norwich as the most physically demanding of the season, which suggests just how much winning the title had taken out of them. 'It was like you'd crossed the marathon [finishing line] and someone's asking you to do another sprint.'

Like everyone I've talked to, Dorigo is enjoying reliving his playing days. He tells me that his most difficult opponents weren't the pacy wingers but the 'clever buggers, the smart players'. Southampton's

Matthew Le Tissier would last ten minutes against him before moving to the other side of the pitch, and then score a hat-trick. 'And people would say, "Oh, Le Tissier had a good game against you." Oh no he didn't!' One of his favourite opponents was Man U's Andrei Kanchelskis because 'he ripped people apart and he never could with me. I was his "most difficult opponent".'

As for Dorigo's – none other than Gordon Strachan. 'I played for Chelsea against Man United with Bryan Robson, Mark Hughes. Hell of a team, but there's this wee ginger guy and I'm gonna smack him. But he'd tuck in and I couldn't get near him. If I went in, I was seven yards out of my position, Mark Hughes would hold the bloody ball up, play it to Strach and he'd have five yards of space in the wrong areas. That's why he was so difficult – he wouldn't take you on. He'd make it difficult for you.'

The memories flood back – his goal at Wembley as Leeds deposed Liverpool in the 1992 Charity Shield; how no one remembers one of his best goals, in the 3–0 home win against Man City in September, because Batty scored a rare goal 'and it was as if God had landed'; a rare mistake in the 4–0 reverse at City's old Maine Road ground. And the player Whitlow dubbed 'the best left-back in the country' has few regrets. He isn't bitter about the money players earn now because he felt he was well paid at the time and was just delighted to be playing football. He doesn't regret not getting the seventy or eighty England caps some suggest he deserved (his old Villa nemesis Graham Taylor picked Stuart Pearce ahead of him), because anyone else would jump at the fifteen he did get. Ultimately, he achieved his dreams, and more.

'When you're a kid, you want to win the league and you want to score at Wembley and you want to play in the World Cup,' he says. 'And fortunately I ticked all those boxes. But winning the league was just fantastic. Six wonderful years here. Not many teams win the league and not many have since. It's a lovely memory.'

Dorigo finally left the club shortly after the Sergeant, being let go when new manager George Graham arrived and injury problems led to his being offered an unsatisfactory new contract. After playing for Torino, Derby and Stoke, and running a property company in the Algarve which was hit by the global economic crisis, he is now an excellent television pundit on channels including Dubai-based Al Jazeera, for whom he covers Italian and Spanish football, and the Asian Cup. 'I've to cover Jordan, Syria, North Korea, South Korea – I go out there and try and look like I know what I'm talking about,' he sniggers as we end an entertaining two-hour talk. 'It's all in the research. Somebody taught me very well. Thank you very much, Mr Wilkinson.'

OO...AH...CANTONA

CHAPTER 21

Eric Cantona – 'Ooh aah'

I don't care about anything.

'We've been through it all together, and we've had our ups and downs (ups and downs!)' goes the song, but being a Leeds fan involves far more downs than ups. A lifetime of misery, false dawns and pain is almost a default mode.

It wasn't quite the rock bottom of recent years, but I vividly remember the horror of turning on Teletext in the autumn of 1992 to read 'Eric Cantona Joins Manchester United'.

I rang Paul Weighell – who was in his office, not roaring off to check out an obscure jazz funk fusion band as a premise to watch Leeds reserves – to splutter, 'Eric's gone . . . and to Manchester United!' What I could never have guessed then was that he'd prove to be such a roaring success across the Pennines, or that, almost exactly nineteen years later, we'd be a few short feet away from each other in a little room.

It's a small colour hotel telly in Glasgow that leads

me to Cantona, when news breaks that the Frenchman – last seen acting, and starring as himself, in the film *Looking for Eric* alongside a former bassist in The Fall – is joining New York Cosmos in the unlikely guise of Director of Football. Yes, Eric Cantona, the so-called 'rebel who would be king', who's never managed, had rumpuses with club after club, and his national team, and who was once photographed putting his finger up Steve Hodge's nose, is going halfway across the world to be a major authority figure in the Big Apple. You couldn't make it up. But then, Cantona's whole life has been a bit like that.

After emails to the Cosmos asking for a one-to-one in NYC ('Do you miss Shutty, Eric?') go predictably unanswered, when the Cosmos arrive in Manchester I manage to blag my way into the press conference – or rather 'media mix zone' (wow) – to meet him.

So it is that I find myself in a wooden Umbro warehouse in Manchester city centre amid a small but hectic media scrum, waiting for Leeds United's mercurial forward, 1991/92. There's a posse of reporters waiting to ask him about his glorious career with Alex Ferguson. We're surrounded by posters of George Best and Manchester pop idols. I'm here to ask him about Howard Wilkinson and Leeds. I feel like a sheep among wolves, a Palestinian among Israelis, a party pooper as unwelcome as our former striker Jermaine Beckford when on 3 January 2010 he scored at Old Trafford to give then League One Leeds an improbable 1–0 FA Cup victory against Manchester United, the biggest football club in the world.

Weirder still, Cantona is appearing alongside Pelé, who turned out for Cosmos in the 1970s in the autumn of his career. It seems an unlikely coupling of arguably the greatest player in the history of football and LUFC's former enfant terrible who, judging by the crackling radio account I heard, was completely out of sorts when he made his LUFC debut in a 2–0 away loss at Oldham on 8 February 1992, when he came on as a second-half substitute (inevitably, for Hodgey).

It was a similar story when I first saw Cantona play in the flesh the following Saturday, when Sergeant Wilko's Leeds were playing IFK Gothenburg in a so-called 'international friendly' of the type that would never take place now, in the middle of the season. There was snow at the edge of the pitch and a bewildered-looking, clearly unfit Frenchman wobbling around the centre circle like a big white duck, firing off baffling passes, like a scattergun without a radar, and looking like he'd never played football before in his life.

However, within weeks he was transformed, and scored the most beautiful goal I've ever seen, right in front of the Kop, against Chelsea on 11 April, when he juggled the ball, flicking it around the defender with the outside of his right foot, and walloped it perfectly into the top corner, the whole movement taking just four touches from receiving the ball to scoring. The cult of Eric had begun, and the sound of 'Ooh aah Cantona! Ooh aah Cantona!' echoed around Elland Road.

Two chancers – from Wakefield, if I remember, calling themselves Oo La La – even made the barmy chant into a dance hit, 'Oo ... ah ... Cantona' (catalogue number 00 AH 1). It's probably a valuable and extremely rare collectors' item now, and unlike most Leeds fans, who probably hit it with a hammer when he left, I still have my copy. It has the balcony speech on the cover – 'Why I love you, I don't know why, but I love you' – and a note reading 'all crowd and speech samples taken from the live recording of the victory parade, Henry Moore Gallery, Leeds, 3 May 1992. If you were there, this is you!' Gulp.

I never fell out of love with Cantona. Unlike some fans, who spat at him when he returned to Elland Road in the enemy red shirt, for me he's always been a bit like the beautiful but unfaithful wife who gave you some wonderful times before running off with the milkman, but who you still can't entirely bring yourself to hate.

As reporters position their recording devices and the expectation builds to fever pitch, my thoughts drift to what others in this story have said about the Monsieur.

For Wilkinson, his untypical signing of a foreign maverick was a case of 'needs must'. Chapman had got a horrendous injury which he thought was a season finisher. By yet another weird twist or coincidence, Cantona was on trial down the road at Sheffield Wednesday. The Sarge remembered him from the French Under 21s, and knew he could play, but, because he'd made earlier enquiries, was well aware of his past. Cantona had a history of falling out with every club he'd ever played for, throwing punches and on one occasion boots in the faces of his teammates, calling every single member of the French Football Federation an idiot to their faces, and revealing that his 'psychoanalyst' had advised him to quit France for England.

'It was a short-term thing, but it's strange how life works,' Wilkinson told me.

Cantona's sixth club, Nimes, wanted a clause in the loan contract that set a date by which Leeds had to decide whether to take him on permanently. 'I think that was the day he scored against Chelsea. The crowd went ****ing wild and Leslie dug me in the ribs and said, "That goal just cost me £1.2 million."'

Gary Speed remembered the French import as 'something we had never come across before', who clicked with Gary McAllister, a football connoisseur, because they were on the same wavelength. 'All of a sudden Gary was saying "what a player this guy is". And he was right. Because he knew.'

Steve Hodge told me you couldn't compare the enigmatic upturned-collared Frenchman to Cruyff or Maradona or the great players he played against because 'for whatever reason' (at one point, it was the fact that he was banned) it never happened for Cantona with the French national team, and he didn't light up a World Cup. 'But you get players who can find something out of the bag and he gave us that at the right time without a shadow of a doubt,' Hodge added.

Tony Dorigo recalled Cantona scoring the best goal he'd ever seen, a thirty-five-yard volley in training, and that far from celebrating and going wild, as any other player would have done, the Frenchman simply shrugged and trotted back as if nothing had happened. Off the field, he remembered how Cantona had once reacted to a barman who had served everyone else before him by rolling up a ten-pound note and flicking it into his forehead. In Batty's 2001 autobiography, written before his retirement from public life, he described visiting Cantona's modest Roundhay semi to find the lawn overgrown and Cantona's young son kicking a ball against the garage door – the same match ball his father had walked off with days earlier when he scored a dazzling hat-trick in the Charity Shield.

The Frenchman seemingly had no regard for material things. Whatever did matter to him was intangible.

There's a flurry of flash bulbs when Cantona strides in. As he takes his seat alongside Pelé I notice he's much jowlier than in 1991/92, with a fuller figure, balding and bearded. There's something of the Roman emperor about him, albeit one with a mischievous glint in his eye. This being Manchester, every eye and lens in the room is focused on Cantona, which seems visibly to irritate Pelé. The Brazilian treble World Cup winner is probably wondering why such a fuss is being made over this younger upstart who never even went to the biggest tournament on Earth (although, to be fair, Pelé never played with Mel or Shutty).

After some corporate guff about Umbro and the 'global power of the Cosmos brand' (oh really?), Pelé introduces some humanity to the proceedings when he talks about being emotional coming to Manchester ('I looked at the pictures of George Best there. We were friends when he was in New York, so I get emotional. That is some story I will not forget') before he hands over to Cantona. All his talk is about Manchester United. There's no 'Why I love you, I don't know why, but I love you' here.

There will be just six questions from reporters, and I'm determined to ask one of them. The deal is that you put up a hand, the nice lady from Umbro brings a microphone over, you say where you're from, and you ask a question.

Every question is addressed to Cantona.

'*Manchester Evening News*. Where does Paul Scholes rank alongside all the players you've played alongside in your career?'

If I could script this moment, I would give anything for him to say, '*Oui*, not bad, but I much preferred lining up with Lee Chapman and Gary Speed.'

One of the questions (about Manchester City's foreign players) is from the *Guardian*. It's interesting, but it blows my cover, since I've gained admittance by claiming to be from the *Guardian* (which I am, but arts, not sport).

It's too late to change my story now.

'Er, another question for Eric. Dave Simpson from the *Guardian*, also working on a book about English football.'

He's instantly suspicious. 'You are from the *Guardian* . . . two from *Guardians*?'

I plough on. 'Twenty years ago next year, you were one of the group of players that won the last ever First Division title, with Leeds United. I wondered how you felt about that experience looking back twenty years. Is it something you remember fondly?'

It's a deliberately worded bomb. The room falls silent and everybody turns to the Frenchman.

Cantona himself looks like he's seen a ghost. Why is this idiot asking me about Leeds? Even in his lengthy autobiography his time at Leeds United barely merits a mention, although there's a tantalizing hint about 'arguments and ruptures that surfaced later'.

Eventually, after an awkward, lengthy pause, he actually answers rather fully, even eloquently.

'Big change,' he begins. 'Because now a lot of foreign players play in England. But when I arrived in England, I played for France. I arrived at Sheffield Wednesday and I spent a week in Sheffield, I think to sign . . . and after a week of training they took the view that I wasn't trying, and I needed one more week of trying. I said no. And I left. Because we played plenty of games during the week and we won 4–3 one game I think and I scored three goals. Which wasn't too bad.'

There's laughter.

'And Wilkinson phoned me and said, "Come here and play for Leeds," and I had a great time there and we won the league. Didn't win for twenty-six years I think? [It was eighteen years since Leeds had won the title.] But now things changed. You play for France and you come to England and you come like a hero. In my time as a foreign player it was very different, and difficult.'

And that's it. I'm not going to be able to ask about Shutty, or the goal against Chelsea, or any of the rumours, but he's been quite revealing, in a way. I'd forgotten that he was one of the first foreign players in English football – certainly one of the first Frenchmen, long before Wenger's Arsenal imported virtually a whole team. I'd been so fixated on how difficult it was for everyone else, I'd never even contemplated that it could have been difficult for him. For a fleeting second I feel a wave of sadness, and wonder if things could have been different, and he could have won more trophies with Wilkinson, not Sir Alex.

There're more questions about Man United, and eventually one to poor Pelé. One of the most illuminating moments comes when someone asks, 'When you put two flair players in the same team, it creates a personality problem. How are you two getting along?'

Pelé (drily): 'Well, my hearing is not so good but I never had a problem with him.'

Cantona (abruptly): 'I don't have a problem.'

But when there's a follow-up question about how the questions are all to Cantona because he's in Manchester – 'but I was at the London press conference as well, and Pele's such a big name in world football' – his clearly not inconsiderable ego snaps.

'We don't care about that. We are not . . . I don't care about that! If it was me, I would not be here at the press conference! I don't care about this press conference. I don't care about that. I don't care about anything. I am happy with my friends and my family, I have a good time. I am passionate about many things. But we are involved in the same project and we want to work together to help New York Cosmos be one of the best. But the most important thing for all of us, for me, Pelé too, is that if we work together we can be stronger. We have great experience, the best in the world. Carlos

Alberto, the academies, we can do something well, but we don't care about the spotlight.'

And suddenly, after one or two more questions about Alex Ferguson, he's gone, as abruptly as when he left Leeds, or indeed prematurely made his exit from Old Trafford, at just thirty-one.

Amid his rant, one line leapt out: 'I don't care about anything.' They are almost exactly the same words used by Gary Speed to describe the Cantona of twenty years ago. And I can't help wondering whether that innocuous sentence may contain a clue to why his departure from Elland Road, and the world of Sergeant Wilko, was so sudden.

CHAPTER 22

Lee Chapman – 'Chappy'

When I scored I used to lose myself for two or three seconds afterwards.

'I watched Arsenal for thirty-five years,' begins the cabbie as the taxi winds its way through Knightsbridge. He followed them when they were still playing at my favourite away ground, Highbury, with its marble halls, cobbled streets, terraced houses sandwiching the frontispiece and magical atmosphere of how football used to be. But especially since the club moved to the giant sponsor-named Emirates Stadium, he can no longer afford to go. 'I can't justify the prices any more. I've got a wife and two kids to feed. I just can't afford it.' He explains that he wrote a letter to then chairman David Dein explaining this, and received an abrupt reply. 'He wrote back and said, "I'm sorry you feel that way but there are sixty thousand supporters who feel differently."'

Which is the bottom line. Unlike Asda, or even the energy firms, football clubs have a captive audience. At worst, they just stop going. But you wonder how long this can go on.

The car pulls up outside a café in Chelsea. I'm here to reunite with Lee Chapman, but this time there will be no late-night bars or Mojitos. It's eleven a.m., and again I see him before he sees me, weaving his way through the waitresses as if they were opposition defenders. The café's busy so we sit outside in the autumn cold, where Chappy explains that he's got to be somewhere else in two hours. 'Annual lunch with the bank manager,' he grins. 'He's taking us out in the West End, so I've got to make the most of it.'

The bank manager will be happy. Not only are Chappy's two businesses – JuJu in Chelsea and Souk in Clapham – doing well, he's just banked a welcome cheque from News International after he, Leslie Ash and even their children had their phones hacked by the *News of the World*; the couple gave evidence to the Leveson Inquiry. Chappy is used to being a target. The tabloids began to focus on him when he started seeing Ash, star of *Men Behaving Badly* and the classic film *Quadrophenia*. They were Yorkshire's Posh and Becks.

Before that he courted the attentions of opposition defenders, and was the target man himself, the spear of Wilkinson's 'relentless machine', the greatest Leeds United goal machine of the last forty years, charged with the ultimate responsibility of putting the ball in the net. Chapman scored the crucial goal at Bournemouth that sealed promotion from Division Two; his thirty-one goals in the 1990/91 season (twenty-one in the league and ten in cup competitions) made him the top scorer in the country and helped Leeds make an impact in the top division beyond their wildest dreams. In 1991/92, his sixteen league goals in thirty-eight appearances took Wilkinson's heroes to the summit for the sweetest triumph over Manchester.

'What killed Man United off was the fact that they were expected to be champions,' he reasons over two pots of tea. 'They were ahead most of the time that season. But they hadn't won the title for twenty-five years, so there was that weight of expectation, and they crumbled. There's this theory that you can be scared of winning. To be scared of losing is one thing, but to be scared of winning is another. It was weighing on them, the great players of yesterday.' Whereas when Chappy arrived at Leeds, Wilkinson had 'severed contact with the past and cleared the history away'.

It worked, then?

'It definitely helped us,' he admits. 'I'd seen Leeds in the Revie era, so to come into that, I did feel a little bit . . . awed. But when I came in, the photos had gone, the pictures had gone, the statues.' He's chuckling. 'But the carpets are still there though, aren't they? That's probably not a great thing.'

I've really warmed to Chapman. Bright and intelligent, he had an unusual entrance into football, deferring a place at university to play for Stoke. He's funny and entertaining too, a lively, opinionated conversationalist with an often slightly askance or off-kilter view that reflects his eventful odyssey inside and outside football.

The six-foot-three hitman didn't need to think twice about coming to Leeds. At Nottingham Forest under

Brian Clough he was a well-travelled goalscorer who'd been at Stoke, Arsenal, Sunderland, Sheffield Wednesday (under Wilkinson) and French club Chamois Niortais, but who was approaching his peak and felt restless. 'When I left Sheffield Wednesday and went to the French club, Forest were in for me then.' He turned Clough down. After the French move went 'horribly wrong', he was kicking himself. 'I thought, "You've blown this. You could have played for a legend." But he came back in for me and I wanted to play for him. I had a great time, won things for the first time in my career [the 1989 League Cup and Simod Cup, and Forest finished third in the top flight that season].'

However, a strong-minded character such as Chappy was perhaps never going to flourish for ever under Cloughie. 'If you haven't any personality or strength, he's fine,' he argues, using the present tense as if the once seemingly immortal, omnipresent Ol' Big Head were still alive. 'But he does treat you like a child. "Young man!" I remember coming out of the dressing room. "Young man! Have you washed your hands?" I was twenty-eight with a mortgage and kids.' He chuckles. 'It gets a bit wearing after a while.'

So he wanted out. But after scoring twice in the Simod final and with a strike rate of one in three, Cloughie was never going to want to let his goalscorer depart easily. The clever Chappy developed a ruse. 'I told him that I'd been hit with a massive tax bill from the French experience and the only way I could pay it was to get a move,' he reveals. 'I was tremendously grateful to Cloughie, but I made this story up, which was how I managed to get to Leeds.'

Chapman knew all about Wilkinson, having netted an impressive sixty-three goals in 149 league appearances under him for Wednesday, and realized the Sarge could get the best from him. Even so, moving from a team that had finished third in the top flight to a Division Two side that in January 1990 was by no means certs to win promotion takes some gumption. 'I knew Leeds was a potentially massive club, and even though I was dropping down a division, and I'd never played outside the top division before, I just had a good feeling about it. And I was right.'

Like others who'd encountered Wilkinson at Wednesday, he remembers him being different at Leeds. The runs were crippling, but not as crippling as they'd been in Sheffield. 'I remember one time we did a thirteen-mile run. People were getting lost because they were so far behind. In the end we had to send search parties looking for the players around all the reservoirs. His teams were incredibly fit, and conditioned throughout the season. But at Sheffield we used to burn out a lot. He'd learned from that by the time he arrived at Leeds.'

It was also a different world from when he'd started out at Stoke, when the old-school drinking culture still held sway. He recalls players coming into training stinking of booze. 'They'd ask you if you wanted any team spirit,' he tells me. 'The "team spirit" was a bottle of Bell's whisky. And some of the older ones would have a glug as they went out on the pitch.' He's incredulous. 'This was on a match day!'

Like Tony Dorigo, Chapman remembers the concentration on set pieces at Leeds as mind-numbing, but vital.

'We'd spend three hours working on the same corner. I'm not joking! But it worked. If you look at football today, how many teams concede goals from set pieces cos of bad defending?'

Leeds do.

'In the Premier League, most of the big teams have this season – Chelsea, Arsenal. Most of their goals are conceded from set pieces, because nobody wants to head the ball. They don't want to get close to a player, and they don't practise. Because they have so much ability and they're paid so much money they don't want to get their hands dirty. But we did. And Howard made sure we did. We scored a lot of goals from set pieces but we also stopped a lot of goals from set pieces, which is the difference between mid table and top.'

Chapman speaks like a Wilkinson disciple.

'How did he get the best out of me? He's a dour character. He likes to think before he says anything, but he had a methodology. A lot of managers send you out there hoping it will go right, but with Howard you knew exactly what was expected of you, and for a player that was tremendous. His job descriptions were incredibly detailed.'

He goes on to reveal that another rehearsed tactic was the diagonal ball to Gary Speed, who had just broken into the team when he arrived. 'He was a raw talent at that stage but incredibly enthusiastic, a lot of power. For a wide player – which Howard played him as at the time – he just had this incredible leap, which surprised people. It shocked teams.'

Other players had suggested that the Leeds team was

effectively run (as teams often are, day to day, apart from the manager) by two or three players, but had been cagey over names. Chapman suggests that he and Strachan, as senior players, and then later Gary McAllister, were the dominant triangle. 'The spine of your team is incredibly important and we provided that spine, on and off the field. There were many times when Gordon would dig us out of the shit, especially that goal against Leicester [on 28 April 1990, a wonderful strike to make it 2–1, the Wee Man's eighteenth of the season in all competitions, which moved the commentator to ask, "Have you ever seen a better goal?"]. Without Gordon we might have never got promotion. We were down and out and Gordon pulled that out of nowhere, an amazing piece of magical football. Obviously I chipped in with my goals as well . . .'

Such as the promotion-sealing header against Bournemouth. Chapman recalls a burned-out pitch and a high-pressure game going nowhere until Chris Kamara 'just came out of the blue. It was one of those moments. "**** the gaffer, I'm gonna go forward!" Boosh! Players didn't ignore Howard very often, but on the sidelines managers have very little impact. One of the jokes was that players on the side where Wilko was stood would be getting that all the game. Not just you getting a bollock-ing but "tell so-and-so", you know. The rest of the players can't hear. So if you got a bollocking it was "sorry, gaffer, never heard you".'

Chapman has a playful, mischievous nature, and he tells me that he and Strachan controlled the banter in the dressing room, which chimes with what his former Forest teammate Hodge said about Clough's teams. 'Everyone laughed at everyone, but in a nice way. You've got to be able to laugh at yourself. Obviously there'd always be one or two players who'd cop for a lot of the jokes.'

He doesn't name names, but does relate a typical anecdote involving Carl Shutt. When he arrived at Leeds, the players convinced him that he was going to be paid a nice sum by the local paper for an interview about his transition from workman to star striker, but he had to look the part. 'We dressed him up as a mechanic in overalls, with a wrench in one hand and a spanner in the other, doing star jumps for the club photographer. Everyone was howling with laughter. But he was great, Shutty. A genuine guy.'

Chapman had a lot of laughs at Leeds, but they'd come on the back of some darker times. 'Arsenal was dreadful,' he admits of his time there in his early twenties. 'Lost in the big city. But that grounded me, and I had to start again. Then I went to Sunderland under Alan Durban, who I'd had at Stoke, and he got sacked, so that didn't go well. I went to France for the money, but the money didn't arrive, so I went back to Cloughie. In a way, Leeds was a reward for all the shit.'

One of Chapman's biggest regrets is that his father didn't see him win the title. He'd died, aged just forty-nine, when his son was starting life at Arsenal, and it hit him hard. 'I was twenty-one,' Chapman explains. 'Death is always horrible, but when it's someone that's close to you . . . It would have been nice to get to know him as a friend, an adult,' he says, revealing a touch of the same wistfulness he'd shown in JuJu about the restlessness, even unhappiness, that drove his urge to score.

Like Gary Speed's, Chapman's father Roy had been a footballer too, for Aston Villa and Lincoln City in the 1950s, followed by a four-year spell at Mansfield. It doesn't seem coincidental that shortly after his father died Chapman's career began an upward climb. 'I had a healthy competitive relationship with my father.' He smiles, softly. 'I always wanted to be a better player than he was. We'd take the mick. He had a better left foot than me, which was always his comeback. "Your left foot's just for standing on." But, yeah, [loss] spurred me on to make something of my career. I took over the torch. It gives you resolve and toughens you up. You've lost your crutch and are very much alone. You think, "I'm the only one who's going to do this." Sometimes you can lean on people too heavily. When they're taken away, you've got to become stronger.'

Within three years, he was scoring goals for Wilkinson by the bagful.

Was Wilkinson a surrogate father to you, as others have said?

'In a way he was,' Chapman replies. 'He had the stability you expect from a father. But I didn't get to know him well.' He played for almost eight years under Wilkinson at the two Yorkshire clubs, but encountered the familiar detachment. 'And I totally understand that,' he insists. 'Cloughie was the same. If you were injured, he didn't even talk to you.' He has a different insight into what others have seen as brutality. 'It's that old-school thing. If you give them sympathy they're going to be injured longer. So you treat them as a leper. I guess it works.

'I'm actually going to have lunch with him [Wilkinson] soon,' he adds. 'I would actually like to know him better.'

In Chapman's 1992 autobiography, *More Than a Match*, he suggests that scoring was in the blood. As a child, the family lived on – 'You could not make this up' – Scorer Street, in Lincoln. Eerily, he had his first taste of title celebrations when his father managed Stafford Rangers to the 1972 FA Trophy. 'I was on the bus with them,' he says with a smile, recalling an event almost exactly twenty years before he did the same with Leeds. 'So I had that buzz. My dad used to take me to Port Vale and Chester. I used to have a bath with all the players. It sounds a bit dodgy now, doesn't it?' He laughs. 'But it wasn't like that. I was in the inner sanctum. I got to like the smell of it. The guys, the characters, the banter. I suppose I grew up in that environment.'

By the time Chapman senior returned to Port Vale as coach, the family were in Stoke, and Chapman became a Stoke supporter. 'They were my heroes really,' he admits. 'I wanted to be on that pitch. I wanted to be one of them.'

Ironically, it wasn't his father that encouraged him to play football, but a friend in Mansfield, who taught him how to play. Soon afterwards Chapman experienced something that would stay with him all his life – the thrill of scoring. 'The buzz of scoring is what football's all about. Even at school when there's twenty or thirty people watching, to hear the cheering . . . It changes the entire game. It's an amazing feeling, always was, and to do that in front of forty or fifty thousand people is just on another level.'

What does that actually feel like?

'For me, when I scored I used to lose myself for two or three seconds afterwards,' he reveals. 'You'd get this massive rush of adrenalin, so when you celebrate you literally don't know what you're doing.' Chapman's celebration, which I witnessed countless times, is ingrained on my memory. More often than not he'd just reel away, arms outstretched, like a giant bird. 'You just did it. Then suddenly everyone's around you. Everyone reacts in different ways but you do lose yourself. It's weird, an amazing feeling. The only thing I really miss is that moment.' A coy smile. 'I was lucky enough to do it a lot of times.'

Before the interview, I sent Chappy a link to a YouTube montage of his Leeds United goals. It only touches the surface, yet is seventeen minutes long.

'It brought back great memories,' he says. 'There's so many that Leslie got bored! But there's some that I'd forgotten about.'

I'd talked with Sterland and Shutty about the number they set up for Chapman, so I was surprised to be reminded how many were laid on by little Strachan. 'Yeah, we had a great link-up, and I made a few for him, where I'd hold it up and he'd come buzzing round me. It was the best period of my career by far, playing with those guys. It was wonderful, really.'

As other players have joked, goals would go in off his head, his knee, even his backside. When I was a child, I used to hover near the goal for corners, but the ball never fell to me. I could never understand it. Yet when you look at videos of a Chapman or a Lineker, they are always there. The ball seems to fly to them, as if it's magnetized.

Eventually, you realize that this isn't a coincidence. This is the goalscorer's art. It fascinates me.

'I knew what they were going to do,' he says of his teammates. 'And the opposition didn't, because they were great players. They won't thank me for saying this but I used to follow them all the time, saying "Don't aim for me, put it there", and I'd get on it. I'd follow Macca, Strach, Speedo or whoever. "Put it there", and then bollock me if I don't get it. And I'd time my runs to do that.'

Can you learn that, or is it instinctive?

'I think it's instinctive, but you have to have played the game a long time. I was thirty-two [in the title season], so there's a lot of experience. And you have to go through that. I was a far better player than when I started, by a long way.'

Fascinating as this rare discussion of the goalscorer's art is, Chapman has another revelation which knocks me sideways. Against Manchester United in the FA Cup on 15 January 1992, he'd fallen heavily on his left hand and broken a wrist. An hour after the game, he lay on the operating table in Leeds General Infirmary. He remembers the pain as the worst he ever experienced, especially as the ambulance – and a painkilling injection – took twenty minutes to arrive. He was told he couldn't play again for at least two months, if at all that season, which led Wilkinson to recruit Cantona.

Were you worried that that might have been it, that even if you had got fit again he'd got himself a new striker?

'I'm always like that,' he admits, revealing a similar

insecurity to that which also fired Gary Speed. 'If you remember the season before, when I went down on the gravel track at Tottenham, I had fifty or sixty stitches and looked like Frankenstein's monster. I remember walking out of the tunnel at Old Trafford the following week and Bryan Robson looking at me as if I was insane. They put this superglue stuff on to protect my stitches. I just wanted to get back, especially for the big games.'

So, in January 1992?

'The thing is, I'm either brave or stupid. Probably stupid. I talked them into letting me play with a plastic cast. We told the referee it had been accepted. It wouldn't be accepted! Because if I'd hit someone with it they'd have known about it. But I wasn't going to hit anyone, because it still hadn't mended. You'd never get away with it now. We conned them! We put a strapping on it so they couldn't see what it was, and got away with it.'

After all the years of dodgy refs, wrong decisions, Chappy's and Sterland's injuries and shocking bad luck, Leeds were due an inch of rope. Chapman returned, and scored, against Luton on 29 February, and stayed in the team for the run-in. 'I had to play with it like that and I had to make sure I didn't fall on it.' To this day a bone protrudes, but he won the league when strictly speaking, as he confesses, 'I shouldn't have been playing.'

Ironically, he ended up playing alongside Cantona, not instead of him, and the pair worked well together. 'It did work. I always felt Eric was better coming on for twenty or thirty minutes, when he created a carnival atmosphere, which helped us. His goals were the icing on the cake, but he did establish us as a force.'

'The thing with Eric, it had to be about him.' As he explains this, I remember the brief tantrum in the press conference. 'At Man United, everything revolved around him; at Leeds it wasn't like that. I roomed with him, and we got on well, but if I came back from dinner at nine p.m. the room would be blacked out, because he'd be in bed asleep. I used to put the telly on so low I couldn't hear it. He was very selfish, self-obsessed. He wouldn't think I wanted to come back and watch TV, but that was Eric.'

There's a funny clip of them together at the time. Leeds have just won the league after Man U lost at Liverpool. Cantona and Chapman are grinning on Chapman's sofa, and an ITV interviewer asks 'Eric, how do you feel?' only to receive a confused look. The interviewer asks Chappy to translate, upon which the big striker says exactly the same thing, but in a cod French accent: 'Ereek, 'ow do yew feel?' He shrieks with laughter. 'I spoke some French because of my time in France, but I was taken aback there. I was in shock cos we'd won the league. The last thing I wanted to think about was to translate. But it was very funny.'

Later that evening, he remembers walking into the Flying Pizza – 'Leeds' version of the Ivy' – with the rest of the team and the entire place applauding.

I have to ask about the rumours, which Leslie Ash herself once denied, saying, 'A horrible rumour arose that I was having an affair with Eric, that I was the reason he left. Of course I didn't have an affair with him! The same happened to two other players' wives, but because I was on TV it stuck with me.'

'I think it came from Manchester,' Chapman says. 'It

started over there about various players' wives and it's bullshit. I wish Howard had nailed it at the time, explained more about why he was sold. Maybe he thought badmouthing him would have motivated him against Leeds. I don't know. But it should have been explained there and then.'

It's water under the bridge now, and he insists it didn't – and doesn't – bother him. Nor did the close attention from the tabloids. 'I've had knocks all my life. It was just one more.'

If Chapman has one remaining grumble, it's the manner of his exit from Elland Road, which sounds rather familiar. 'Howard called me in. I thought he was going to offer me a contract but he said, "I've decided to call it a day." And that was it, that was all he said, after eight years together. I was a bit disappointed with that. He could have been a bit warmer, but he didn't get the credit he deserved, and if we have lunch we'll talk on a different basis. I suppose if you make an exception for one you've got to do it for all of them. It was his job to be like that.'

Ironically, Chapman played under Wilkinson again, on loan from Ipswich in 1996, when he only played two games after being sent off for catching West Ham's Marc Rieper with an elbow. 'It wasn't malicious, I just caught him. It was a shame; I half thought I could get it going again. But it's never a great thing, going back. It should have possibly been left alone.'

After retiring, he returned to Leeds to open a northern branch of his London members club Teatro, which didn't last. 'Peter Ridsdale talked me into that,' he insists. 'They invested a lot of money, telling me they'd bring the whole of Leeds and the players in, but it didn't happen. I found out they had a travel agency and were taking people into other restaurants, not mine. They'd forgotten they had a fifty K investment!'

But unlike some of his teammates, he's had no trouble reinventing himself to find a new life after football. 'I went to sixth form college and did four A levels and was going to study chemistry and business studies, but deferred my entry into Manchester University,' he explains. 'I'm almost managing now. I've got forty people working for me, and it's like managing a team. Same psychology.'

Football management didn't interest him because he'd seen friends try their hand and find themselves at the mercy of wealthy owners who knew nothing about football, for whom the game was a costly, unbusinesslike hobby, like buying an expensive boat. 'You're not in control of your own destiny because you're sackable. What I'm doing now, I'm in charge. The buck stops with me, and I can sack myself.' He's smiling. 'It's highly unlikely.'

A regular face around Knightsbridge, he admits he misses the days living in Boroughbridge and going out in Harrogate and in the country with McAllister. 'With his first wife Denise, who sadly passed away . . . happy days. It was a wonderful four years and Leeds are the team I look for, with Stoke. But it was a dream of mine to be the top scorer in a title-winning team, and luckily it happened, and it will always be there.'

Chapman may have grabbed all the headlines, but next on the list is someone who was a £140,000 rookie but who scored arguably the most important goal of all.

CHAPTER 23

Jon Newsome – 'Newsy'

I remember watching *Match of the Day* afterwards and
Gary Speed saying, 'Look at your face! You look like
you've just been sent down!' . . . I remember thinking,
'If I score again, I must remember to smile.'

I track down Jon Newsome via former Leeds striker
Brian Deane, who suggests he is now 'selling cars near
BDTBL'. It's not an expression I'm familiar with, but
turns out to mean Beautiful Downtown Bramall Lane.
A subsequent Google search tells me that the
Automarques showroom where the former centre-half
is working lies just yards from where he scored one of
the most famous goals in Leeds United's history.

When I first see him he's parking a huge white
Mercedes, but we relocate to a small office, which has a
picture of him in his playing days hanging on the wall.
He's an adult now, not a callow youth (and says to me
with a grin on his face, 'If you ever want a car . . .'), but
otherwise he looks instantly recognizable as the twenty-
one-year-old defender whose pivotal, game-changing

header at Bramall Lane on 26 April 1992 took the score to 2–1, swinging the match Leeds' way, as the Whites conquered Sheffield United to deliver the title to West Yorkshire.

'I suppose it was the final hurdle to overcome,' he begins in a trademark Sheffield accent. 'It was a very unusual weekend. The fact that Man United were playing at Liverpool, and Rushy had never scored against Man United; our early kick-off; there were all these things. Really windy day, Bramall Lane being open in the corners, wind everywhere. The ball at the time was an Umbro ball, which was a bit floaty. The bonus for me was the innocence of youth. I'd not been involved first half of the season, I'd been injured, got into the squad, played a few games and thought, well, you know, "It's a big game." Looking back, I don't think I realized how big a game it was. But yeah, great to score, being a Sheffield lad, at Bramall Lane . . . it's everything you dream of really, and then to cap it off Brian Gayle scored a calamity own goal. Chappy scored an o.g. Our first goal came off Rod Wallace's hip . . . it was one of those days, two hours of madness, and you come in and you think, "We've won the championship. How did that happen?"'

He doesn't need prompting to turn his attention to the gaffer. 'Those words "trust your swing" really stuck with me. A very good analogy. Howard was a very deep man. And I think he liked those kind of things. He saw himself as a bit of an intellect; he portrays himself as that. Don't get me wrong. He could shout and bawl and throw teacups like the rest of them. But you need that to manage a group of men who are all different.

'It was a fantastic dressing room: bit of old, bit of youth, some big leaders and a big togetherness. Fabulous set of lads really.'

He suddenly seems miles away, back in 1992, and sums up his feelings with a lovely line that is unnecessarily modest but humble and humbling: 'I find myself extremely fortunate that I was hanging on to the shirt tails of getting inside that.'

He'd always dreamed of being a footballer. 'It's my earliest memory. I grew up all over Sheffield, really. I started playing when I lived at Chapeltown; my parents bought a post office. You never know whether you're going to be good enough. I had quite a few knockbacks in my early teens. I dint know if I was going to get into the City Boys, which was the shop window.'

In those days, he wasn't even a defender. Scratching round to find a role that suited him, he played midfield, then centre-forward. 'The first time I played in defence was in the Under 16s, which was the big year, your last before leaving school, and they said, "You're playing centre-half." I said, "I've never played centre-half." "You're playing at centre-half today!"' By this point he'd been a striker for Sheffield Boys, South Yorkshire and Yorkshire.

'You look back and I'm not sure how I overcame the knockbacks,' he says. 'It's something within yourself. I was quite a determined youngster. I was, like most footballers, verging on being arrogant, but actually quite insecure, because you're always looking for somebody to pat you on the back and say you've played well. It's part of your make-up.'

He did manage to get into the City Boys (as a centre-forward) and was offered and signed schoolboy forms at Sheffield Wednesday. In the last year of school he played for the Wednesday youth team in the local league, and at the end of the year was thrilled to discover he'd been awarded a two-year YTS deal. 'I played a lot of reserve games, about sixty, and youth games. I was a Wednesday supporter as a kid.'

His father had taken him to Hillsborough in the mid to late 1970s – the same time I started watching football – when Wednesday were in the Third Division. 'But they started improving. I remember people like Terry Curran; Mel Sterland was coming through as a youngster. Mel was a great player, great guy as well, fabulous footballer, one of if not the best to come out of Sheffield. Big character, great lad.' Back then, Newsy could not have possibly imagined they'd end up on the same side.

He managed to turn professional shortly before Wilkinson left for Leeds and 'Big' Ron Atkinson gave him his chance. 'He was successful at Sheffield Wednesday, but I personally didn't feel I was getting an opportunity. I played about seven or eight games under Ron. Then he gave me a year extension on my contract, but I never got back into the squad in eighteen months, until the final game of the season the following year. He played me at Oldham on the plastic pitch. I think we got beat 3–2. I don't know why he did that. I think, rightly or wrongly, it was a bit of a sweetener, but they offered me a new contract and I turned it down. I wanted to play on a Saturday afternoon, at a lower level if I had to. It was the club I supported, but I just wanted to play football. He didn't take that very well I don't think.'

The news that Newsome had turned down a new deal made the local paper, where it was seen by the ever eagle-eyed Mick Hennigan, who had already watched Newsome at reserve games and had sat talking to his parents.

'There was a coach called Clive Baker who'd looked after me since I was young. Fabulous guy. He once said that the year I came through was the best influx of kids he'd ever had: David Wetherall, Marlon Beresford, Graham Hyde. Howard will have been aware of this. Mick Hennigan came and said, "The gaffer wants to see you at Leeds . . . tomorrow!" They took me and my father out for dinner, offered me a contract that far superseded Sheffield Wednesday's. I was on considerably less than Mel!' He chuckles, recalling that he signed on for just £400 a week. 'At the time it was half decent money. It wasn't fortunes, but it was incentivized, and I was happy to sign it.'

He remembers Wilkinson asking which other Wednesday youngsters hadn't signed new deals. 'I didn't think anyone had. I remember him turning to Mick and saying, "Right, go and get the lot of them!"'

While Hennigan tried to tempt the others, Newsome was sworn to secrecy about his signing. In the end only David Wetherall came as well. 'But it was possibly the best move either of us ever made.' They didn't know each other well and were polar opposites; like Mike Whitlow, he affectionately refers to Wetherall as a 'geek', who wore white socks and flip-flops. He was a chemistry student whom Wilkinson – ever the educationalist – let finish his Sheffield University degree. He graduated with first class honours. 'David was a very intelligent young lad,' Newsy says. 'While we were scrubbing boots he was studying. We came as a pair. We were pals, but chalk and cheese.'

While Wetherall stayed living in Sheffield, Newsy moved to Leeds and became big pals with Gary Speed. He says he'd no idea that Wilkinson was mounting a title challenge, and remembers the concentration on small increments I'd talked about with Sergeant Wilko: first clean sheet, first point, first win. There was never any talk of winning the division.

Newsome contrasts Wilkinson's calm approach with that of Danny Wilson, his manager eight years later, when he was back at Wednesday. 'On the first day of the season he [Wilson] was talking about how we could beat Man United and win the league. I walked out of the room thinking, "The guy's off his head." And he was, because we got relegated that year. Howard was all about small goals, but ones that are achievable. Very understated – fabulous, really.

'Forty points!' he exclaims, suddenly. '"Get past forty points and you can start looking up," he'd say. "You don't stand at the foot of Everest and look at the top." I didn't play for anyone else like him. You could tell he'd been a schoolteacher. I was used to it, because I'd grown up with him.'

The differences between the Sarge and many other managers became more apparent when Newsy roomed with Steve Hodge, who told him how at Forest, under Brian Clough, they never discussed opponents. Whereas Leeds would have 'meeting after meeting'. He recalls one time, when they were away to lowly Scunthorpe in the League Cup, Wilkinson preparing his troops for the game by purring about the abilities of the young Scunny left-winger. 'It was as if he should be playing for Real Madrid. There was nothing this kid couldn't do. You go out thinking you'd better be on your game. Maybe he was warning of complacency, but people like Steve Hodge would be used to Cloughie saying, "Think about how we're going to play. You're not here to worry about them.'"

As ever, when Newsome played, Wilkinson was an unknowable, detached figure, although he reveals that he's got to know him better since. 'You bump into him now and it's different. Before it was manager/player. Sometimes when managers do get too close to players it causes problems.'

Training was hard, but not as hard as when Wilkinson first arrived at Wednesday and had them running on the moors. 'In the snow. But Howard was a runner, he loved his running. But you look back and marvel at how fit you were.'

He singles out the man who'd been his youth coach as a kid. 'Some people didn't get on with him, but I've got a massive amount of respect for Michael Hennigan. As kids, you name it, we did it; different regimes. Brilliant. As an apprentice you're always at the club. We used to spend hours and hours at the club.' He sounds beautifully wistful as he talks about 'doing little jobs, sorting out things for the first team'. Like his friend Gary Speed, he thinks the demise of the old apprentice-ships has been a great loss to the game. 'I think today's "scholars" don't do jobs, but I don't think scrubbing baths did us any harm. It's good grounding.'

There was fun at Leeds, though, and Newsome remembers occasions when the players would let off steam by racing their cars out of the ground. 'I was in a Golf. We'd say, "Let's go and have a drink somewhere," and shoot off in the cars.' One day, on the notorious Armley Gyratory, his car just spun away from him. 'I completely wrote off this Golf. Smashed it to pieces. They were all laughing their heads off. There was a lot of fun at times. The coppers turned up and the whole Leeds team were stood around this car.'

When it came to safer social pursuits, he backs up others' suggestions that Strachan was the orchestrator, 'a big part of getting the lads together. He was very much a family man. When I first came to Leeds, he invited me out, with him and his wife, for a meal. Six months ago you were stuck in the reserves and all of a sudden you're having dinner with Gordon Strachan. Fantastic really. He made me feel a part of it.'

When he first joined, in the summer of 1991, Newsome was troubled by an injury in pre-season. 'They couldn't find out what it was. Eventually it got sorted.' So he didn't make his league debut until 2 November, when he came on for the last seven minutes against Wimbledon. 'I think my first game was the game before, in a cup match,' he says, 'and I came off at half time. I was knackered!'

But after Wimbledon he didn't feature again for a whole three months.

'You wanted to play in the first team; also you're aware whether you're ready or not. It did me a favour in that I got some games under my belt, got fit. The last thing you want is to play before you're ready. Howard never said why he'd signed me or what he saw in me.'

It must have been intimidating for a young lad of twenty-one, trying to get in a team of seasoned internationals.

'It is, but you've got to do yourself justice. You've got to be able to cross that white line and believe that you are there because you can do what you're there for,' he argues. 'At the end of the day, you're competing, but you're a team, and that was a really good squad. Socialized together. Cracking times.'

Newsome's chance – and fate – called again on 7 March 1992, when he was thrown on for the last twenty minutes away at Tottenham after Mel Sterland had to withdraw. He remembers it like it was yesterday. 'Twenty minutes to go. "You're going on at right-back. Go on and make a name for yourself, son!"' Right-back was an unfamiliar position, but Newsy recalls the first ball coming over. 'A seventy/thirty challenge in my favour. I just put my foot through it and blasted it into the corner, and Gordon Strachan came over and said, "Son, we don't do that. We're better than that on this pitch." And I thought, "Shit."'

Then Leeds had a corner, and someone suggested he go up. He asked Speed where Sterland stood for corners. 'And he said, "Stand on the penalty spot. You're going to score now. You're gonna score, News!" He was laughing. But I was proper pumped up, and the ball came over.'

What happened next was straight from *Roy of the Rovers*.

'You just pick the flight of the ball up and it wasn't going anywhere else but on my head, and in the back of the net it went.' He smiles at the memory. 'I remember just standing there, thinking, "I don't believe this." And everyone's jumping on me, screaming and laughing. I remember watching *Match of the Day* afterwards and Gary Speed saying, "Look at your face! You look like you've just been sent down!" It was just shock. I remember thinking, "If I score again, I must remember to smile." I did, honestly.'

The rest is history. The following month, Sheffield United's John Pemberton fouled Batty on the edge of the penalty box. McAllister astutely pondered his options, and floated the ball beyond everyone bar Newsome, who stooped in unchallenged and nodded in at the far post. The photograph of him celebrating – one arm up, the picture of youthful ecstasy, being hugged by Speed and Fairclough – is one of the most iconic of the era. He's seen it a million times but I've brought it along again, to celebrate his second, and oh so crucial, goal for Leeds.

'I remember getting up and I was just elated.' He also reminded himself this time, 'You'd better smile here.'

He vividly recalls the victory celebration and bus parade, and dropping the trophy. 'Ha! It nearly went over the edge as well, and I remember the photographer smashing his head on the bridge outside Elland Road. The press were on the upper deck of this open-topped bus, in front, taking photos, heading to this railway bridge. We're all "Get down! Get down!" and they thought we were taking the mickey. Then at the last minute they've all put their heads down except one of them and it's nearly taken his head off. Blood everywhere, they had to call an ambulance. We were laughing our heads off, which we shouldn't really, but you're just caught up in the moment. We'd won the league. It was unbelievable.'

For Newsome, winning the 'best league in the world' had been a triumph of 'a big impetus, self-belief, a team working . . . and fitness'. And Wilkinson. '"Trust your swing. Do what's got you here."' He gazes fondly at the photograph. 'It took the pressure off really.'

He missed the 4–0 collapse at City on 4 April but remembers another highlight of the run-in, Cantona's sublime goal against Chelsea, when Newsome returned to the team (as a 77th-minute sub) at Elland Road. 'It was a bit of flair – it worked, dint it? At the time he did what he was brought in to do. Knowing the guy, he needed to feel wanted, and he was wanted, and he thrived on it. I didn't room with him or anything, just chatted to him as much as anyone else.' But otherwise, he downplays Cantona's contribution and – being another true Wilkinson disciple – his own, which included a tremendous tackle to take the ball off Ian Rush in the goalless draw at Anfield, when the Liverpool legend had the goal at his mercy. 'The real people who made it happen were the lads who played week in week out,' he insists. 'I played seven games, a couple of substitutes. You feel like you're gatecrashing a party at times. I played a role, but those lads slogged it out.' It's true, but without that goal, and the crucial match winner against Tottenham, maybe, just maybe, the title might have slipped away.

'I didn't play forty-two games that year,' he continues, modest as ever. 'If I had, I'm sure I'd have felt different. My medal's on a bookshelf with some of my stuff. A medal's a medal, and we were talking recently about old players who sell their medals, but memories are memories.

'Alex Ferguson was gracious in defeat – although not at first. Gary McAllister often tells a funny anecdote about the day when the title was won, when he was sat on the sofa watching the Liverpool–Man United game on TV with Chapman and Cantona. He had the match coverage on a screen and presenters Ian St John and Denis Law in his earpiece. "After the game Fergie comes on and says, 'I want to make something clear. Leeds haven't won the league. Man United have lost it.' So I say, 'Look at his face, the red-nosed bastard!' and Denis Law in my ear says, 'Gary, Fergie can hear you.' I'm not saying Fergie holds grudges, but I played against him many times after that and he never looked in my direction once. He's since mellowed – he looked at me once!"'

Later, Ferguson did admit that Leeds made fewer mistakes and confessed that 'losing it has had a numbing effect on us and I don't know how we'll overcome it, but we'll find a way'.

Newsome played seventy-two times for Leeds (plus fifteen games as a sub) until 1993/94, when he found himself in and out of the side, which he suspects was down to his inexperience. 'I also felt at Leeds, especially later on, that no matter what I did you were never sure whether you're going to play the following week. I think sometimes you're an easy target – drop the kid, he's not going to knock on your door.'

He admits that he was sad to leave, but adds, 'When a manager says to you "We've had an offer from Norwich City, do you want to go talk to them?", what does that say to you? I didn't see it coming really, no. It was the summer, close season, got a phone call, went down there and they made me more than welcome. The manager had made his decision. I didn't even know what they'd paid for me until the press conference after I'd signed.'

It was a million pounds, which cash-strapped Leeds must have seen as amazing business considering they'd got him for next to nothing. Did the fee bother him?

'It was a bit of a millstone. I think fees can affect some people but all clubs value you at something. It didn't make me different as a player. I played my best football at Norwich. I was the record signing. Club captain. I flourished under that.'

By 1995/96, Norwich's own perilous finances saw Newsy sold to Wednesday for £1.6m, and he returned to score at Elland Road when the Sheffield outfit won 2–1 during the 1997/98 campaign, by which time his old mentor had gone. 'It was quite funny actually because I had a few boos. I've no idea why, so it was good to score in that way. The keeper made a good save, it fell to me and I was there.' He scored fourteen goals in a total of 205 league appearances. 'I've never forgotten those centre-forward's instincts.'

Then, when he was twenty-nine, he damaged his knee and it was all over. 'The club was going through a bad time. I had an operation. It didn't really work. It was last chance saloon. The club said they'd stick by me and give me the chance to get fit over the summer, and then while I was on holiday they sent me a letter saying they wouldn't stick by me, and they were not willing to offer me a new contract, or a week-to-week contract, which kills you then, doesn't it?'

On the other hand, he knows that he was very lucky. 'At the same time there was a young lad called Dave Billington at the club and he had to retire at nineteen. Fifteen years ago I'd have bitten your hand off for the career I had.'

Newsome took his coaching badges, managed in non-league (Gresley Rovers) and wanted to stay in the game, but he got divorced and wanted to devote some time to his two children. 'Which I couldn't have done and stay in the game. You can't be disappearing on a Friday afternoon and coming back the early hours of Sunday morning.'

Working as a financial adviser 'bored the pants off me. Then I ended up doing this. I've got a great carry-on now. You come out of football and you get your life back. I play golf, go away for the weekend with my girlfriend and my kids. I miss playing. I miss being fit. Nothing will ever come near playing professional football, but I fulfilled my childhood ambitions. I'm forty and I've got hopefully a lot more to come.'

When I ask about his happiest memory, he doesn't hesitate. He points down at the photo and says, 'That goal.'

It's the happiest memory for so many of us. I can still remember the sensation of supporting a League Championship-winning club that came from the bottom reaches of the Second Division, like an electrical charge you want to last for ever. And at the time, it felt like it should. In 1992, Leeds United stood on the precipice of another Revie dynasty.

What could possibly go wrong?

Two
Downfall

CHAPTER 24

The 1992/93 Collapse

Whatever went right the previous season went wrong
the season after.

A common view, still espoused in pubs and books, is
that Howard Wilkinson went mad, sold Cantona and
lost the plot. But I wonder if it's that simple.

In the summer of 1992 he strengthened the squad,
paying £2m (his highest spend on a single player at the
time) for Arsenal's David Rocastle, a possible long-term
replacement for the ageing Strachan. Scott Sellars was
brought back from Blackburn for £900,000, and Leeds
began the new campaign in irrepressible style, triumphing 4–3 over Liverpool in the Charity Shield, as
Cantona scored a hat-trick. However, a 4–1 defeat at
Middlesbrough in the third league game, although
followed by another Cantona hat-trick in the 5–0
demolition of Tottenham, set alarm bells ringing.

Wilkinson's near-watertight defence, which conceded
less than a goal a game in 1991/92, was suddenly leak-
ing. Sterland was still injured – to no one's knowledge,

permanently – which meant centre-half Newsome and others filled in at right-back. Of equal if not greater significance was the change at the start of the season to the back-pass law, preventing goalkeepers from handling the ball. It had a major impact on the way Leeds United played. As Gary Speed told me, 'The back-pass rule affected us particularly, because the centre-halves used to stroke the ball back to the keeper and Lukey used to launch it up to me and Chappy. Suddenly we weren't allowed to play that way any more.'

In Wilkinson's view, in addition to losing Mel, the change was a 'disaster in Chrissie's [Fairclough] case'. For his central defensive partner Chris Whyte, though, 'Adding a change like that shouldn't make you go from top to bottom. We just didn't gel as a team. The same players. The same enthusiasm. But you lose five per cent and it makes a difference. We weren't the force we knew. We used to camp in the opposition's half. For some reason, suddenly it wasn't happening.'

Meanwhile, away at Rangers in the European Cup, a McAllister volley stunned Ibrox. Then Lukic, dazzled by the floodlights, punched the ball into his own net and Ally McCoist gave the Glasgow team the lead – a scoreline that was repeated in the second leg at Elland Road. Shortly afterwards, Cantona was sold to Manchester United as the season fell to pieces, and Leeds followed the First Division championship by finishing a lowly seventeenth.

What on earth had gone wrong? Had time caught up with Leeds? Steve Hodge says it might have done. 'A lot of the players around my age – twenty-nine, thirty, thirty-one – had peaked as a unit. We got off to a bad start. The defensiveness was probably stiffening in the summertime and maybe Howard brought in too many midfield players. I'm not blaming the back four for it – as a team, defensively we struggled. Being knocked out of Europe didn't help, but you can't let that affect your whole season. In those days you played knockouts so there was a gamble that you might get beat early in the Champions League. Then you're left with two or three players unhappy in the reserves, and that's the way it panned out.'

Wilkinson defends his transfer policy. 'I signed Rocastle and Sellars to complement the midfield. But that went belly up. I signed David Rocastle not to be a player who didn't play, but to be a squad player. But because we didn't start the season well, instead of becoming a strength he became a problem because people were moaning about why I didn't play him. Tony Dorigo started to get this problem with his hamstring. David Batty had been to see me in the summer. He wanted a more expansive role. He wanted to be the passer and everything else. Against Ipswich [in October, when Leeds lost 4–2] I had to play him at right-back. In order to prove me wrong he got booked and gave away a penalty.'

For many, though, Cantona was the issue. 'Winning the title took a lot out of the team,' Lee Chapman says. 'But Howard tried to change the way we played, to play through midfield. I still think if we'd played the way we did the season before we wouldn't have won the title, but we wouldn't have been fighting relegation. From what I hear, Eric went to see him before the season began, saying he wanted to be more involved. I remember thinking, we'd won the title playing a certain way, playing from the top, satellites around. Suddenly I was making runs and it wasn't coming. They were playing tip tap – that wasn't how we won the title. And unfortunately Howard has to take responsibility for that. I don't know if he was trying to accommodate Eric. Eric didn't like the way we played, but you can't change a whole team.'

'There were two things that happened,' Wilkinson points out. 'One, our results showed that we weren't as good as when he [Cantona] didn't play. Secondly, the team weren't ready for him. We were a team of players who made a star team. The team he joined were a team of stars. There were other factors . . . Factors which meant he had to go.'

Gary Speed said much the same when I spoke to him: 'Eric was a volatile character. There'd been undercurrents. He had a mysteriousness about him. I got to know him a bit, and he was definitely a nice guy, but you never knew which one you were going to get. You could be with him all day in training and the next day he'd walk straight past you. And then we played QPR away, and Eric wasn't playing. We were all in tracksuits and he came down in jeans, and his coat, and bag. Apparently he'd said to Howard, "I wanna go home." And Howard's said, "Here's your passport, **** off." And he got up out of the meeting. You wanted to say "See you, Eric" or "Don't go!" but you knew that was it then.'

Shutt remembers how he felt. 'If Howard hadn't come down on him, he'd have lost the dressing room, big style. The way Eric was being, to Mick or whoever, he was being disrespectful. There'd be times when he was left out and Eric would be getting his stuff and ****ing off, saying he'd got an injury.'

The manager, it seems, will always get the blame, but you won't hear that from Leslie Silver. 'It's been said to me so often,' he told me, 'that Howard will be remembered as the man who sold Cantona to Man United. That's so unfair. The last thing he – or we – wanted was to lose Cantona. But Cantona was a different sort of character. An individual. He had one ambition, to play for the biggest club in the world. He didn't like directors. He didn't like managers. He considered himself to be a superior being. He was the most magical footballer, but an egomaniac. He decided where he wanted to play. But I think Howard had a problem with Cantona from day one. Once Cantona had made his name – particularly at the Charity Shield – Howard had an impossible job.'

Silver is backed up by Bill Fotherby: 'Howard was a disciplinarian – "at set pieces you stand there" – and of course Cantona couldn't stand that kind of thing. He'd walk off the training ground, causing problems.' And as Mick Hennigan points out, 'Remember, at Leeds, Howard's the man. We've got Batty, Strachan, McAllister, Speed. Everything's geared on work, effort, pressing, that ferocious start. That's not in Cantona's make-up. So players are looking round and he's not doing it. Whereas he goes to Man United, a younger team which has been defeated twice by Paul Hart's FA Youth Cup team, but nearly all their lads make the first team, and Cantona pulls all the strings. Cantona is the conductor. When he left, he was a Protestant who became a Roman Catholic.'

Alan Sutton says that 'Howard grew to hate Cantona. That strut and the collar up. Things turned very bad. In the first season Eric was happy coming on as sub. Second season he wasn't. In the end they were terrified that he'd ride off on his motorbike and they'd lose a million pounds.'

In the end, it appears finances did play a major part. 'We needed a right-back, and Howard asked me to have a word with Martin Edwards about Denis Irwin,' Fotherby told me during our chat. 'He said there was no chance, but says, "Bill, would you consider selling Cantona?" I said, "Oh, you must be joking. Impossible! He's the star of the show here." Now we were due to pay the French club [Nimes] another half a million for him in the next month, and of course as a club we didn't have any money. We didn't let people know that. He said, "Look, can you just ask Howard. We've heard certain things." I knew – although I didn't expect the uproar – the supporters would go crazy, so the deal was done before twelve o'clock. It was a relief to Leslie Silver about the money, although we would have found a way, somehow.'

Silver is adamant that 'We didn't want him to go to Man U. We'd have rather he go to Bristol than Man U! But in the final analysis the player makes his own choice. He was on a short contract. He only went for

£1.3 million. We were unhappy about it. That was the turning point of the downturn.'

There was bitterness among some players. Carl Shutt recalls that 'When he came back to Elland Road to play against us I just twatted him. I remember his face, startled . . . it gave me great pleasure. There's nothing worse than when you're working your balls off to get into that team and you get someone like that.' But as Gary Speed told me, 'Eric's exit affected us, but only for a short time. There were a lot of things.' Failure to win away from home all season long was of course one of them. 'The home form kept us up otherwise we'd have gone down. The longer it went on, it became psychological.'

Hodge agrees with this. 'At home, with the crowd behind us, we could still dominate teams physically. Away from home you're under more pressure, and we didn't have teams pinned in like at home. But to go the whole of the season without winning an away game was absolutely ridiculous. It was sad to see us capitulate so quickly.'

In Tony Dorigo's eyes, 'the expectation was a factor. Once you've won it, do it again. But the way the season progressed was horrific. What was going on? We tried everything. Different training. Different warm-ups. Whatever went right the previous season went wrong the season after. It became a difficult place to be around, cos everyone was trying to work out what the hell was going wrong. Before, I wasn't allowed to give an opinion. Suddenly, the manager wanted everyone's opinion. Alex Ferguson has been very good at getting people around him, and for me that was an issue. Mick was a hundred and ten per cent effort, always there. But maybe there should have been others, to shoulder the burden. Howard was such a dominating character, but on the way down he was carrying the whole world on his back. He wasn't looking too clever. I felt terrible, cos you could see the world on his shoulders.'

'Looking back, I should have rebuilt the team sooner,' Wilkinson admits. 'I think obviously people have a shelf life. Whatever it takes to win a title, it's going to be harder at thirty-two, thirty-three. I should have signed a right-back, but we were still counting money and in those days there was no way of knowing Mel's injury was as bad as it was.'

Wilkinson did rebuild the team, selling Batty to Blackburn (which Speed described as 'weird, but I think Batts wanted to go'), bringing in Gary Kelly from the youth ranks at right-back, and recruiting new players. In the next two seasons he finished fifth. But off the field developments were brewing which would prove catastrophic for manager and club.

CHAPTER 25

The End of Sergeant Wilko

It just unravelled at the top, and it started to seep down through the club.

In one sense, the seeds for the modern era of English football were contained in the 1990 Taylor Report, which recommended that the likelihood of a crowd disaster such as the one that happened at Hillsborough in 1989 would be substantially reduced by the introduction of all-seater stadiums. The old standing terraces were duly replaced with more expensive seating and CCTV, all of which began the slow drift away from football as a predominantly male working-class pursuit to a more family-oriented, more gentrified pastime.

However, the major change was the formation of the Premiership in 1992, commencing just weeks after Wilkinson and his team became champions. In return for exclusive broadcast rights, the clubs would now get an unprecedented windfall that would help them lure some of the best footballing talent to England. Rupert Murdoch's BSkyB tabled an astonishing bid of £304m to secure the rights to games that were previously shown on terrestrial television or not at all. The change, and the sudden injection of big money, brought an end to the traditional three o'clock Saturday kick-off for all matches, an influx of foreign players and new flair to the English game.

With Cantona, the final piece in Manchester United's jigsaw, the Reds ended a twenty-six-year wait for the title in that 1992/93 season and began a period of dominance of English football only briefly interrupted by steel magnate Jack Walker's lavishly funded Blackburn Rovers' title in 1994/95 and Arsenal's in 1997/98.

Suddenly, changes were afoot in boardrooms around the country, as clubs – initially Tottenham, Newcastle and Manchester United – raced to become public limited companies and to access ever more cash to spend on transfers and sky-rocketing wages. It was the start of a stampede towards today's billionaire owners, international conglomerates and shady offshore owner-ships, and away from the relatively underfunded locally based businessmen, the likes of Leslie Silver, whose smaller businesses had previously been enough to fund clubs.

The effects were felt particularly at Leeds, whose finances had been stretched to breaking point by the three-year rise to the title and who were suddenly play-ing an ever more precarious game of keeping up with the Joneses.

On the field, despite recovery in the league to those two fifth-placed finishes in 1993/94 and 1994/95, and more European campaigns, Wilkinson's demise was heralded by his young team's 3–0 reverse against Aston Villa in the 1996 League Cup Final at Wembley, where the manager was booed from the field by the same fans who had cheered his team's glory just four years earlier.

Then on 7 September that year, at Elland Road, the visiting Manchester United delivered the final blow to Sergeant Wilko, Cantona inevitably scoring the final goal in a 4–0 beating.

Did it all come down, in the end, to money?

'Finances were stretched,' Wilkinson admits, 'people started getting interested in our players. Batty was the first problem. Blackburn offered him mountains of money. They got into his head. There were rumours about Speed. Gordon – Coventry offered him dopey money. McAllister? Our top pay was six K a week. But we were all right. After promotion we went fourth, first, nowhere, and then two top five finishes. If you did that today with a promoted club you'd be a miracle worker. So it shouldn't have been as disturbing a factor as it was. But things started to develop at the top.

'What people didn't realize because you don't tell 'em is that Leslie was funding the club. We'd decided that we needed to get success to turn things round, at which point the process would be reversed because revenue would be coming in. We'd have our own youngsters coming into the team from the academy and he could start to recoup. Then he got burgled. Violently burgled. Which was a real blow to him. They took Sheila upstairs, got Leslie downstairs, and said, "You don't wanna know what's going to happen to her if you don't tell us where . . ." That shook him rigid.'

Silver knew he was a target. 'I'm not a high-profile character, but I'd made a lot of money with my business. So I'd been mentioned in the paper, as a "millionaire". I'd been chairman for thirteen years. I was in my seventies. I thought, "Bloody hell, enough is enough."'

As Wilkinson recounts it, Silver, Fotherby and Peter Gilman 'fell out in the boardroom, the three of them, over becoming a public company. That rumbled on for a year. So the rock – Leslie – understandably started to be not as comfortable in his own skin about what was happening. It just unravelled at the top, and it started to seep down through the club. I still don't know what went wrong at the Villa game. I thought it was the opportunity for another high point. A lot of the players hadn't won at Wembley apart from the Charity Shield . . . No, I still don't know.'

On the morning of the League Cup Final, Dorigo pulled his hamstring ('It was devastating – I was in tears') and Wilkinson decided to play Gary Speed at wing-back. It didn't work. 'That game was the end for me,' Speed told me. 'Villa played five at the back, with wing-backs. Villa did it every week and were good at it. We'd never even practised it.'

Dorigo could only watch from the sidelines. 'The stuffing got knocked out of us. I could see Howard's face . . .'

For Alan Sutton, the way the crowd turned on Wilkinson 'was horrible. He was in front of me on the bus, with his wife. His head was in his hands . . . and it seemed to affect him a lot after that. When you get to know someone, you know how they are, and I think that really hurt him.'

'It wasn't a nice walk,' Wilkinson says. 'But then it's comparative, isn't it? It didn't affect me for a long time, but it added to this growing problem with selling the club.'

Leslie Silver had simply had enough. 'Bill Fotherby was pushing me to turn the club into a PLC. I knew to do that you had to have a trading record, and Leeds United's trading record was horrendous! Anyway, we got an offer for £37 million. At that time we were £10 million overdrawn at the bank, which I was securing. So the bank overdraft was paid off, the shareholders got £17 million, which was the only time I ever made money from the shares, and there was £10 million left to spend on players. Bill was chairman for a few weeks and he loved it. I made two big mistakes in football. One was allowing Peter Ridsdale to remain on the board, and the other was that deal. On one hand you've got local people involved, then the city of London steps in.'

Wilkinson recalls that Peter Gilman tried to stop the sale. 'I remember a game at Coventry and Peter got me in the tunnel. I was almost pinned up against the wall. "Do you realize what's happening . . . that these people . . . do you realize?" It was such a shame, because the three of them were a great team.'

But, as Bill Fotherby confirms, there was no real option. 'Leslie wanted out and football was changing. It wasn't the size of your local man's pocket any more.

It was PLCs, international, big business. I got a company called Caspian to take over. They were worth £800 million. As far as I was concerned, Leeds United needed that kind of backing. It turned out later that they didn't intend to stay. They wanted to up the shares and move on, that's how it turned out. I thought they were genuine. "You'll be chairman, Bill." I thought I was sharp but I wasn't sharp enough for them.'

Wilkinson knew that his future was in doubt 'because clearly there was unrest in the fans, but there was a suggestion – more than a suggestion – that the new people were going to bring George Graham in as manager. It was not a nice time. The board didn't know he was lined up for the job, they only knew what was in the papers. But I knew because I had friends in management and they told me. But even when it happened Bill Fotherby in particular fought tooth and nail to keep it status quo.'

'They came up from London,' Fotherby recalls, 'and we played Blackburn on the Tuesday night. They came up in force. They tried to get me to finish him and I wouldn't. "If he goes, I go." We won 1–0 and stung them upstairs, and I put my arms around him in the dressing room and said, "Fantastic, Howard."'

The end, however, was nigh, and it was becoming all too apparent. Sonia Hennigan told me, 'A friend of mine was involved with social work and she commented a lot on how tired Howard looked, towards the end. He had put so much into it for so long, I think he was showing signs of exhaustion.' Her husband knew it was all over too. 'After the Man United game, Alex Ferguson said something like, "I'm not sorry that we beat you, but I'm sorry about the scoreline". Something like that . . . and someone's mentioned "Howard's still here". It means he's in his office. I come home thinking "Something's not right there", and it weren't.'

Sergeant Wilko has no regrets, it seems. 'By that time I was not enjoying going to work. I'd tried to resign, twice, before the season and then after the start. After the Manchester United game Bill said, "Howard, let me sort it." He phoned me on Sunday morning and said, "I've told them that I've sacked you." So he did me a favour. A big favour.'

George Graham duly came in. Mick Hennigan lasted only one game with him, away at Coventry, before the new manager said, 'You can come and clear your desk.' 'I think he said he was sorry,' Mick says, 'but I never went back, not even to clear my desk.'

Bill Fotherby remained, briefly, but as he tells it, 'Then they started spending money like nobody's business. They had to wait for me to resign to bring in Ridsdale but then they were borrowing at 12.5 per cent, which was a killer. It was a very sorrowful ending for me and it still hurts me. Everything we achieved under Howard Wilkinson has been overshadowed by Ridsdale. We built Leeds United up and they killed it.'

The tragedy is, as Wilkinson is keen to point out, that a new generation of young Leeds players were ready and waiting to pull on the famous white shirts. 'We were about a year and a half away from bringing through [Paul] Robinson, Woodgate. I'd already played Kewell and Harte. I'd persuaded Leslie for the money for Lee Bowyer and Nigel Martyn. Alan Smith, McPhail, Woodgate, we'd got them as kids, worked with them twice a day and in school holidays, got 'em living up there. It was fantastic. Unfortunately, football being what it is, everything's going like clockwork and the clock springs start to break. I was frustrated because I felt that that crop of players could go on and be like Manchester United.'

It didn't happen. George Graham didn't stay. Assistant-turned-manager David O'Leary played Wilkinson/Hart's youngsters, but surrounded them with hugely expensive signings. At one point the club had six strikers. Failure to qualify for the lucrative Champions League in successive seasons resulted in the biggest financial meltdown in British football history, followed by two relegations and administration, from which Leeds United are still to recover.

But the glory of 1991/92 refuses to go away.

Epilogue

That title was undervalued in the sense that those players who won it had to perform at the very maximum of their limits, for all those games.

It's 29 October 2011, and Leeds are honouring the twentieth anniversary of the title with a reunion dinner. Bizarrely, it is six months early and many of the Last Champions can't be there.

A more significant reunion takes place on 3 December, as Leeds host Millwall at Elland Road, when Strachan, McAllister and even a returning David Batty lay a wreath for Gary Speed, whose death at forty-two has shocked the club, and the nation.

Speed's untimely passing triggers an outpouring of grief unparalleled in modern football. Amid the financial excesses, meltdowns and madnesses of today's game, perhaps the universally loved, unaffected personality a shaken Wilkinson accurately describes as 'the perfect ambassador for an often imperfect profession' epitomized football's rapidly disappearing innocence, or lost soul.

Nowhere is the sadness felt more keenly than in Leeds, where the crowd pass around a huge banner with those words from 1990 – 'Go on Gary Speed, get one yourself, son' – and sing the once swashbuckling young player's name repeatedly over a montage of the Welshman's goals. Twenty years after the title celebrations, the city is reunited again, in grief.

And perhaps, when the tears dry and memories again grow fonder, that was what it was really all about in 1991/92. Not the football, which was wonderful, but the unity and togetherness which saw a group of players, and an entire city, come together to achieve something that was improbable.

Two decades on, the club is back where it was before Wilkinson arrived, struggling in the second tier with protests outside the ground. Following Simon Grayson's sacking, promotion specialist Neil Warnock is the latest to attempt to follow the Sergeant and revive the ailing giant he describes as 'the fourth or fifth biggest club in the country'.

After leaving Leeds, Wilkinson became the FA's Technical Director (from 1997 to 2001) and nowadays is 'busy, busy' with the LMA, the FA and UEFA. But when I started my journey, there was a measure of frustration in the voice of the last English manager to win the league as he pondered how he would be remembered. 'Good managers are good managers, great managers are rare,' he said. 'Was I a great manager? It doesn't matter what I think. It's for other people to decide. Unfortunately in sport, greatness is measured by trophies. In that sense, if you don't amass loads and loads of trophies, by definition you can't be great.'

He didn't amass loads and loads of trophies, but he achieved the one that matters most with players who should have found the task beyond them, and in doing so pulled off a football miracle. That he didn't do it again should be immaterial. In the Bible, David wasn't required to slay Goliath twice. Nobody ever asks Neil Armstrong why he never went back to the moon.

Twenty years after he placed the Leeds United flag on football's summit, he will say only this: 'I was very good at making the most of what was available, and I used methods which now are commonplace.' A leader to the last, he gives the credit to his troops: 'You've got to be careful about being immodest, but that title was under-valued in the sense that those players who won it had to perform at the very maximum of their limits, for all those games. If anybody earned the title by doing as well if not better than they could do, they did that. But there is no measure of that. All you get is a medal. I thought they deserved more credit. Not for the title win, but for the fact that nobody gave them a chance, and how much they had given, in order to earn it. And they had earned it.'

It's a cold evening, and I feel the urge to return to where it started, Elland Road. As I drive down there I'm thinking not of £200,000-a-week fancy Dans, Ferraris and financial meltdowns but of special bonds, Vinnie's tears and Chapman's goals; of Mel and Shutty and Mick Hennigan and others who laid their bodies on the line to haul their team to the top of Everest.

And if I close my eyes, I can see those floodlights. And

suddenly there's the Sarge, urging his troops forward as Whyte plays it to Sterland, who races down the wing and hits a perfectly weighted diagonal ball to Speedo, who heads it back to Chappy, and it's a GOALLLLLLLLLLLL!, and we're all jumping and the world is drenched in sunshine.

And then I open my eyes, and Elland Road is dark and lonely; there's no cheering, and no Speedo. And I wonder: could it ever happen again?

Appendix: Leeds United's First Division Results 1991/92

20 Aug	Nottingham Forest (h)	W	1–0	McAllister
24 Aug	Sheffield Wednesday (h)	D	1–1	Hodge
28 Aug	Southampton (a)	W	4–0	Speed 2, Strachan 2 pens
31 Aug	Manchester United (a)	D	1–1	Chapman
03 Sep	Arsenal (h)	D	2–2	Strachan pen, Chapman
07 Sep	Manchester City (h)	W	3–0	Dorigo, Batty, Strachan pen
14 Sep	Chelsea (a)	W	1–0	Shutt
18 Sep	Coventry City (a)	D	0–0	
21 Sep	Liverpool (h)	W	1–0	Hodge
28 Sep	Norwich City (a)	D	2–2	Dorigo, Speed
01 Oct	Crystal Palace (a)	L	0–1	
05 Oct	Sheffield United (h)	W	4–3	Hodge 2, Sterland 2 (1 pen)

19 Oct	Notts County (a)	W	4–2	Chapman, Hodge, Whyte, McAllister
26 Oct	Oldham Athletic (h)	W	1–0	Kilcline og
02 Nov	Wimbledon (a)	D	0–0	
16 Nov	Queens Park Rangers (h)	W	2–0	Sterland, Wallace
24 Nov	Aston Villa (a)	W	4–1	Wallace, Sterland, Chapman 2
30 Nov	Everton (h)	W	1–0	Wallace
07 Dec	Luton Town (a)	W	2–0	Wallace, Speed
14 Dec	Tottenham Hotspur (h)	D	1–1	Speed
22 Dec	Nottingham Forest (a)	D	0–0	
26 Dec	Southampton (h)	D	3–3	Hodge 2, Speed
29 Dec	Manchester United (h)	D	1–1	Sterland pen
01 Jan	West Ham United (a)	W	3–1	Chapman 2, McAllister
12 Jan	Sheffield Wednesday (a)	W	6–1	Chapman 3, Dorigo, Whitlow, Wallace
18 Jan	Crystal Palace (h)	D	1–1	Fairclough
01 Feb	Notts County (h)	W	3–0	Sterland, Batty, Wallace
08 Feb	Oldham Athletic (a)	L	0–2	
23 Feb	Everton (a)	D	1–1	Shutt
29 Feb	Luton Town (h)	W	2–0	Cantona, Chapman

03 Mar	Aston Villa (h)	D	0–0	
07 Mar	Tottenham Hotspur (a)	W	3–1	Wallace, Newsome, McAllister
11 Mar	Queens Park Rangers (a)	L	1–4	Speed
14 Mar	Wimbledon (h)	W	5–1	Chapman 3, Wallace, Cantona
22 Mar	Arsenal (a)	D	1–1	Chapman
28 Mar	West Ham United (h)	D	0–0	
04 Apr	Manchester City (a)	L	0–4	
11 Apr	Chelsea (h)	W	3–0	Wallace, Chapman, Cantona
18 Apr	Liverpool (a)	D	0–0	
20 Apr	Coventry City (h)	W	2–0	Fairclough, McAllister pen
26 Apr	Sheffield United (a)	W	3–2	Wallace, Newsome, Gayle og
02 May	Norwich City (h)	W	1–0	Wallace

Bibliography

Auclair, David – *Cantona, The Rebel Who Would Be King* (Macmillan, 2010)

Batty, David – *The Autobiography* (Headline, 2001)

Cantona, Eric – *My Story* (Headline, 1994)

Chapman, Lee – *More Than A Match* (Stanley Paul, 1992)

Clavane, Anthony – *Promised Land* (Yellow Jersey, 2010)

Hodge, Steve – *The Man With Maradona's Shirt* (Orion, 2010)

Jones, Vinnie – *Vinnie, The Autobiography* (Headline, 1998)

Kamara, Chris – *Mr Unbelievable* (HarperSport, 2011)

McAllister. Gary – *Captain's Log* (Mainstream, 1995)

Mourant, Andrew – *Leeds United, Player By Player* (Guinness, 1992)

Mourant, Andrew – *The Essential History Of Leeds United* (Headline, 2000)

Rowley, Les and Wray, John – *Where Are They Now* (YFP, 2005)

Saffer, David – *Champions 1991/92* (Tempus, 2003)

Sterland, Mel – *Boozing, Betting & Brawling* (Green Umbrella, 2008)

Strachan, Gordon – *My Life In Football* (Sphere, 2006)

Wilkinson, Howard – *Managing To Succeed* (Mainstream, 1992)

Acknowledgements

This book would not have been possible without the drive and encouragement of Kevin Pocklington, my agent at Jenny Brown Associates, and Giles Elliott at Transworld. I'm enormously grateful for the support and editor-like eagle eye of my partner, Emily. I thank Daniel Balado-Lopez, copy-editor par excellence.

I will be forever grateful to Paul Weighell for rekindling my dormant interest in Leeds United (painful as it has subsequently often been), and to James Brown, Tim Southwell and Iestyn George for sharing the innumerable highs and very few lows of the Howard Wilkinson era at Leeds United. I thank Harry and Kevin Lister for taking me to my first visits to Elland Road as a child.

I am grateful to all who provided contacts along my journey, from Paul Dews at Leeds United to various anonymous sources: you know who you are. I acknowledge Anthony Clavane, author of the fine book *Promised Land*, for providing me with the phrase 'The Last Champions' – whether or not it appeared anywhere before – by using it as a chapter heading which took hold in my subconscious as a title long before I realized where I'd got it from!

I particularly wish to thank all the players, staff and wives who gave me such fascinating interviews, and subsistence during and after them. I hope you all enjoyed sharing the memories as much as I enjoyed hearing them. To those players I did not manage to track down or who preferred to keep their counsel on this occasion, my door is always open for a future edition of this book.

Last and definitely not least, I am tremendously grateful to Howard Wilkinson, not only for the initial exhaustive (and hopefully not too exhausting!) interview but for assistance with contacts and queries along the way. I of course thank Howard along with the chairman, directors, staff and the players for bringing the title back to Leeds in 1992 in the first place, thus making this book possible and giving the city something that will never be forgotten as long as there is Leeds, and as long as there is football.